# Ill at Ease Overseas

Stephen Koral

Dedicated to Mum, Dad, Mel, Danielle and everyone I've met on the road.

# CONTENTS

# ACKNOWLEDGMENTS

Chris Burrows – Cover Editing
Rachael Williams (The Copyediting Co.) – Proofreading and polish

*The World is a book and those who do not travel read only a page.*
Saint Augustine

# CHAPTER ONE
# SOUTH AMERICA

**Saturday, 22nd October 2017**

I am an ex-backpacker that can't quite seem to let go of the fun of past adventures. There's nothing more I'd like to do than fill my backpack full of scruffy old clothes, leave England full-time, stay in cheap hostels and jump around new countries. Alas! Adult stuff like a mortgage and responsibility hang over me instead, therefore these days I pursue travel to the death as a hobby whenever I can. Living like this presents its fair share of problems — money is always one of them. I find myself regularly living in my overdraft with weeks to go until the next payday, having dealt with another financial hit from a huge purchase on *Skyscanner*, or having just blasted my month's wages away somewhere on the other side of the world. Money at least comes and goes, but the finite resource of free time to undertake the trips is probably the largest burden. I travel within my holiday allowance from my job, limiting me to few weeks out of the year where I try to maximise the time by cramming in multiple stops during the day and then partying at night, often with flying visits to several countries on the same trip. After a fortnight of culture, sunburn, beach parties and jungle trekking, I'll catch myself landing home at 2AM from a huge flight and having to be up for work just a few hours later, trying to resume normal life through blurry eyes and jet lag. I genuinely need a holiday after my holiday to unwind sometimes; I live in the mindset of "I'll sleep when I'm dead", but now in my mid-thirties I'm kidding no one about my ability to spring back after a few hours' sleep. There's more: I tend to visit new countries on every trip as I'd like to try and do a hundred of them before I die. As such, the list of "safer" or standard tourist destinations for someone from the Western Sphere have dwindled away, often pushing me further off the beaten track. I've done many of the traditional getaways; over a year spent backpacking around Asian countries, months in the States, ticked off most countries in Europe. I'm now left to tackle places that sometimes have large distances without any major civilisation, no hospital facilities and, in some cases, no working police force. These bring outright problems which are compounded once out there: losing things, injury, being threatened by an angry local, or simply getting lost. I found getting off the beaten path isn't all remote beaches and reconnecting with nature — sometimes it's sleepless nights, diarrhoea and danger.

Some of the lesser problems experienced are perhaps a little more familiar to most, leaving the usual comfort zone at home by trying new foods that risk an upset stomach or meeting new people with whom you share no common language. It may be awkward and difficult to deal with the cultural difference, or perhaps finding that your room for the night is a significant drop in standards to what you're used to at home. Often these new experiences are ultimately net-positive because it'll either be a memory you'll cherish, or you'll realise how good you have life back at home in contrast and you'll grow from it. This is what drives me on; to experience new ways of life and see new things that many haven't. And sometimes I will just be awake on a remote, deserted tropical beach at 5AM after a night of partying in far flung bars, watching a sunrise, and that'll be the moment that I know it's definitely been worth the hassle to get here.

I was at it once again, throwing myself head first into my love of travel, currently embarking on a custom holiday built by me and my partner after many a night spent hunched around a laptop in preparation. We tend to avoid pre-packaged holidays in favour of a more customised time away, rather than being stuck in the same place for two weeks at a resort, but this style of travel does come with its own risks. In this case, it was a trip which had us travelling to several destinations across South America, responsible for getting ourselves around a continent renowned for its high crime rate and associated risks. Aside from a handful of friends who had travelled there previously and imparted their experiences on me, most of our information about the continent had come from the research we had done online. Now, I am aware that looking online for information has to be taken with a pinch of salt as the internet tends to leap to the extremes on a topic — if you've ever typed symptoms of an ailment into it before you'll know what I mean. Search results for a headache will tell you it could well be a tumour you've got there. Mild cough? That'll be lung cancer. To an extent it's the case with travel too, and I had read multiple horror stories about life in South America. Travel forums would start with pictures of beautiful white sand beaches or lush green jungles, then lead to stories about cartels, tourist stabbings and murders in broad daylight. Sure, Rio de Janeiro looks nice on the photos, but amongst those streets, some forgotten travel forum I visited said that there are packs of kids from the shanty towns called Piranhas who roam around using blades to slash clothes from passing people, often leaving the victim without anything to wear, hoping a wallet or jewellery might get swiped in the process. Stories of pedestrians getting caught up in gang shoot-outs. Lengthy prison sentences from kilos of cocaine being planted on transiting tourists. I know it probably does happen, although being caught up in it is rare; yet these extremes do have a habit of lodging in my brain to bother me when I'm trying to enjoy myself out there.

You can read the internet as much as you like but it'll only prepare you a tiny bit for what's actually in store, and there was a lot to get our heads around. We hadn't been to any of the continent's countries before, we knew nobody who could help us out if we got into trouble, and neither of us fluently spoke either of the main languages used on the continent —— to be honest we even struggled to pronounce some of the place names. Fortunately, we weren't going in totally blind. I had spent collective years backpacking and was relatively experienced in dealing with troublesome situations — like street scammers for example (a blanket "No" approach will suffice if a seemingly friendly stranger tries to fire up a conversation, particularly in the touristy areas) — and my wife Mel, a native of Indonesia, has excellent communication skills across several languages (unfortunately, just not the ones commonly used in South America). In the past we had each successfully navigated our way around multiple Asian countries without any major issues — although large swathes of Asia are arguably a lot safer and therefore easier to travel around than South America on the whole. It was surreal to think I was now married to her too, on our first trip together since tying the knot, flying to Peru now with an actual wife sat next to me. I could see her ordering herself another of those small plastic bottles of free wine often available on long haul fights and it made me laugh seeing her get stuck into them. She turned to me and smiled (her teeth had turned slightly purple from excessive red wine consumption) whilst the second consecutive film of the Ice Age franchise began on the screen in the headrest in front of her. I knew I was onto a winner marrying her. There's a huge story of how we'd met in Indonesia and developed feelings during a protracted time revolving around the country's legal system (I'm pretty sure there's a whole book available about it). Meeting her had totally changed the solo-traveller dynamic I was used to. On my previous travels I'd get away with my drunken wild misadventures, completely carefree, living in the mindset of: if anything happens to me, I'll deal with it. I was partially responsible for her these days and having concern about someone else in the potentially dangerous areas we'd be visiting over the next few weeks was still a relatively new concept for me.

# PERU

## Lima, Peru — Saturday, 22nd October 2017

Excusing a brief smile at passport control, my very first interaction with a bona fide South American was with our taxi driver, ferrying us over to our *AirBnB* from the airport as we sat in the back seat of his van. Airport taxi drivers from around the world must often find themselves acting as a sort of diplomat to first time travellers to their country, being the first point of contact to the newly arrived wide-eyed tourist who probably has many questions ranging from local customs to what restaurant is good in town. In my experience, a good taxi driver doesn't just take you from A to B, he'll impart his knowledge on you as part of the service (equally, he'll know when to shut up and let you ride in silence if you're not feeling particularly talkative for whatever reason!). Very much like our taxi driver now as a case in point; a greying man in his sixties called Roberto, a retired air traffic controller from the airport we'd been picked up at in Peru's capital Lima. He'd obviously done this before, seemingly knowing what I was about to ask, and had prepared his answers. I would find out over my time in South America that fluent English speakers are not common, so meeting Roberto right off the bat was unusual in that he spoke it with some proficiency. I hoped our talk with him would calm the nerves of the earlier internet searches, but within minutes of our introduction he was filling us in with his gruesome stories.

"Such a mess," he said, telling a story about his life. "Blood, brains, all over the dashboard and front seat. I saw my wife lying there, dead."

His wife had been car-jacked in an incident that had gone horribly wrong, having resisted attempts to have her car stolen, only to receive a bullet in the head. This happened during Roberto's time living in the Brazilian city of São Paulo before he moved to Peru, so he had recently been flying back regularly to Brazil for the court cases.

"They sentenced that motherfucker only last week after months spent in the court room. He is going to jail for fifteen years now, a result in a case like this is rare."

His grim story was set to the backdrop of down-town Lima at midnight as our little van chugged along the unlit streets to our destination, passing stuff you definitely don't see at home in rural England like an intimating group of ruffians stood around a barrel fire. Most buildings had thick metal bars across their windows. Roberto had made the move to Lima as living in São Paulo had been too painful with the reminders of his lost wife, but by the looks of things, Lima at night-time didn't look much better. Vast stretches of the roads were in a terrible state to drive on and were largely unlit, the only light available outside was from headlights of other cars. The van shook as we crossed huge pot holes in the roads, leading us deeper into the city.

We'd been chucked in at the deep end going straight into a South American city; being around central Lima at night wasn't exactly easy on the eye and from what we could see out of the van windows, not very safe either. A bastion within the city for those who aren't too keen on getting stabbed on their first night is the coastal district of Miraflores, where our *AirBnB* was located. One could argue Miraflores is the most affluent district of the entire capital, which is itself the wealthiest city within the country. Look, I'm all up for an adventure and getting out into the thick of it, but you have to be sensible sometimes and staying anywhere else in Lima with its high crime rate and people starting fires on the street could wait for another day. Approaching Miraflores was a significant change from what we had seen so far; the security bars across shop windows were no longer needed as in their place was a notable presence of armed police patrolling, both in cars and on foot. The small, slightly dilapidated buildings we'd seen frequently in the centre were replaced with apartment blocks mixed in with vibrant bright red or yellow buildings styled after Spanish architecture, an interesting hangover from the country's colonial past. Our *AirBnB* happened to be in one of the nicer buildings I had managed to see through the limited view in the dark, a trendy apartment block high up on Miraflores' cliffside on the South Pacific coast. Roberto knew the host of our stay, a lovely elderly American retiree who had been waiting outside her apartment for us to arrive. They conversed in Spanish for a few moments whilst Mel and I stood outside of the taxi, checking we'd collected everything and gathering our bags from the trunk. As this was going on, a faint noise in the distance which sounded like two gunshots echoed around us. Picking up on the noise, Roberto interrupted his conversation with the host, turned to us and in a joking way said, "Don't forget you two, you are in South America now!".

### Lima, Peru — Sunday, 23rd October 2017

Whilst the gunshots of the previous night was a noise I certainly don't hear at home, I had awoken to another foreign sound at the crack of dawn. Birds. But foreign ones. What sounded like thousands of them, singing with loud exotic calls, echoing around the city for miles and bursting in through our bedroom window. It was like all of the birds had perhaps flown into the city from a nearby jungle overnight and taken advantage of the quiet city streets of the early morning. Jet lag had us awake at the crack of dawn anyway, never mind all the screaming birds outside the window, and with nothing else to do other than lie on the bed quietly so as to not wake the host of our

*AirBnb*, Mel and I made the decision to go and enjoy an early exploration of the city for the first time in the daylight.

Everywhere was closed. Sure, the sun was barely up, so you might expect that. We were to also learn it was the country's census day, and by law every resident had to stay at home to wait for some government people with clipboards to visit and count them. Haven't these guys heard of census by internet? Or even by post? The only full day we had planned in the capital and absolutely nothing was open, nothing to even get a bit of breakfast. Well, if we had any concerns about the safety in the city then it didn't matter today as we were positively the only people around – save for a few armed police on patrol. This was the affluent area of the city after all, so of course it made sense that the rich are protected by armed police on the street, although I did wonder briefly whether these guys were only here to enforce everyone remaining at home for census day.

With nothing to do in a city emptied of people we walked for miles, stomachs rumbling as we passed a closed *KFC* and *McDonalds* — both with 'Cerrada Por Cencus' scrawled on cardboard placed in the front window. The struggles of being tired and hungry were lessened as a pleasant blue sky appeared when the sea's haze lifted from the coast, leaving Miraflores an agreeable place to spend our morning. The district offered a picturesque park, hugging the coastline with deep green grass, palm trees and nice views looking out to the ocean. Despite Lima's position on the map as a coastal city, much of it is on a higher ground relative to sea level, up to a hundred metres high in parts, meaning that getting down to the beach from the residential areas leaves a steep drop to negotiate, fortunately there are a few walkways available that allowed us to get to sea level. Sat on the beach, being at sea level today was something that had been on my mind for the upcoming part of the trip as our plans tomorrow had us heading directly inland and up into the extremely high Andes Mountain range, and travel advice pointed us to avoid flying direct from sea level into the mountains if we could help it. You don't have to heed the medical travel advice but going against does increase your chances of encountering issues; many of the popular places for tourists in the Andes are so high up they can cause altitude sickness, which is essentially the body going into shock before it has time to adjust to the thinner atmosphere and the decreased availability of oxygen within it. Our main draw to the country was of course Machu Picchu, the famous citadel built by the native Inca people around 1450 AD, a full hundred years before any of the European settlers arrived to begin the process of creating modern day Peru. Machu Picchu is arguably the most difficult of all of the Seven Wonders of the World to access due to it being tucked away in Andes, and almost all tourists have to make their way high up into the mountain town of

Cusco first before descending toward the world wonder. Alternatively, those with more time to burn can attempt the Inca trail, a twenty-six mile hike in the wilderness to the site at a slightly lower altitude, a route that was originally used by the native Inca people centuries ago. Kudos to those that attempt it; it's a hard four-day slog that you need to be physically fit to endure, along with tackling whatever weather nature conjures up, not to mention the variety of blood-feeding insects that accompany the journey. We didn't have the time, nor Mel the inclination, to attempt four days of walking and camping with mosquito bites on our ankles, so a flight direct to Cusco suited our schedule and skin. Cusco however sits at a height of 3,400 metres above sea level, the highest destination of this South America trip, or any trip I've ever been on for that matter. I'd had a think about where I'd been on my previous travels and realised, I hadn't been anywhere even remotely near that height. Altitude sickness starts from 2,500 metres onwards with symptoms of drowsiness and a terrible headache, and can eventually lead to death if the body hasn't adjusted properly to the altitude. A lot of the advice I could find online had a bias towards mountain climbers — 'only increase altitude a few hundred metres a day' sort of stuff, written for those who have the time to adjust over it gradually and with emphasis on being careful about physically exerting themselves because, well, they're climbing a mountain. We were flying directly to well beyond any altitude either of us had been in our lives, whizzing past the chance to adjust incrementally by having booked our trip before we'd even given any thought to any of this.

All was not lost with our direct journey into the skies, and the miracle of modern medicine offered a solution in the name of *Acetazolamide*. In a nutshell, it cleverly tricks the body into thinking it's breathing in excessive carbon dioxide, and so to counteract that, the body begins to produce more red blood cells to carry the "less" oxygen available, whilst also subtly increasing breath rate and depth. The body naturally begins to create the additional blood cells needed once at higher altitudes, but it's a slow process that takes several days, which is obviously no good if you're already well beyond the 2500 metre mark. Providing the medication has been taken a couple of days before arrival to anywhere with extreme altitude, you're there with a fighting chance, body raring to go, pumping the necessary extra red blood cells around those cholesterol encrusted veins you have. Of course, as with any medication, it comes with side effects; although mild for myself, my fingers and toes tingled excessively. My knee caps ached and looked like they were bulging a bit too, but I was probably being a bit paranoid about them as I couldn't remember what my knee caps looked like before taking the medication. Either way, tingling fingers and big knees was preferable to choking to death up in the clouds tomorrow.

The rest of our time in the capital was quiet and spent aimlessly walking around the deserted streets of the city, then later relying heavily on our wonderful *AirBnB* host for sustenance to carry us throughout the day once she had woken up. If you're not familiar with *AirBnB* then I can't recommend it enough. Regular people like you and me can rent out available bedrooms in our houses for strangers to come and stay at, a bit like a homestay. For the holiday maker, their luck might come in and get an entire apartment to themselves, but from our experiences in the past it is usually a spare room of the tenant's house. It's admittedly not usually as relaxing a stay as it could be compared to having your own hotel room (I worry about waking my hosts up when getting up for a wee in the night or coming in drunk in the late hours. Walking around naked is an absolute no!). But, don't knock it until you've tried it. If you're only somewhere for a night or two and want to mingle with the locals to get their insider tips of the area, often at half of the price of a hotel, then *AirBnB* is worth a shot. Given that nothing was open, we'd have almost certainly had a miserable day spent hungry if we had stayed in a hotel; instead, we were fed and watered by the host, and it was time spent conversing with a local, too. People started to peer out of their homes towards the evening once the clipboard men had left, so shops did eventually open their doors, but by this time Mel and I had managed five hours sleep across two and half days and were ready for an early night. It had been a calm but somewhat anticlimactic first full day on the continent I supposed, but we still had plenty to look forward to in the coming days.

## Cusco, Peru — Monday 23rd October 2017

A small propeller aircraft touched down at Cusco International airport early on a clear Monday morning, carrying two excited but slightly nervous travellers in the form of me and Mel. The plane had flown inland from the Pacific coast for a solid hour, passing several villages and farms scattered across the endless arid beige mountains and hills below. We were now located roughly in the centre of the Andes, a mountain range that runs a whopping 4,300 miles like a spine along the entire western side of the South American continent, stretching from the southern tip of Chile to almost reaching Venezuela's Caribbean Sea coast. I had spent the flight worrying about the altitude and nervously anticipated the aircraft's doors as they opened, exposing both Mel and I to the thin air to discover whether the medication had properly worked for us. I could certainly feel an instant change in the air when stepping out and disembarking from the plane; it was noticeably harder to breathe and the passing breeze seemed to dry my mouth out. I normally slather on lip balm constantly even at sea level, but here I had taken to practically eating the stuff as the dry air sucked out the moisture from my lips. I didn't feel an instant altitude sickness headache forming though, so I took it as a good sign. The key is to take it easy on the first few days at height because altitude sickness can be difficult to shift after it has kicked in. There's no real remedy other than to head to lower altitude once the symptoms start, and as you might well imagine, skirting around death would cause all sorts of travel disruptions to our tight travel itinerary. We did wonder if we should have the remainder of the day holed up at our hostel with a ruck of protein bars to give our bodies time to adjust, but once within Cusco, we found it far too enticing not to go and see a little bit of it. As a compromise, we planned to drop our bags off at our hostel but then have an easy day of light walking around the streets of town.

Deep within one of the many narrow streets of the city our taxi stopped outside our hostel. The morning air was fresh, cool but pleasant to be in. We passed through a quaint white painted archway with flowers growing around it, the building appeared to be some sort of converted old Spanish colonial building, and then into a small courtyard that was surrounded by the hostel's dormitories. I've stayed in some real shitholes on the road over the years, but this hostel appeared well looked after, with friendly reception staff and a generally relaxing atmosphere all round. I hoped the quality and peaceful vibe continued on into the dormitories, because if you're a hostel virgin and not in-the-know with how they work, a stay in some can be pretty rough going. Mel hadn't been to one before and, with her higher required baseline of standards compared to mine, cautiously agreed to try a stay in one. I prayed our time here would be clean and calm because I'd be hearing about it regularly from her throughout if it wasn't. It had been a while since I had even stayed in one myself to be honest. They had been my de facto places to stay during my solo backpacking stints, but I do have a bit of a love / hate relationship with them these days. With these budget accommodation places it is sometimes hard to get a good night's sleep as they can get rather rowdy, and even if there's not a party going on somewhere in the building, several other strangers snoring, tossing and turning in the same room is guaranteed to disrupt sleep. My main gripe is that I'm now ten years above the average age of the rest of the guests now (most tend to be around the mid-twenties mark), reminding me of my fleeting bygone youth. They're also usually backpackers on extensive trips, free to go wherever they like the following day, travelling wherever the wind takes them; meanwhile, muggins here is on a tight itinerary trying to cram in as much as he can with his mere fortnight away. I don't need a reminder of these things. Positives for hostels are they're cheap and great to meet the other travellers to spend the days doing activities with, or at the very least to meet drinking companions, so this is why I endure them. Also, a unique offer for hostels in Peru, they provide a special free tea for guests. Coca — the infamous plant used to make cocaine. A whole tub of the raw leaves sat there unguarded at the reception desk for us to help ourselves to.

Coca tea is consumed similar to the way we drink tea at home, simply as part of Peruvian day to day life — there's no milk added to this one though, it's literally just the leaves from the plant and hot water. It's perfectly legal, and I would soon notice it was available everywhere around Cusco. The plant is indigenous to South America and a lot of land has been dedicated to cultivating it since humans realised the leaves can get them off their tits, although the high from cocaine is completely different to the mild buzz from drinking it as a humble tea. That'll be because cocaine is heavily processed in contrast; kerosene, or less commonly diesel is used to strip the good stuff out of the leaves and then it is scooped up and compressed, therefore it is effectively like snorting hundreds of the leaves at once. It's a weird brew in its natural form, there was almost a fishy aroma released once the hot water met the leaves. The actual taste wasn't too offensive, similar to one of those piss-weak *Earl Grey* teas that people seem to enjoy instead of a proper strong brew back home. I found the first one rather refreshing, so I helped myself to another as we waited for the receptionist to type away at her keyboard during our check-in.

One of the benefits of being male in Western society is that we generally don't have to take as much time as women to get ready to go out. Imagine having to waste an entire hour getting ready every single morning before going to work! I can literally wake up, shovel my breakfast in, brush my teeth, press one out and be on the road to work within ten minutes. Similar preparation time is spent going on a night out or other such events. It's ironic that I can be ready within minutes, but this efficiency up being wasted anyway because, ultimately, I still have to wait for Mel. I have spent countless hours sat in my ironed shirt and trousers, waiting on the bed or downstairs whilst Mel puts makeup on and does her hair. And then when I think she's finally done and we're ready to leave the house, she'll spend ten minutes choosing what shoes to wear. Mel wanted to "freshen up" before we spent any time wandering around Cusco, which usually means I've got at least an hour's wait ahead of me. I was slightly miffed as I was keen to get out onto the streets and explore, but luckily there were more cups of the coca tea to keep me occupied as I flicked through the local channels on the dorm's TV. I watched something on the news about yesterday's census as a video segment appeared of people walking round with clipboards like we'd spotted in the streets of Lima yesterday. I flicked over to find a badly acted soap opera; interesting at first, but it was all in Spanish and I had no idea what was going on, so I eventually gave up and, after yet another cup of tea, lay on the bed watching the ceiling for the remainder of the hour.

As it happens, Cusco is quite a gorgeous city. I think technically it's classed as a city anyway, but rather has the vibe of a town with its cobblestone streets and rickety orange-tiled rooves, bright white painted buildings and alleyways to be found nestled within. And, of course, not to forget the short distance from vast expanses of countryside and the scenic panoramic views of mountains in the backdrop. It was a world apart from the built up and frankly scary-in-parts true city that we had just left in Lima. One of my favourite things to do when I get to a new place is to take that first walk around, soaking up the sights and vibe, lacking any direction by just happily exploring. In this manner, we found ourselves at the town's main square, Plaza de Armas, which is steeped in history as it served as a hub for both the Spanish during colonial times and the ancient Inca empire before it. If you're expecting to learn more about the in-depth history here, I'm afraid you've picked up the wrong book. I'll admit — as I've become older I have garnered a mild interest in history about certain places or people; indeed, places like Plaza de Armas have a rich and complex past, but I'm still not quite at that point where I find some main square on the other side of the world interesting enough to get into all of the specific details across its hundreds of years of existence. If, like me, you're more inclined just to appreciate the scenery in places like this then you can fill your boots. There are small areas of grass or benches to sit on to watch the huge fountain spurting water, a huge chapel with intricate detail in the brickwork, cafes, restaurants and shops surrounding the square along with the stunning mountains in the distance. And, of course, like anywhere in the world, it's just fun to sit on the grass and people-watch the passing tourists.

I enjoyed my time soaking up the atmosphere, but the experience was spoiled slightly by constantly being approached by street merchants primed for sales of trinkets and other such crap for tourists. Look, I know they have to make a living somehow, but could they make their living elsewhere? If I want an amateur painting of an alpaca, I'll go to an art stall, or rather, draw one myself. If I want a pack of ciggies, I'll go to a shop. Fruit? I'm sure I walked past a grocery store five minutes ago; I certainly don't want an already-peeled orange that's covered in flies. I know there are tourist traps all over the globe, and I'm not just having a dig at the lads in Cusco, but sometimes you want to relax and enjoy a place without the constant hassle of sellers trying to grab your attention, who only end up annoying you. Actually, you know what — whilst I'm at it, the actual shops are shit here, too. Mel wanted to buy a few t-shirts for her family so she dragged me around a few of the claustrophobic shops (something I positively detest at the best of times) and I actually became annoyed with what was on offer. The big thing for t-shirts here is to take a big brand, logo or whatever and try to fit it around something to do with Peru. It would be nice if their puns worked even slightly, but there's absolutely no pay off. *Llama Marley* accompanying a drawing of the country's native llama animal, but with dreadlocks and smoking a blunt. Maybe there's somehow a link I am missing there between Peru and the whole reggae movement, but I am definitely missing it here: *Guns'n'Llamas, Red Hot Llama Peppers. Peru Wars* written in the *Star Wars* font was one that I found particularly offensive. Underneath it, a Princess Leia guinea pig and a llama version of Han Solo. Anything huge in pop culture, there was a Peru based t-shirt found somewhere. Although irritated by it all, I felt absolutely primed stomping through these shops looking at the crap, and it seemed like my good feeling was being wasted being amongst it all. I asked Mel if she wanted to go for a jog around the town this afternoon maybe, and with her confused expression to my question I realised I was probably buzzing from the several cups of coca tea I had ingested throughout the day. Unsurprising then, that the tea is so popular with the locals.

When coca is consumed, along with the high, it is supposed to act like an appetite suppressant, but it takes a lot for me to suppress my love for food. I was entirely ready to engage with a local meal. I'm generally not fussy with food and will try anything once, although as I've got older I have become squeamish with seafood (performing an autopsy on a large prawn at the dinner table, cracking its head off and hooking the tube of faeces out from its gut is something I can miss these days), but generally I'm game for anything. I've eaten some unusual stuff abroad over the years; a crocodile burger in Australia, fried crickets in Thailand and Hákarl in Iceland (a delicacy made from fermented Greenland shark which was the single worst thing I've ever tasted — disclaimer: this was in my youth before I realised shark shouldn't be on dinner plates), so I was open to the idea of trying something equally weird out in Peru. Mel on the other hand, considering her Asian roots where extended family members in the rural areas of Sumatra have been known to consume Man's Best Friend, her personal tastes are aligned to what we might consider "normal" food in the West. We picked a restaurant and sat on a little balcony overlooking the main square and were presented with a menu. I couldn't help but notice that what would be a beloved family pet in England was on offer on today's specials: guinea pig. These furry little rodents are native to South America and are both kept here as pets and consumed as food. Mel settled with llama steak, another native animal but recommended by the waiter as "good as cow". I judge the Sumatrans for eating a species we keep as a pet, but I guess I'm not any better as I ended up choosing the guinea pig for my first proper meal in the country. A handful of previous travellers to Peru I know said they'd tried it, but it had been a "choose your dinner" experience, selecting it live from a hutch and taking it away from its mates like how we do with lobster in posh Western restaurants. Not one of them commented on the experience highly. I was really disappointed with it too, although thankfully mine was already stored in the freezer when I'd selected it off the menu. Firstly, it retained too much of the shape of guinea pig when it came out onto the plate, like one had been thrown directly into the fryer — even the hairs had curled up and remained on the skin. I could almost forgive the presentation, but the taste of the meat had an aroma of wet straw, much like that of a rabbit hutch, and there were only about five gristly bites on the whole thing. Mel's steak looked amazing. Real chunks of meat she was biting into, juice dribbling down her chin, meanwhile, I looked on enviously with my charred rodent. Ah well, another cup of coca tea it is then!

### Cusco, Peru — Tuesday, 24th October 2017

The following day we decided we'd push a little bit further beyond the centre of the town. Having been here a full twenty-four hours without headaches or lethargy forming was a good sign that we'd avoided altitude sickness, giving us some encouragement to explore far beyond the small area of town we traversed yesterday. During our time on the main square, we had noticed looming in the nearby hills what looked a miniature version of Christ the Redeemer in the distance, similar to Brazil's famous big statue of Jesus with his arms stuck out. The pair of us thought that seeing Peru's smaller counterpart up close would make a nice warm up for the real thing, which we were due to see in a couple of weeks, and it'd be a decent day's activity spent walking to see it in lieu of doing anything else. It was certainly going to be a decent physical excursion though, we didn't have a proper walking route planned and were going to wing it, but more notable was the day's temperature. The town's air easily dips to near freezing at night, yet surprisingly manages to get quite toasty in the daylight hours, especially so when the sun cracks out through the clouds to accompany the already dry air. Mel enjoyed the sun's presence as it helped to create a more dynamic light for better photography, but it also made merely existing for long periods of time outside much harder than it needed to be.

The roads out of town were winding steep paths and narrow alleys with stone brick housing either side, usually painted bright white. Groups of school kids ran past in these alleyways on their way to school and often said hello to us, or we'd come across 'must have' photo opportunities like old native folk wearing traditional clothing walking around leading llamas on a rope. It didn't take long upon leaving the outskirts of the town and bordering into the countryside to realise we weren't getting near the statue without paying an entrance fee. Many of the routes leading up into the hills appeared to halt pedestrians with barriers across the road like it was some sort of national park or something. We hesitated around one of the barriers for some time deciding what to do, and whether we could risk jumping it, when we were approached by a couple of old men with donkeys on leads who seemingly appeared out of nowhere. Through broken English they appeared to be offering free entry to the area if we paid for a ride on their donkeys first to lead us there. I was tempted, but when I was told we still had seven kilometres to go I didn't want to put a poor donkey through the ordeal of carrying me that far. Determined not to pay a penny to see this statue, we continued on attempting different routes and eventually spotted an unmanned side road leading off into the hills, looking roughly like it was going in the direction we needed. Stood at the bottom of the road gazing up at the steep ascent and beyond, we began to comprehend the scale of the task we had created for ourselves. We'd not really been at it long, yet our journey to this statue seemed to be getting longer by the minute and we were quickly depleting the water we'd brought with us. There'd eventually be a shop or something up there to restock up on though, I was sure, and with that gamble we pressed on.

It was approaching midday and the direct sun began to beat down on us, bringing the temperatures up to the mid-twenties along with it. I was already thirsty. Strangely, there were many mountains around us in the panoramic views of Peruvian countryside that were much higher than our altitude and these were caked with snow. I say "strangely" because I'm confused how the whole altitude and snow thing works. Ben Nevis back in Britain is the highest mountain we have, and aside from a few weeks in the middle of summer where temperatures sometimes reach above freezing in the day time, it always has snow on it (it has been known to snow in early summer there!). This is at the comparatively wimpy height of 1,345 metres, so why the hell weren't we hiking knee deep in snow now at Cusco's 3,400 metres? No, apparently in Peru, the snow likes to form exclusively on the mountains that are pushing beyond the Earth's troposphere. I'd brought a jacket, half expecting it to be chilly, but it wasn't needed and was just more weight to carry, making me even hotter. Not that I'm complaining; I'd rather be warm than cold given the choice for an excursion like this, but I definitely should have brought more water. Another quirk of the high altitude was that it gave the sun a ring, almost a faint rainbow right around it like a halo, and I had never seen anything like it before. Obviously, it's something to do with the sun's rays bouncing off the thinner atmosphere or something — I don't know, I'm not meteorologist, as I'm sure the entirety of this paragraph indicates — but it looked pretty cool anyway.

Carting the tarmac required to make a road this far from Cusco must have been viewed as a pointless endeavour and it eventually petered out, leaving a rocky path in its stead, all the while taking us further up the rolling yellow hills and deeper into the Peruvian countryside. The last of Cusco's buildings were long gone and there was no one else around either, save for two female tourists around our age who coincidentally happened to be walking in the same direction as us further ahead. We were able to eventually catch up with them to ask if they were heading to this statue, hoping we'd be able to confirm we were heading in the right direction. They hadn't even heard of the statue — and were in fact going to a waterfall. It didn't take much conversation for them to realise mine and Mel's lack of plans and organisation, so they kindly asked if we wanted to join them for the day. Aside from a map they were carrying, they each had a huge bottle of water in a clear plastic container which glistened in the sunlight, that alone was enough to convince me to follow them like a little magpie that spotted something shiny, in the hope of having some for myself. Plus, I will take seeing something natural like a waterfall over a statue any day of the week. We spoke to our new friends and they told us about their lives. Both were backpackers, one from Canada and another from Switzerland, having met only a couple of days ago themselves at a hostel. Both had been travelling the continent for a year. Lucky gits.

Our group would need to stop every ten minutes or so as at least one of us would need a short rest to catch our breath in the thin air, trying to find shade under the occasional tree if one was available. Our friends took these breaks as an opportunity to pull some stuff out of their bags, usually a map and a compass to get their bearings. These guys looked like they'd come well-prepared for a hike, more so compared to me and Mel who'd only managed to bring jackets we weren't going to use and not enough water. After a moment of studying their equipment in silence, one of them pointed out the direction we needed to go — continuing over a nearby fence that happened to look like it might be part of someone's property, up more hills and further away from town. Without hesitation the two new girls began the climb over the fence. Mel and I looked at each other as we followed with our climb over, deciding if we should be going this far. I was at a crossroad — not literally, as I was now trespassing in someone's field, but figuratively — going on a bit of an adventure in foreign countryside is what I live for, but I suspected having no water would be an issue eventually, and every step took us further away from Cusco. Trespassing was the least of my concerns; Mel and I were now on a full on hike. Was this wise?

A dog's bark began to echo soon after climbing over, amplifying the suspicion that we were trespassing, and continuing further led us to a small collection of houses where the bark sounded like it might have been coming from. A villager in a traditional style shawl stood in the field at a distance from us, staring over in our direction. The four of us stopped and looked back, pondering the direction of where our next steps should be as the dog's bark continued. Attempting to break the awkwardness and diffuse any annoyance of our trespassing, Mel shouted across, "Hola señorita!" The words echoed across the mountains, but the figure didn't move and just watched us, saying nothing back.

"Say it again Mel, maybe she's deaf."

"HOLA SEÑORITA!"

Nothing but stares. We edged closer, the dog now visible on a chain and still barking at us. An "Hola señorita!" one last time from Mel. It became clear upon our approach that it wasn't in fact a 'señorita', but rather a man who looked really confused at Mel calling him a woman, likely explaining why he hadn't responded. He was actually really friendly once we got close enough; an old local man in a poncho, seemingly not bothered about the four wandering foreigners on his land, shaking our hands as soon as we got close enough. We stood around for a few moments smiling at him, and although he didn't speak English, he understood the word "waterfall". He pointed us in the direction and happily it almost matched the way the compass was telling us to go, so off we went.

I regretted not taking my opportunity to ask the 'señorita' for some water, as I could feel the blood in my body turning to paste. I was tempted to drink from a natural stream we found shortly after our encounter with the local, as was everyone else. I collected some in my empty water bottle for an inspection and honestly, I had never seen such clear water around in nature before. It was outstanding. Normally back home, water found outside is as brown as a turd with all sorts of shite floating about in it, but here it was as clear as bottled water from a stall. I took a swig, furthering my inspection. The only thing which was slightly off was the taste, which had a hint of decomposing leaves but was almost certainly fine to drink. However, as good as it was, I decided against swallowing it just in case I risked triggering the squits so early into the trip.

I couldn't remember the name of the waterfall they'd said earlier, I didn't even know where we were. Mel and I were totally in the hands of the strangers we had met. I'd have to guess the way back to Cusco now even if I decided to turn around. What I didn't know at the time was that we were heading to Balcón Del Diablo (translated as "The Devil's Balcony"), a small landmark of the area featuring a red rock cliff with a waterfall and small river underneath it; a nice quiet spot that had certainly been worth it after our couple of hours spent hiking to reach. The girls went off to explore and take photos, having found a little cave below the waterfall. I lay on the grass at the base of the waterfall by myself and just listened to the water running — it was a moment of absolute tranquility. It crossed my mind that I don't do things like this enough in normal life back home, just lying in the middle of nowhere with my mind half switched off, listening to the nature around me. My life at home is normally non-stop; commuting, work, talking to people all day, commute again, a couple of pints with Mel and the lads if I'm lucky, a bit of TV or writing to end my day, then a few hours' sleep; rinse and repeat. This actually felt like real down-time by this waterfall, and I very nearly fell to sleep with the first true peace I'd had in as long as I can remember. If the girls had forgotten me and left me there, I honestly wouldn't have been that bothered about it. They did, however, return and one of them cracked open a flask of coca tea that had been saved as a surprise. Fluid, but with stimulants in it too! The day couldn't have got any better.

Having assumed we'd be the only people this side of the 'señorita' from earlier, I was surprised to see another group of people appear from the bushes on the other side of the river who made their way to a small clearing in the foliage; a group of five white guys with an older native gentleman. I watched with curiosity as they set up a small gazebo and then the white guys, obvious to me now tourists, sat around the older gentleman whilst he spoke to them. They were too far away for me to make out what was being said, however the Canadian girl in our group informed me they will likely be undertaking a spiritual cleansing session, with the aid of a psychoactive brew called ayahuasca — the high from which would put my coca tea to shame. She had plans to do it in a few days elsewhere in the country and knew a bit about it. The main ingredient, called dimethyltryptamine (or DMT for short), gives a psychoactive high where the user trips hard for hours on end. It's a naturally-forming compound in many plant species around the world, but is found in high concentrations in a native species of vine in South America. The Indigenous peoples of Central and South America have taken it for centuries and each tribe, from Peru to Costa Rica, apparently have their own methods of preparing and administering it. For example, they may mix with another substance to alter the high slightly or go from mild to high doses. The end result is usually the same. It's not just a trippy experience like on LSD or magic mushrooms; people often cite ayahuasca trips as life-changing events where they look at themselves from a different perspective, mulling over their past and dealing with issues they have struggled with for years, often resulting in highly positive experiences. A proper ritual will last for days, and as the DMT hit wears off from day one, another dose will be used to top up again.

Signs that ayahuasca is working begins with vomiting and diarrhoea, then the intense tripping starts where you can pick away at the very fabric of reality, uncovering repressed memories and learning about yourself in ways you never thought about before. I can't quite wrap my head around a trip being that intense; the most 'out of it' I have ever been was trying mushrooms once as a teenager around my friend's house and experiencing amusing mild visuals, but mostly spent the evening with my mouth open, stroking a footstool having mistaken it for a dog. I watched on across the river as the old native bloke, known often in these rituals as a shaman, presented a container from his backpack and the white guys passed it around and drank from it. What a place to do it; coming out to South America is one thing to try such a mind-bending experience, but to do it after big trek in the hills away from the city was pretty mind bending in itself. Getting the doses wrong can be dangerous (although I presume rare for the experienced shamans) and of course, with the unpredictability of hallucinogenic drugs, they're not guaranteed a good trip at all and it can be a terrifying few hours. They lay down on the grass under the tent in silence for some time after their drink, not really moving much after that. I wanted to watch how they'd react, but it was getting on in the day and the girls said we should make a move back towards home. Dark clouds were brewing beyond the mountains and I hoped the little gazebo the lads were under was enough to protect them from getting soaked and ruining their experience.

We managed to beat the storm to Cusco before the rain came down, on a much easier walk downhill back to the town. I never thought that getting to 3,400 meters would be noticeably easier to breathe! Entering the first restaurant we could find on the outskirts of town, I consumed a large llama steak, (which had lodged in my mind from yesterday), and my body weight in water. We parted ways with our two new friends after swapping details with them, agreeing it had been a chance encounter which had worked out great. I imagined me and Mel still stuck up in the hills if the timing had been off for meeting them, soaked with rain having only just reached the statue, or lost and struggling with dehydration. With just a couple of hours left before nightfall, I nipped off for a quick pint in Cusco's only Irish pub whilst Mel went shopping around town for more rubbish t-shirts emblazoned with llamas on them. The Irish pub, just off the main square, claims to sell the highest pint of *Guinness* in the world — I had to try it. When I got there, it was the canned shite that's fizzed up with that electrolysis thing that's mounted on the bar. If you have no idea what I'm talking about then don't worry about it; it's a gimmicky way for bars to sell *Guinness* in a can, passing a small electrical current through it before it's served, fizzing it up ever so slightly and it is supposed to emulate the way a draught pint tastes. It doesn't, as it has still been sat in a can for months. I was impressed they had a load of native IPAs to try though, so all wasn't lost. I felt drunk off a single pint — for all of the downsides of high altitude, it evidently makes a piss-up cheap.

## Cusco, Peru — Wednesday, 25th October 2017

I awoke like a kid on Christmas morning: far too early and unable to get back to sleep with excitement, but instead of presents, I had an organised quad-biking day with a local activities company. The company were taking myself, Mel, and a large group of other tourists out of the town and into the countryside where we'd get to ride around on four wheels in a region called the Sacred Valley within the Andes, so-called because of the fertile soil which benefited the native Inca peoples many years ago and considered highly sacred because of it. I had been on a quad-bike only once before, in my early twenties, as a passenger to an eleven-year-old girl driver who was delivering hay to cattle on her parents' ranch in the Australian outback. It's a long story. She wasn't a particularly good driver as you might imagine, in fact the ride often dipped into terror in the moments she managed to leave the ground from hitting bumps in the fields. I'd survived the experience; moreover, it hadn't put me off having a go on a quad-bike myself all these years later. Riding one is quite exhilarating for the uninitiated, they're almost the same amount of fun as being on a motorbike with the wind in your hair, but with all the safety and stability that comes with four wheels — because let's face it, you can be a great motorbike driver but it's the other idiots on the road that will kill you. On today's excursion, those four deep-tread wheels allowed us to get around both on the highways and then off into the expanse of Peruvian wilderness. They're surprisingly quick too; we were hitting speeds of 40mph at times, which is noticeable when not protected inside a car chassis, leaving insects and kicked up pebbles from the vehicle in front to relentlessly hit me in the face. We flew across the countryside and down winding roads, cutting through little villages, over streams and around huge lakes. Despite the backdrop of snowy mountains like yesterday on the trek, it was quite dry and dusty on the tracks, passing through large expanses of yellowing vegetation and soil that had dried to the point of turning to dust which the quad- bikes kicked up. I think this whole quad-biking thing might have been pretty new to the rural Peruvians too, as some of them looked startled as a long convoy of quad-bikes tore through their towns. That said, in hindsight, were they startled, or were their faces displaying annoyance that their quiet little villages were being disrupted by gangs of tourists tearing through on noisy machines? If it is indeed called the Sacred Valley, then it certainly didn't feel all that sacred with our loud petrol engines and beefy tyres tearing up the place.

Villages within the Andes mountain range are few and far between, however, the Sacred Valley still appeared to remain fertile in modern times as multiple farms and ranches lay between the settlements in the vast countryside. The tour group pulled into one of these large ranches in the back end of nowhere, and the instructor told the group to pick a bench and sit down in preparation for lunch. Everyone obliged and formed in random groups, leaving the quad-bikes clicking as their engines cooled under the bonnets in the ranch's yard. Mel and I happened to sit on a bench with a couple of lads from Texas who, like many of the tourists we had encountered, had been backpacking around the continent for an extensive time. Straight off the bat they were telling us interesting tales of close calls and dodgy incidents from the past few months — I of course wanted to know the worst one of the lot.

"Lima. Trying to buy drugs last week." I liked their openness. They told me a story where they had been drinking at a bar in the capital and became friendly with a stranger. After a few hours of drinking with them, the stranger mentioned he knew a dealer who could get cocaine if they wanted some, which they did, so they all met in an alleyway behind the bar some time afterwards. It was dark outside by the time the dealer arrived. The dealer didn't originally realise that he would be selling to two foreigners and not Peruvians, so he did what any rational individual would do in this situation when the truth became apparent; he pulled a gun out and had it right up to one of the Texan's heads. The stranger translated to the Texans in a panic that the dealer was shouting about not liking surprises.

"We honestly thought we were going to die right there and then," one of the guys chipped in. "It was only because of the stranger managing to talk this dealer out of shooting us outright that we didn't. I thought it was a scam, but this stranger seemed genuinely scared we were gonna get a bullet."

"We still managed to buy the coke, we sorta had to at this point, and for about a tenth the price from back in the States," the other guy commented. "It was fuckin' good quality! We had too much left so had to flush it at the hostel before our flight to Cusco yesterday!"

I honestly don't get the drugs abroad thing. To each his own when it comes to taking it, I'm firmly in the camp that if it's your body, it's your right put into it what you like — providing you're aware of what it's doing to your body and the consequences. No one should have the right to say someone else is a criminal because they choose to take drugs. Foolish maybe, like the small chance those guys on ayahuasca yesterday lost their mind whilst being miles from civilisation; but that's their choice. But there's no way the high the Texans experienced on cocaine would ever been worth the risk of getting shot or arrested. What's the best case there, they get high for a few hours, versus all the stuff that could have gone horribly wrong? So, the dealer didn't end up shooting you in the head? Great. What about the police catching you instead? Prisons in South America are some of the most brutal in the world, risking years inside one of them because they had to do some coke with their beers? Just stay well clear kids, or at least take your heroin in your home country like a normal person.

After an early evening spent picking out dust from every crevice from the day's activities (I was astonished how much dust a single nostril can retain!), we met up with one of our friends from yesterday's trek at our hostel's bar. The full day of excitement had taken it out of Mel and she didn't touch her cocktail much, whereas me and our friend managed several in a short space of time. I know I was moaning a bit about hostels before, but I had missed the fun vibes of being in one; strangers from all over the planet hanging out, forming plans and bonds by taking on a new country together. This particular hostel had an excellent bar area along with pool tables and areas for drinking games, which is always a nice bonus if you can tolerate the noise from the dormitories. We started mingling with others in the bar after the alcohol levels in our blood picked up and met couple of American lads who invited our group over to have a game of Beer Pong which I reluctantly accepted. I never really got the idea of Beer Pong — you want to impede my drinking with a game? Beer Pong is such an American idea too; I honestly think it's a way to drag out a drinking session without actually drinking. We have a drinking game in Britain, and that's called getting drunk. Plus, now I've started having a pop at it: the ball of Beer Pong is hardly hygienic is it? Handled by everyone having a try of the game, and when the pissed-up idiot can't get it in the cup it bounces off the rim and rolls along the floor and around all the shite people have brought in with their shoes. I could have had three pints in the time it took us to finish a single game. With two cups left and tensions high between everyone on both teams (except for me, who couldn't give a fuck), the ball ricocheted from the edge of a cup and rolled right across the room. One of the American lads spotted it rolling away and informed the crowd that he had seen it "roll six feet under the bar", which made me laugh on a compete tangent because Americans still use imperial measurements. They battled the British for independence; went against our royalty, laws and even fought against our tea. And yet to this day they still use King Henry's foot as a unit of measurement. Mel sat at the sidelines trying to enjoy herself, watching on as several drunk people searched for a dirty ball that would soon end up in someone's drink, but she couldn't get into the mood and so decided to go to bed.

There was a group of about twelve people from Europe and the States who continued to drink at the bar after the game, among them two young Dutch girls. They were friendly and talking about their time here, telling the rest of our group that they had already spent an entire week in Cusco. The city was certainly nice but any more than a few days here, I imagined, would be too long. I asked what they had spent their time doing.

"You've not been to the nightlife yet, have you?" one of them said.

"Other than to this bar and the one with the fizzy Guinness in town," I replied, "then no." My interest was piqued.

"Well, we've found a really good nightclub, it's so much fun there. We're gonna go again tonight, you guys should join us." I was definitely up for this; the experience of foreign nightclubs is definitely one of the reasons I come to places like this. My new group of friends seemed keen for it too. However, simply joining the expedition was not so straight-forward as there was a fly in the ointment: my absent wife who was residing in bed. I had to either let her know that I wanted to go out to a local nightclub with a group of people I had only just met and risk her saying "No" to it or — and hear me out here — leave her to a much-needed rest and not have her worry about me off around town and up to my mischief somewhere. I opted for the latter, letting the multiple pints of ingested beer make the decision for me. The beer said it would be a shame if I had to sit back in the room and watch more TV in a language that I didn't understand instead of making the most of this opportunity for my last night in Cusco. Just after midnight, I was in a taxi filled with strangers driving across the city heading to God knows where.

I had no idea what Peruvian nightclubs might offer and did, for a moment, question how safe it was, as wherever you are in the world, nightlife can attract troublemaking clientele. Cusco felt safe, but we were still in the same country as Lima and the night-time there had been pretty scary so I couldn't be sure we'd experience a trouble-free night, even as part of a group of people. The taxi dropped us off on a narrow side street on the far side of town somewhere. Registering my surroundings through drunk vision, I found it reassuring to see two bouncers waiting at the top of a flight of stairs checking I.D., meaning they weren't just here for show. The Dutch girls nodded at the bouncers who recognised them as we passed, leading the way down the stairs into a small room that housed a busy dance area packed with people and flashing lights. I was honestly amazed to see a DJ belting out some half-decent dance music alongside, I shit you not, four men on stage dressed in traditional Peruvian clothing (woven ponchos and such), playing panpipes in front of microphones in time with the music. I'm not sure whether this is a standard thing that they do across the country or just at this particular nightclub, as it was certainly an odd combination; traditional wind instruments alongside a groovy electro dance beat, but it worked really well and the mix got the crowd bouncing.

Throughout the crowd I spotted a handful of tourists, but the majority of the four hundred punters were local young people, mostly lads, some of which were a bit persistent with the European girls in our group. As a male looking for a partner, you might slowly move up behind a dancing girl and start dancing too. This may lead to a term called "grinding" if she is interested, which is when she will gently rub her arse on the lad's groin area, in time with the music. It is something that happens in nightclubs across the globe. I'm not judging here, but it surely is the most primitive, baseline method to meet a partner that we have as a species. I've mostly been hopeless at it anyway trying to meet girls in the past; I dance awkwardly and so tend to rely on my personality outside the club in the early hours when most of the girls had been grinded away by the better-looking lads. Still, it's a very successful method for some fellas from what I've seen over my years spent in the nightclubs. The key part is understanding the etiquette to it; if she is interested she might stay around for a grind, or if not, she slinks off into the crowd and the male leaves her alone. The lads in Cusco would get a bit too close before the girl has even had time to establish who was behind her, and then follow them as they tried to move away. I might be thinking of the wrong film set in South America, I think its *City of God*, but there's this proper red-head guy hanging around with all the badass main characters. He looks odd, in a place where everyone has a great tan and dark hair, there's this redhead guy with strong ancestral genes lingering from the colonial days who must be really conscious of looking like a big ginger out in the tropics. We had one on the dance floor, initially attempting to talk to me several times in pure Spanish and then aggressively grinding behind the girls in our group, to the point where he quickly became an irritant. South American gingers must be as rare as hen's teeth. I'm told in nearby Argentina, gingers are considered bad luck by the general population and are often treated rudely as a result. If the rest of them are anything like this knob-head we had on the dance floor, I could see why. He began to upset the girls, so, acting like the tough guy that I definitely am not, I asked him to leave, pointing quite clearly for him to go. I spoke in English but I think he understood. He shouted at me in Spanish as a means of protest, but eventually left us to it and went back his group of Peruvian mates across the dance floor.

I managed several pints of the decent local beer and a few hours of dancing to some crunky Peruvian panpipe electro music. The Dutch girls were right; it was a good nightclub. I don't think worth staying here a week for, but still, there was definitely some fun to be had within these walls, and I didn't doubt the town had other hidden places like this around. The pints I had drunk had built up, so I let my new chums know that I was off to the toilet and would be back on the dance floor with them shortly. The coca tea leaves which were usually available for free in public buildings weren't anywhere to be seen in this club, as it appeared the patrons preferred the harder stuff — something I realised when I happened to walk in on several shady lads huddled together doing a drug deal in the toilets. I've walked in on deals taking place before in various pub toilets back home in England and it doesn't faze me, but I wanted to give any hard drug-related activity the widest possible berth in South America, especially when it concerned several dodgy native lads in a narrow toilet, and those Texan lads' gun story I'd heard earlier in the day still fresh in my mind. I thought it was best to leave these lads to it and come back later when they'd left, but then I wondered how that would look; seeing a deal going on then turning around and leaving may have seemed suspicious. A couple of them looked up and noticed me anyway so it was too late now, I had to go through with having a piss. Trying my best not to look like an under-cover copper, I shuffled through the lads, up to the urinal and unzipped my fly. I stood there for a moment, nothing happening, not even a drop. I began realising one of my worst fears was coming true — I had stage fright from being watched and couldn't urinate. This had only happened once before, when I was on a project out at sea off the coast of Indonesia with a group of men from the country's navy. With two hours spent off shore I needed to use the toilet, so the navy insisted I did it off the back of the small boat we were on. Stood astern of the boat with my cock out facing towards the vast Java Sea with the pressure of several tough Indonesian men looking on at me, I just couldn't get the wee to come out despite desperately needing to go. The fact no piss came out and I knew people were watching makes the situation worse and I find it even more difficult to piss, and there comes a point where I just have to give up and move on. To the onlookers it must have looked weird: I get up, stand with my todger out for several minutes without weeing, put it back in my fly then just sit back down. I was in the exact same position now, with several Peruvian dealers watching me not go, thinking to myself, 'Please work, even a few drops just to convince them I'm cool!'. Breaking the tension, the toilet door was forcibly pushed open by my ginger City of God mate from the dance-floor barging into the room. He started shouting about something, it could well have been directed at me by the look on his face, I have no idea to be honest. The dealers looked aggravated by his actions and instantly leapt on him to begin beating him up. I wasn't sure what was going on aside from the fact I knew I still couldn't piss, but as eyes had been taken off me I took my opportunity to shuffle past the fight and leave. I got back to the dance floor, told the group I'd had enough for tonight, left the building and nearly urinated myself on the bumpy taxi ride home.

I initially tried to be quiet getting back inside my hostel room, but it's hard when you're so drunk and come in barrelling towards the bathroom to use the toilet. I was greeted by a frosty "And just where have you been all night?", at four in the morning. I tried to justify to Mel that I could have spent the night by her side making sure she was okay, but it's likely the only time in my life I'd ever be in Cusco and I assumed she'd want me to have fun and enjoy the night-life. She definitely didn't want me to do that. I had a five-minute-solid wee, enjoying the lack of eyes on me, then crashed out on my bed with most of my clothes still on.

## Aguas Calientes, Peru — Thursday, 26th October 2017

"Oh fuck… what's the time…?!" Bright sunlight poured through gaps in the curtains, startling me as it did and thrusting me up out of my slumber. I grabbed my phone in a panic having realised I hadn't set an alarm last night before bed, and seeing it was nearly eleven in the morning was a problem. I shot up to a spinning room whilst Mel was still asleep. I nudged her, accidentally rather hard being in a panic, instructing her to wake up right this instant. With our combination of her developing a sickness overnight and me very hungover (or rather still a bit drunk), we had both overslept and were pushing the time for our lift to the train station for our onwards journey deeper in the Andes. Ah — the rushed, hungover stuffing of items into my backpack and racing out of the door onto my next destination — how I'd missed doing this in my old glory days of backpacking! No time to shower or brush our teeth.

"Have we left anything in the room?!"

"I don't think so!"

Room door slammed shut, keys thrown at reception, grabbing a handful of the coca tea leaves to blow the cobwebs off as we left (and just in case they didn't have it at the next destination!), and we were off on our way. The day ahead travelling was longer than we had anticipated; a couple of hour taxi ride followed an equally long train journey through the Peruvian Andes with us both not feeling too hot.

The town of Aguas Calientes (translating simply to "Hot Water" in English) was our last stop before Machu Picchu. It's a small town nestled in a picturesque mountain valley with a river running through it, and since the town was founded a hundred years ago the local economy has been primarily fuelled by passing tourists trying to get to the neighbouring world wonder, evidently even more so in the age of international travel. For those not attempting the Inca trail, it's the last place you'll find a bed and hot food before reaching the landmark. With a tropical warmth and humidity compared to the higher altitude of Cusco, noticeable once stepping out onto the streets from a long train ride, the town offered quaint wooden buildings up to three stories high, squeezed in between each other. Some of these were cute little restaurants and trinket shops, often with balconies overlooking the town. Multiple wooden bridges crossed the river which split the town in half. There were also sign-posts for hot water springs available to swim in, hence the name of the town I guess, and every part of it looked enticing for a first-time tourist. It would have made for a great afternoon spent exploring if we'd been in any fit state. Fucked if we could be bothered though, both Mel and I arrived as rough as toast for our different reasons and so we only saw a fraction of it all on the walk to the hotel, hoping to aim straight for a bed.

Waiting for us at the hotel's reception was a short middle-aged native man dressed in striking traditional clothing (who looked like he might have come straight off the stage with the panpipe crew from the club last night), along with another tourist couple also from England. He'd come as an extra as part of a package we'd booked to the site which gave us a room in town and a local who'd escort us around the site tomorrow. I thought he'd just be meeting us in the morning or something. What was he doing here now? I couldn't honestly be bothered talking to him as he had come out of nowhere and began interfering with me getting straight into my bed. He shook our hands and sat us and the other couple down at the reception's foyer, imparting advice for the big day tomorrow in his slightly unusual grasp of English. "Bring shoe that's soft inside"-style information. The preparation talk didn't take too long to be fair, but just before departing the swine dropped a bombshell informing us that we had to meet him at the town's bus station at 3am. I was absolutely pained by the thought of meeting at that time, it probably meant waking up as early as 2AM too as Mel would need her usual time to get ready. She'll be damned if she hasn't got her make up on for those *Instagram* snaps for something as epic as a Wonder of the World. As rough as it all sounded, if it ultimately led to an interesting early sunrise walk around Machu Picchu to beat the mass tourist crunch, I was game for it, I suppose.

### Aguas Calientes, Peru — Friday, 25th October 2017

3.05AM. It was dark outside as we stepped outside from the hotel, and we were both tired. I brewed a strong concoction of the coca tea hoping it would be enough to combat the overall lack of sleep I'd had since arriving into the country. Coincidentally, we happened to set off through the doors of the hotel's reception at exactly the same time as the English couple that we'd briefly met with the guide last night. I was secretly worked up about this as it made me have to politely force a conversation with them, which I really couldn't be bothered with at this time of the morning. As the river cuts straight through Aguas Calientes, crossing to each half of the town means you are reliant on the several bridges scattered over said river. Mel and I walked in silence listening to the annoyingly sprightly English couple whilst following the river through the town, our brains so tired and pickled that even picking which bridge to cross to the bus station required some thought. I soon noticed a long row of people sat on a road parallel to the river, fifty people at least, trailing along the kerb to the bus station. At first, I thought it was perhaps lots of homeless people, then I realised they were dressed too much like tourists. I asked one of the people sat on the floor, "What's going on here?"

"This is the queue for the bus station to Machu," he laughed, "the buses start in two hours my friend!".

It turns out we weren't going for a night walk around the site, then to clock a nice sunrise over some ancient ruins — we were going to sit on a kerb for no less than two hours to beat the other five thousand visitors that descend upon the site every day. The bus is the only reasonable route there; the alternative is a two-hour steep uphill trek which Mel definitely didn't like the idea of. We sat down at the end of the queue, feeling a bit defeated about the situation. Our guide soon showed up as promised, said hello, squeezed onto the kerb near us, sat down and fell asleep.

I hadn't really come prepared for a two-hour homeless man simulation, so with nothing to occupy me I just sat there on the kerb with my mouth open staring at the moths bumping into the streetlights. A welcome bit of entertainment came an hour into our wait as two stray dogs appeared in the middle of the road and started shagging almost directly in front of me. The street erupted in laughter and people threw over bits of food for them, the dogs both trying to eat and shag at the same time. If reincarnation exists, I'm coming back as a stray dog if this is the life they get to live. Mel lay on the pavement trying to sleep as my mind began to wander with boredom, and some more time passed with nothing to do other than watch the moths again. These moths were significantly bigger than the ones we have at home, but no matter the size, they still act the same around the world over — goth butterflies that are obsessed with bashing their heads against lights. Did you know that moths aren't just attracted to lights? They love beer as well apparently. Mix a bit of beer with a banana, stick it to a tree and watch the greedy little shites flock to it. Well, that is if they have mouths to begin with — did you know some are born without mouths and live only a day? These moth facts are as about as entertaining as my time spent sat on that kerb. It was dismal. The numbers of people arriving increased by the minute, poor tourist suckers finding themselves joining a now lengthy queue that went on for hundreds of people — I admit it was mean-spirited, but I found it rather funny to see their faces drop upon realisation of the long queue of individuals that had made it here before them. Some had arrived independently of any tour group and obviously had not been made aware to get here really early, and would pace up and down for some time either looking stunned or wondering if there was a way to cut in.

Mel's stomach rumbled, not with hunger from missing breakfast but due to her ongoing illness causing an urgent need to take a shit somewhere, and she asked the guide if he knew of a toilet. He said no problem and told me to wait there — I wasn't sure if that was an attempt at a joke — and that they'd both be back in around ten minutes. In their spot left a gap next to me in the now ridiculously massive queue for the bus station. I peered out along the line and several hundred tourists sat on the kerb, a row of faces looking as fed up as mine which trailed off down the street and beyond into the darkness. Two agitated French women had been hovering around in my vicinity not long after Mel and the guide had left — I could see what they were up to, and they soon moved over and straight into the gap. I was just about to tell them that the spot was taken, but angered fellow queuers took the lead instead, shouting things like "What are you doing!", "You can't cut in!", some were even concerned enough to outright shout "Fuck off, idiots!". The French women didn't move and put up quite a fight for their new spot, their weak argument being they had lost their friends and wanted to wait here for them. It became so heated at one point that a big Indian man behind them in the queue stood up ready to deck them out. Their audacity was almost admirable as it took some balls to stay there for a full three minutes enduring abuse and insults. They finally buckled and retreated to the back of the queue, fading into the darkness as they walked away never to be seen again.

At 5AM, we finally embarked on one of the first buses to depart from the station and it was such a good feeling to be off that bloody kerb. The old bus weaved uphill several miles to the site, bypassing hikers who must have found the long queue of people this morning far too intimating to try and join and decided that walking was quicker. Multiple tourists poured off several buses and rushed up to large iron gates leading to the entrance to the site, with their passports ready as a condition of entry. The site is essentially the ruins of a rich man's estate, specifically the Inca emperor Pachacuti from nearly six hundred years ago. As you can imagine, time and mother nature hasn't been kind to the brickwork, leaving all of the remaining walls worn down. Most are only at waist height. Many of the foundations of the general layout are still there, including the rows of terraces that were used for farming to support the seven hundred and fifty inhabitants, so you can still get a feel for what it would have been like there. It's situated high on large hill in a valley and there was low hanging cloud that day, partially blocking any complete vistas for us, but those first few minutes once we got onto the site, plus what the clouds allowed us to see still left us awestruck. The ruins and scenic mountains in the background poking up to the clouds looked striking and several llamas had been let loose to do their thing around the site, giving that extra Peruvian stereotype for the tourists' photos. The guide, as genuine, friendly and valuable as he had been with his insider tips on getting us here early, had quickly became a nuisance. As far as I was concerned, we had been awake since stupid o'clock to beat the crowds, now was the time for our photos before the bulk of tourists arrived in the background, and just to soak it all up whilst it was still quiet. This wasn't on his schedule, and he sat us down on a wall by the entrance and spoke to us for twenty minutes about the site. I wasn't hugely interested about the finer details like the names of the people who lived here on exactly what year, what the bricks were made out of; I could read up about in my free time if I really wanted to know this, but I didn't want to be rude to a man who was clearly passionate about this subject. After a few minutes I stood up and asked if we could walk around whilst he talked, he told me to sit back down on the wall and listen, so I timidly sat back down. A massive group of photo ruining tourists walked past us, free to go wherever they wanted, meanwhile I was learning from the guide that fifteen different types of potatoes used to be grown in the courtyard. This is not what I wanted to be doing.

Mel's sickness turned out to be a Godsend; she needed the toilet again so we had to interrupt the guide and leave him with other the English couple. Unsurprisingly, there are no working shithouses around an ancient Inca ruin so it takes a bit of a time to get to a toilet at the main entrance and come back in through the gate. Bowels emptied and site re-entered, our group had moved on from the wall we had left them at, and we couldn't find them after spending about 0.05 seconds of bothering to look, so we were free to go off and do our own thing entirely.

Although the entirety of Machu Picchu is spread across a huge eighty thousand acre site, most of where the ruins lie can be seen within a morning. This still takes a few hours of walking though, often up steep steps and along hillsides, so being physically fit is a must (or, at the very least, unfit but determined!). I imagine Peru's government, who own the site in modern times, are keen to retain some of the authenticity and so are reluctant to modernise too much, like levelling paths with tarmac, or installing toilets and handrails. Instead, you're often left with a load of uneven rocks lumped together to create a pathway, or big treks up hillsides with nothing stopping a rather steep fall down. Sections of the site are impossible to travel in a wheelchair, and I could see those who were overweight were struggling to navigate around in general. I was impressed to see a large American lady attempt a big climb up to an area called The Sun Gate. This is situated up what feels like a small mountain – it got the blood pumping even for a relatively fit person like me as it took nearly an hour of uphill walking to reach. The trek also required concentration on where my feet were being placed as the rocks weren't always level and misplaced footing could have resulted in a long fall. Once reaching the top, it gives an excellent view, possibly the best view anywhere here as you are able to see the main sections of Machu Picchu's ruins nestled among the landscape. The large American lady, who was red-faced and clearly not having fun on the climb up, surprised me and eventually made it to the top. She clearly had to let everyone in her proximity know that she was having a hard time as we'd hear the occasional "God damn rock in ma' shoe again!" or "Not more damn steps!" as she'd turn a corner and see the path continued further upward, but overall it was a fantastic effort from her. I was impressed with Mel too, who had managed the climb in her sickly state with only minimal complaints. We stayed for some time at the Sun Gate to soak up the view once we had found the remnants of a wall to sit on, enjoying the coca tea once again as the pockets of thick morning cloud dissipated, giving way to a clear view of the mountains surrounding the valley. Though there had been a notable increase in tourists since we had arrived (we could see them still piling in from the main entrance even all the way up here), many couldn't be bothered with the trek up to the Sun Gate so it's certainly a little hidden gem if you don't like crowds of people.

There's a rather mystical beauty about the place. Part of it, I think, is thanks to the distinct lack of modern developments anywhere nearby other than the entrance; it's literally just ruins set far out in the South American countryside. Compare that to the Pyramids of Egypt, which is practically neighbours with a *KFC*. It takes a couple of days to get to this remote part of South America, even when relying on modern transport, and because of all this it does actually leave visitors with a feeling of stepping centuries into the past. No toilets or gift shops and their litter, nor annoying sellers and their Peru Wars t-shirts. I know it's not particularly friendly for those with accessibility issues, but the lack of handrails and tarmac paths definitely helps to retain its ancient charm. Ah — accessibility issues, I realised hadn't seen the American lady for some time now at the Sun Gate so I assumed she'd had enough and made her way back down the hill. Midway on our descent we came across a small gathering of people who were busy looking down a steep embankment to the side of the pathway. We of course hovered around for a bit to see what the fuss was about. They were focused on a recently flattened strip of vegetation which went into the valley and into some trees at the bottom. One of the people informed us that a poor American lady had lost her footing and rolled down the hill, flattening anything in her path. I guess a reduction in authenticity by installing handrails wouldn't have been such bad thing after all; especially if it prevents terrible accidents like this. Luckily, one of the crowd of bystanders said he was the lady's husband, and also mentioned he was a doctor, so if they did manage to haul her up I'm sure she'd be fine. It's a shame she wasn't married to a crane operator, though, as that would have come in more useful.

We poked around the ruins for some time after getting back to the base of the site, discovering many small roofless rooms, or multiple rows of neatly formed walls used for farming. Whilst it was interesting being within the ruins themselves, we agreed we had enjoyed viewing them from the Sun Gate rather than being down amongst it all with the steady increase of tourists. We'd had long day despite only being lunch time, and we'd seen all we had the energy for. It left us with a few hours to kill before the train back to Cusco, so with nothing else left to do, we decided to pass the time back at Aguas Calientes. Getting back was considerably easier; rucks of tourists were still piling in the other direction which meant our return bus was virtually empty.

I leaned over from a restaurant's balcony to overlook the main street. We had found a great little bar at the side of town and I had discovered a primary spot for some people watching. I was dazed from tiredness but nevertheless quite relaxed with a beer in hand, observing all the tourists below slowly returning from the ruins, that is, until being snapped out of my moment by the sensation of a sudden sharp pain on my elbow. I looked down and was aghast to see a little insect on it. What the hell? I quickly whacked it, killing it, but leaving a splatter of blood around the murder site. Then I saw on the rest of my arm there were six or seven other little blood marks across them where it seemed like a feeding frenzy had taken place. To my horror I had been silently attacked by sand flies. I had almost believed the existence of these little blood feeding flies to be nothing more than myth; I had met other travellers before who told me about being attacked by the little bastards in high numbers. I wondered whether people had them confused with mosquitoes or something, having never actually seen little flies land on me to suck blood before, and certainly having not been bitten by one myself as far as I was aware. This is considering I have spent a good couple of years in the tropics across my lifetime too. Well, there's a first time for everything — I had let my guard down and become a buffet for them sat on this balcony. Mel was unscathed. Blood suckers don't seem as attracted to Mel as they do me; when out in Asia she will rarely get bitten whilst I'll have ten itchy bite marks on my ankles alone. I joke with her that they prefer me over her because I'm the exotic one in the tropics, and whilst there might be some truth to that with unacclimatised people supposedly producing more attractive scents to mosquitoes in hot weather, the joke's on me because the lumps they leave itch like buggery for days, never mind the risk of disease they carry with them as well. These sand fly bites somehow managed to be even worse than a mosquito's as it left a much harder and itchier lump. Panicked, I went to my go-to source of third-rate information and anxiety fuel: the internet. According to it, the itchy lump on occasion may host a little parasite called Leishmaniasis that has now set up home there, transferred via the fly's feed. This parasite can cause all sorts of health problems like swollen organs and death, leaving me with something to just mildly worry about in the background over the coming days as I waited for symptoms to develop. I really take issue with these blood-sucking parasites; aside from the fact their horrible little tongue things have entered my body to extract my blood, they are then using my blood to create more of the little bastards. Your blood is used to make more of them? Congratulations, you're now technically 33% its parent. It's a horrible system, and I hate it.

We took a train back to Cusco, arriving during a rainy evening, back to the same hostel before our excursion. Even whilst out on the road, there's something endearing about returning to a hotel or hostel if you've been away from it for a little while, coming back to a familiar layout with the familiar faces working at reception, or indeed the fellow patrons. In this case, bumping into the two Dutch girls from my first Peruvian nightclub experience two nights ago. They both recognised me as I entered reception and, almost surprised by my sudden presence, went for hug to greet me. Mel looked a little startled that two seemingly random strangers had greeted me in this way as she'd not met either whilst being sick in bed. I couldn't believe they were still in Cusco, but when quizzed about it, they had now both lost their passports and were stuck here until they could get back to the Dutch embassy in Lima. All was not lost, they told me, as they still had that nightclub to enjoy and were in fact about to head out shortly, but were just waiting for a friend that they had met in Cusco "who has ginger hair" to arrive. In the remote chance my mate from the nightclub toilets was currently on his way over, I decided retiring to bed was probably my best bet, plus we had an early flight to catch tomorrow.

# BRAZIL

### Foz do Iguaçu, Brazil — Saturday, 23rd October 2017

I had enjoyed my time in Peru, but I was ready to move on after a week there and to be honest, both Mel and I had been looking forward to Brazil more out of the two countries. Brazil offered more iconic items on the bucket list; the city of Rio de Janeiro alone had two world-renowned beaches and the Christ the Redeemer statue to name a few. Before our time in Rio though, we had a two day stop at a town called Foz do Iguaçu in the south of the country. There wasn't a great deal of literature available online about the town; *Wikitravel* offered a few paragraphs, and some other sites offered basic details, but nothing substantial for tourists to get stuck into. Being situated in South America, I expected a small sort of town, possibly suffering from bad infrastructure, unsafe to walk around in parts, definitely rural. It just showed my preconceived ideas of the continent really, and how wrong they were once there, instead we found a clean and attractive town that was actually quite developed. Big, deep black newly-tarmacked roads, rows of attractive middle-class bungalows of different sizes and colours with big gardens and exotic flora surrounding them, and multicoloured tropical birds sat on telephone wires chirping away; all reminding me of the suburbs of Australian towns I had visited on previous travels which is something I did not expect to find. We encountered a few more English speakers than in Peru, one of which was our bedsit owner, pointing out it was quite safe to go walking around in the daylight, but to be careful beyond the main boundaries of the town. Taking her advice, a late-afternoon walk around the streets left me delighted to spot stereotypes of the country such as groups of kids playing football barefoot in the streets, vibrant graffiti sometimes featuring the national flag emblazoned along walls, and a small garden party with the native samba music playing in the background. One particular Brazilian stereotype I was keen to get involved with was the country's love of grilled meat. We stumbled across a Brazilian steak house during the walk and it was everything I could have hoped for. Disappointment like guinea pig was nowhere near the menu, it was all proper food — a pile of steak with fried eggs on top, fried bananas, chips, rice and veg. As much as I had enjoyed Peru, the food had been a bit hit and miss and this first meal here in Brazil had topped anything I had eaten on the trip so far. They say the way to a man's heart is through his stomach, and my love for Brazil would only grow from here.

# Foz do Iguaçu, Brazil — Sunday, 24th October 2017

The borders of Brazil, Paraguay and Argentina meet in the same region of South America, in a specific area called The Three Frontiers, with each country separated by the confluence of two large rivers. Between the rivers there cascade an incredible 275 waterfalls across a two-mile strip, so seeing this impressive creation of nature had been the reasoning behind our two-day detour to the south of the country. As I mentioned earlier, there wasn't a great deal about the town or surrounding area available to research and at first it wasn't entirely clear whether or not we'd be able to see the falls within walking distance from Foz do Iguaçu (the town name itself translates as mouth of the river Iguaçu). We'd later learn that we'd need to take a fifteen-minute taxi out of town to the south-Brazilian border to see the falls via a particular tourist viewing site. The language barrier appeared, giving us troubles with several taxi drivers who couldn't quite understand where we wanted to go, nor the prices for taking us there. Unbelievably, we happened across one taxi driver who spoke German so Mel was able to communicate with him, as she speaks German like a big show-off. It was quite interesting to learn that there was a huge community of German speakers in the town; descendants from people who moved over from Europe after World War Two. Many of the younger generations have never actually been to Germany despite using the German language for their entire lives here, at least within their community, and many like the taxi driver carried admiration for a motherland that they had never been to. I sat there listening to Mel and the driver talk about this all, not understanding a single word but still appreciating it. I love language, it really fascinates me how you can make a sound out of your head that is enough to convey a thought or idea to someone else, more so in this instance that two people from complete other sides of the world — an Asian and a South American, using a language from Europe to talk to each other.

The driver dropped us off at a large car park near the border and bid us auf wiedersehen. Once past the ticket booth, I wasn't quite expecting such a large site featuring a modern café and toilet facilities, packed with tourists, set in a clearing in the jungle which ran along one of the rivers. None of this had popped up when I was trying to do research about the area. Due to travel restrictions on Mel's Indonesian passport which prevented her from getting a visa on arrival in neighbouring Argentina (interestingly, the option was open to me on my British passport despite tensions still existing between the UK and Argentina over Argentina's claim over the Falkland isles), we were limited to viewing the falls exclusively on the Brazilian side. Not that it mattered; we could see the majority of the falls from where we stood as most of the water appeared to fall into Brazil from Argentina. How many different angles do you need to see a waterfall from, anyway? A pathway ran along a clearing next to the large river which collected the waterfall run-off, with water impressively falling from a hundred metres high in some places, creating a fine mist; enough to make my clothes wet if I stood around gawping for too long. Sections of the site were wholly impressive, at times I could see perhaps 40 or 50 separate waterfalls in a panoramic view all at the same time. I had never seen anything like it before.

Occasionally, a small wooden viewing platform would appear that could take tourists off the main path, leading them directly above the river where impressive views of either the falls or the huge drop to the river below could be witnesses. As there wasn't many of these platforms available, time on them was valuable and queues were often formed with people waiting for their turn. Keen for some photos from one of them, Mel and I duly fell into line with everybody else. The queue moved slowly, but it was understandable as other tourists here had spent several minutes queuing and so wanted to make the most of their time. During our wait, a young blonde woman pushed in front of everyone, forcing her way to the platform without looking behind and started focusing on her camera by taking photos of the falls. The queue was outraged, myself included. They say British people invented the idea of queuing and these days it's ingrained in our culture — like drinking tea or glassing a football rival in the pub (that's right folks, in Britain, 'glass' can also be a verb). One way to really piss us off is to push in when we're queuing. I was furious — I think the French chancers from the bus queue for Machu Picchu were still fresh in my mind.

"There's a queue here, mate!" I shouted at her amongst the torrent of angry Portuguese she was already getting from the Brazilian majority of the crowd. Of course, when she spoke back, quelle surprise, she was also French.

She replied back to the crowd, "But I do not like to queue!", and her arrogance really twisted my tits. I think I would have been less annoyed if she had just insulted us all instead. The French being French continued shortly after as we waited in line for a bus back to town, and I could see a French couple eyeing up a way to jump the queue. I've noticed the only way to keep French people in line is if they literally have tight narrow metal fences to keep them in, much like cattle. The rest of us had queued in a narrow waist-height barrier for the bus, maybe no more than half a meter of width across. The French couple walked all the way around trying to find a way to cut out the queue, realised they couldn't, and by the time they started their way back through the entire route of the cattle barriers, the bus had driven off without them. It was an absolute delight for me to see from the rear bus window. The falls were great, I would just rather use words in my book to moan about French people.

With our activity ticked off the list, that afternoon we found ourselves drinking at a bar in the centre of Foz do Iguaçu on a busy main road. I loaded up a map on my phone out of curiosity, just to have a look at the immediate area we were sat in. Despite finding the idea of borders ridiculous — lines drawn in the dirt that you can't cross without a little book containing a picture of your face in, utter madness! — still, I find myself oddly interested in them and how they've been formed by people over the years. Three countries meeting in the same area certainly warranted a quick scan across *Google Maps* whilst drunk in a bar.

"Hey," I said to Mel, "Do you wanna see Paraguay?", noticing how close we were to the border. "It's a ten-minute walk to the river, and we'll be able to see the country right across it!"

She agreed to the idea, although a little apprehensively. There's a slight edge to being out and about in South America, a point that I'm sure I've conveyed enough in the paragraphs above, but it felt particularly prominent being within the first 24-hour period of a new country having not fully assessed the culture yet. That said, other than my weird two minutes in a Peruvian nightclub toilet, we'd not really encountered any major safety issues so far on the trip. Plus, didn't our bedsit host say it was mostly safe in daylight anyway? Paraguay didn't appear to be too far from the high street looking at the map, so I was sure we'd be fine. Plus, there's nothing like that feeling of unjustified confidence once you've had a few beers.

It only took a minute or so of walking, leaving the bustling high street as we started our approach to the border, to find our surroundings become eerily quiet. We seemed to be the only souls around. None of the buildings appeared occupied; some were municipal, some residential, there was even a small Brazilian navy base, but they all appeared shut. It was a Sunday in a Catholic country, which might have explained the calm. The only indication there might be others around was loud thumping dance music in the distance towards the border, and what faintly sounded like a load of people having a decent party. Was there a bar nearby here, perhaps, or some sort of border rave going on that we could crash in on? We carried on a few more minutes expecting to see the river separating the two countries, hoping for an impressive view to go with it. It wasn't the case; there would be yet more road to walk down, taking us further and further away from the safety of the high street. Maybe I had misjudged this "ten-minute walk" I had told Mel about. There was one last house before the road turned into a country lane — a small rickety bungalow which was in massive need of some DIY. A couple of red-neck-looking types sat watching us from the porch, drinking bottles of beer whilst their kids played on the doorstep and among the trash and breeze blocks lying around in the garden. Neither of them took their eyes off the two obvious exploring foreigners walking by.

It's quite easy to forget when inside built-up areas such as towns in the tropics they can only be a stone's throw away from dense jungle. We were soon on a small dirt road with thick vegetation all around us that partially blocked out the sunlight. We were beginning to feel like this venture might not be the best idea, with a subtle hint of dread. The road had a slight declining slope which encouraged me to press on, thinking it must lead to either the riverbank or this party we could hear, however it didn't matter to Mel at this point who'd had enough and didn't want to continue. The thumping music echoed around us, making it hard to pinpoint the exact location, but it did seem to get louder as we moved closer to the border so surely, we must have been on the right path? I left Mel on the road briefly as I scouted ahead down a steep embankment through some bushes to try and see if we were anywhere near the river. It was fairly difficult to navigate dealing with both the declining slope and vegetation, likely home to a few poisonous snakes or spiders, and yet despite this, I valiantly pressed on until I managed to stumble into a clearing that was in fact someone's back garden. Several dogs came running towards me, barking aggressively. I put my hands up shouting "Whoa whoa whoa!", ready to boot one of them if they got too close. A fat, shirtless man followed the dogs from out of a bungalow with a baseball bat in his hands and shouted, "NO FURTHER!". I guess he could tell I was a tourist if he had shouted at me in English. I apologised and backed off and up the hill with the dogs snarling at my feet, but even they weren't daft enough to follow me back up through the bushes, my heart was pumping flat out from this exercise and adrenaline. It wasn't quite enough to deter me just pushing on a bit more once back on the road though, and my persistence eventually paid off as I got to see a small glimpse of Paraguay. Unfortunately, Mel was too short to peer through a small gap through the bushes and trees, so it had all been a waste of time for her. She wasn't missing out on anything special if I'm being honest — I could just about see a few young lads riding around in circles on motorbikes on some docks across the river, setting firecrackers off whilst others were swigging beer and falling about looking drunk. The buildings that I could see seemed to be dilapidated, possibly as part of an abandoned industrial estate, certainly not looking as nice as anything we'd seen from the Brazilian side of the river. The party noise could well have been from those lads; it was hard to tell as I was struggling to get a good view of anything through the jungle. Mel was done with it here and, underwhelmed by our experience, we decided to turn around and leave.

The feeling of being alone was finally broken by a car that began approaching from further down the road. Unusually, the car's engine sounded like it was in high revs, as if the car was moving considerably quicker than you might expect on this sort of narrow country lane. It didn't sound right at all. As we were quite far from safety now and to hear a car approaching our direction quickly, we decided our best course of action here was to panic and run back up the hill. I shouted over to Mel as we began sprinting, "Just pretend we're joggers in case anyone dodgy is coming!". This quickly thought-up plan would not work on two counts: both of us were in Hawaiian shirts and sunglasses, totally not dressed right for any jogging; and secondly, as if being a jogger would make any difference to any would-be assailant. Choosing flight over fight turned out to be justified as the car had sped right up to us and, once it joined our position, intimidatingly trailed behind at our running speeding instead of passing us by. I glimpsed behind and was horrified to see the car was packed full of young, scary ruffian types sporting the classic "I'm going to cause trouble" attire; big gold chains and caps on backwards. We had strolled too far out of the safe area, and I had encouraged my wife to do it like an idiot. Giving the best jogger impression we could muster up as sweat poured out of us, we managed to make it to the last house with the red-necks still outside, and at that point the car started to slowly overtake us. As they crawled past with music blasting out of the car windows drowning out the dance music across the river in Paraguay, all eyes within the car were staring at the two sweaty tourists in floral shirts. I just kept thinking to myself, "Go on, please keep driving past!" They sped off after about a minute of following us, onwards towards the main high street. We ran straight back to the main road, relieved to see open shops and people going about their business.

We sat on a wall by the high street, giving ourselves a moment to catch our breath.

"Paraguay, my ass," Mel said as soon as she composed herself, clearly quite annoyed. We both agreed after the rapid breathing allowed us to talk properly that the little excursion there would be the last time we were going to wander off the main path in these sorts of places again.

## Rio de Janeiro, Brazil — Monday, 30th October 2017

We'd timed two nights in Foz do Iguaçu well, as we might have run out of things to do had we planned any longer there. In contrast, we had given ourselves over a week at our next destination, Brazil's famous coastal city of Rio de Janeiro, where we had plenty to check off our list. Of course, we wanted a few days idling on the two world-famous beaches, Ipanima and Copacabana, plus a guided venture in the potentially dangerous shanty areas — or, to use the correct term for them, favela. Plus, no visit to Brazil is complete without seeing Christ the Redeemer. Mel squealed with excitement as we could see the towering statue off in the distance through the taxi window from the airport, taking blurry photos of it as she simply couldn't wait. If you're not familiar with all of the details then it's a white, 38 metre reinforced concrete statue of Jesus stationed on a 700 metre mountain right at the edge of the city. It looms prominently over the streets and is visible in most places, ironically overseeing the goings on within one of the most dangerous cities in the world. Blurry photos could wait as far as I was concerned, we were going to see the thing up close in a few days.

Rio was a different world from Lima. It appeared clean, the streets packed with people dressed in trendy clothes amongst expensive high street outlets and, most notably in comparison to Lima for the moment, the ride was smooth as there wasn't a single pothole in sight — although this all may have been attributed to our taxi ride from the airport passing through one of the city's more affluent districts. I was well aware that all of Rio doesn't look this good, and there are heavily impoverished expanses surrounding the city where the quality of life of residents is extremely poor. The people of Rio are split into two main communities, the haves and the have nots; the relatively wealthy who live in the areas that are generally based more around the lowland by the coast, and the poor who reside in the favelas areas up on the hills surrounding the city. There's a strong sense of this duality of life here. It's evident when people from the favelas enter other parts of Rio, as they stand out with scruffy clothes, often sitting idle on the streets, sometimes begging; whereas it's generally not safe for outsiders — both tourists to the city and locals from Rio — to enter the favelas. That's not to say all those that live in the favelas are dangerous, but there are dangerous people that can be found in there. Murders, car jackings and gun crime do happen around the city, not just within the favelas, and it's an endemic problem for the majority of the developed areas of Brazil. Travel advice often mentioned that muggings can occur at any time, even in broad daylight, and sometimes with the use of guns. If you were to ever find yourself in this situation, unless you really value your wallet, you are advised to comply with everything said, removing all items from your pockets, and try to remain looking down at the floor in case the mugger thinks you're trying to remember their face to report to the police afterwards. Then after they've left with your valuables and your life intact, you can piss your pants or however else you feel best to process the mad minute you've just had. It's worth saying right here and now that there's nothing worth stealing from my wallet. Best they'd get from mine is two bank cards (that I would instantly cancel), a Morrison's More card (they wouldn't be able to cash the points out here — I checked), and a dusty old condom (the latex has likely perished as it's been in there since I've been married). I suppose a would-be mugger doesn't know this though, and it's a risk he's willing to take in case there is something worthy buried inside. It was quite hard to fathom that I could be a target anywhere here, especially as I passed through modern trendy shops and cafés of the city, which gave off safe beach resort vibes like I'd maybe find in Europe rather than somewhere that I could have my life threatened for an old condom. It was also far hotter than Lima, or anywhere we'd been on this trip, easily reaching the low thirties before midday even though we were by the coast.

Rio has two main beaches; the shorter Ipanema, the ever-so-slightly trendier of the two, which runs on the south of the city, sits in contrast to the five-kilometre-long Copacabana that runs concave to the east of the city. Together, they make up a large section of the city's coastline. I'm not usually the biggest beach fan, but they were both stunning and I could see why they were world-famous — it's not just for the long stretches of white sand only a couple of minutes' walk from the city centre; there are convenient small bars scattered where the city's concrete meets the beach's sand, along with the scenery of palm trees, picturesque hills poking out from the haze generated by the sea in the distance, and, well, just the vibe of the place. Locals were playing football barefoot in the sand, whilst others had set up barbecues. Attractive men and women walked by, sometimes wearing next to nothing. I actually became annoyed by how attractive they all were, feeling short-changed growing up as part of a genetic cul-de-sac in rural England and the horrors it had shat out, myself included. Tanned models of perfectly formed flesh passed us in ridiculous quantities on both Ipanema and Copacabana, and it aggravated me greatly.

### Rio de Janeiro, Brazil — Friday, 3rd November 2017

Mel's Indonesian skin had turned a lovely shade of golden brown from a couple of days spent on the beach, soaking up the rays of Brazil's high UV index. My skin on the other hand had turned a reddish-pink, acting as an indicator it was time to get out of the sun and get started on the activities we had planned. First up on the list was Christ the Redeemer. Much like our Machu Picchu tour, it required an early rise at the crack of dawn to beat the crowds, although thankfully not quite as early this time and with no daft queues or French people. The view once getting to the base of the Redeemer was impressive by itself — perhaps it is a rarity in the world to find a view on a mountain pressed right up against a city that is based predominantly at sea level. I certainly can't think of any other examples. Rio's many buildings were scattered for miles to the city's jagged coastline, and beyond that lay a panoramic view of the ocean, occasionally dotted with small inhabited islands. And, of course, the statue is the icing on the cake; it really does look impressive sat atop it all, looming over the city — Jesus with his arms spread out in a T-pose, visible from almost anywhere as an homage to the big sky wizard's only child. To give it credit, whether you believe in the meaning behind it or not, it is an incredible feat of engineering. Religious people certainly love their expensive tributes to God, don't they? I honestly don't think us atheists would ever spend money on an extravagant symbol of our beliefs like a huge statue, even if we did settle on a symbol we could call our own. It just seems like such a religious thing to do, waste money on things like this — massive churches and temples fed from donations of God-fearing people — instead of spending it on needy causes around the world like feeding the hungry or putting a roof over the heads of the homeless. When the collection plate goes around at church, I make the effort not to put any money in and to give the money directly to a charity afterwards. Donating out of spite.

I'll find myself in church occasionally. Mel enjoys visiting as her roots are from a highly religious country — our relationship took some years to get to the level where we became comfortable with each other's vastly different beliefs. The early days of our relationship saw heated debates on religion, usually started from low-hanging fruit for atheists like how Noah's Ark is impossible and frankly a load of old bollocks, or what the fuck are dinosaur fossils about if the world is only six thousand years old. These days we've learned to deal with each other's beliefs though, mainly by not discussing it, although I will occasionally attend church as it means a lot to Mel when I do. I'll let you in on a secret though; I genuinely enjoy the downtime I get in church. Whilst the sermon is going on, I switch off to what is being said and enjoy the quiet — an entire hour to myself without the hassle of life beyond the church walls, time spent thinking about the important things in life like what I might want for dinner in the evening or what new TV series should I start on. It's odd; I find myself in churches two or three times a year and actually enjoy my time there.

I have an analogy I use whilst explaining my thoughts about religion to people, and you're going to get to read about it briefly now as I've started on the subject. My little dog back at home sometimes sits on my lap and watches TV with me and recognises animals running around when a bit of Attenborough is on, and he'll instinctively begin to bark at the TV. He's smart enough to perceive the images on the TV, but not smart enough to realise the images aren't of a real animal, never mind even begin to understand the intricacies of how a TV works, as his little dog brain isn't advanced enough. I think human minds are the same here, just on a different scale. We can see the world around us and understand it to an extent, but the human mind isn't developed enough to understand the inner workings of the universe. So, like the dog who reacts by barking at what he can merely see, humans in the past had created the idea of a God, a being who made the world around us, just as a simple explanation we could wrap our forever-developing minds around. It's quite possible the human race will never be smart enough to figure the real workings of the universe out — hey, it might actually turn out to be some sort of conscience that has created it all, like a God I suppose — but some of us are at least trying to understand the truth of universe and not leaving it to some fairy tales from the Bronze age to explain everything.

I wondered how those in the city's surrounding favelas felt about the amount of money that had been spent on an extravagant symbol of religion when it could have gone towards genuinely improving living standards for actual people struggling in the shanty areas instead. A visible reminder that money is there to be spent when it suits; in this case raised by the Catholic community of Brazil, who are even doing a whip round for another, larger statue in the south of the country to be called Christ the Protector. I'd soon find out myself about the opinions of people from the favelas, as the time had come for mine and Mel's visit inside one later that afternoon. Some basics about a visit — you can't just walk up into one as they largely remain dangerous places for outsiders, particularly tourists. Your first port of call is to find a reputable tour guide who will provide a safe escort for you once inside. Each city in Brazil has several, separate favelas and each one varies on quality of life and general safety. Most favelas were once outright violent slums with daily bloody shoot-outs between gangs, that is until the Brazilian government introduced what it calls the Pacification Programme in 2008, which involved having groups of armed enforcement officers storm in to establish a presence in each one. Any resistance from gang members or anyone who disagreed was dealt with swiftly, often using deadly force if necessary. Whilst this has generally worked for many of the favelas around the country and they are now much calmer places than they once were, the government is yet to address the lack of sanitation, overcrowding and poor educational standards for the residents. With all this in mind, we'd done our research and booked through a reputable company found online that set us up with a guide who was native to the favela, plus a local translator. Some of our "entrance fee" went into the pockets of the gangs who run the area; with this we were granted safe passage through and, as our translator put it, it made us "untouchable" being accompanied by a local. The original favela we were meant to visit was now inaccessible, as only the day before our arrival a group of tourists were mistakenly shot dead by police by entering with a guide who was a complete chancer. This had moved our visit to the Santa Marta favela. This all might sound risky and potentially more trouble than what it's worth, more so to me as we listened to the long list of "dos and don'ts" from the guides at our hotel before we embarked on our short train ride to the favela. Our local guide was called Rodrigo; a short young man with a vibrant blue shirt who spoke Portuguese very quickly, and our translator a tall man called Luiz with curly hair and completely round glasses, who I couldn't believe was wearing an anorak with clothes underneath on yet another day of low-thirties temperatures. Luiz looked like a bit of a defenceless computer geek even without the anorak, and I thought to myself if shit goes down here then Luiz would surely be the first target out of the group. It's fair to say I was apprehensive when the time had come to leave the comfort of the main touristy areas of the city and venture out into the unknown, however with Luiz's curly hair, glasses and coat I oddly found comfort in the thought that if someone this geeky was happy to enter then we'd surely be fine.

A thin barrier crossed the road at the base of the hill up into the favela. It looked like it lifted for vehicles, but as it appeared rusted and covered in dirt it likely hadn't seen a passing vehicle in some time. To me, it looked like a clear indicator that passing this meant entry into the favela's boundary and off Rio's "safer" streets. We followed Luiz and Rodrigo's lead around the side of the barrier. There was some nervous excitement about the next few hours, but the heat alone just made me feel uneasy too; the uncomfortable surrounding air having journeyed inland and away from the coastal breeze and into the hot, humid, dense city. The favela's buildings changed from being Rio's leafy suburbs nearby with their apartment blocks and balconies, turning into simple one-storey concrete or breeze-block bungalows, or corrugated metal shacks. Whilst basic on the material front, they were improved somewhat by being vibrant paint and graffiti, which covered many external walls of the favela — often in striking red, orange, bright purple, with widespread use of yellow and green for the Brazilian flag. The residents going about their business eyed us with some suspicion as we walked past. Some residents had the trendy gear like their non-favela counterparts had, but more often they didn't, instead having holes in their clothes, mismatching flip flops or looking like they had missed a few meals. I couldn't quite believe that the differences were so striking on either side a of a literal mere barrier.

We soon entered a small courtyard area of sorts, or rather, a clearing amongst the mass of cramped housing, encountering some of the scariest people I had ever seen in my life. I have been to some dark and weird places on my travels over the years, including a brief visit to a crack den in Los Angeles and an extended period visiting an Indonesian penitentiary. As you might imagine, these places were full of rough, dangerous men and even these didn't somehow seem as intimidating as the chaps here in the favela; several huge guys with skin heads and scars, some with full facial tattoos — most of whom were occupying themselves with a humble game of cards. A table positioned amongst the men caught my attention; it had on top of it massive boom-box which blasted out loud Latino rap music and next to that what appeared to a be a hand gun. A man sat by the table keeping an eye on it (literally, as this other eye was missing). A couple of them looked up at us as we passed, but most were interested in the card game.

"This is unusual for them to leave such a gun out on display," began Luiz, "this might be because of the recent tourist shootings in the other favela; there is some tension in the air." Great. This group of men were the gang that were "in charge" of the favela, although I wasn't quite sure what sort of role they played these days since the Pacification Programme; were they still peddling drugs, and if so how does it fit with Pacification Programme? Do they protect the residents from other gangs? How many other guns do they have? Do they act like a council for the favela? I wondered how much impact The Programme actually had on the slums beyond safety, and how much these guys have allowed it to change their home. They were clearly still the big dogs around here, their presence stationed with the obvious loud and visual clues, strategically placed in this clearing before the many little roads weaved off into the mass of housing further into the favela. Perhaps it was all for image these days. Either way, it worked for me — they are what I would consider the God tier of stage fright if I had to try and pee in front of them. I'm getting cramps in my abdomen even thinking about them now.

Luiz explicitly told us not to photograph anywhere around the gang as our earlier protection payments would likely have been stuffed where the sun doesn't shine, followed by a good kicking. Luiz had picked up on mine and Mel's nervousness and informed us it's an easier ride beyond here as the entrance is considered the worst part of the tour. The gangs control the favela's lower land as it is considered more valuable. In fact, the further up the mountain we reached, the less desirable the land becomes, so the poorest residents living right at the very top are the ones that get the great views of the city's skyline. I could see in terms of practicality that perhaps lugging your shopping up there was quite the walk, as there were no main roads as such and only steep pavements which weaved through the mesh of housing. It would take us at least half an hour to walk from the base of the hill right to the top. I guess from a gang's point of view, if a neighbouring drug gang or police are raiding your favela then the nice views aren't that important if you don't want to be weaving for half an hour downhill to get to where the action is.

After leaving those scallywags at the bottom of the hill we began to meet the other, and certainly more approachable, residents of the favela. Living in their poor surroundings, it was admirable seeing some residents taking pride in what little they had, one woman I saw brushed up litter outside her small single-room house, whilst others had done intricate paintings along the walls outside or had created miniscule gardens outside their premises, in an effort to try and spruce the place up. The favelas are home to many millions around the country, yet the buildings are technically illegal residences because they aren't "officially" registered by the state, so this means the residents are illegally here too. This makes finding a job hard, and contributes to the high unemployment rate, also compounded by factors like poor education and the lack of transport out of the favela to jobs within the city. This evidently left many residents idle with bags of time on their hands. Claustrophobically tight alleyways often had people stood around between the buildings, and I did find the first encounters up close with the residents somewhat intimidating as I squeezed past them, although occasional friendly smiles and accompanying handshakes would eventually begin to chip away at my fears. Some residents appeared a little wary of us, as we were them. I couldn't help but feel this was made worse by standing out in my brand new t-shirt, shorts and trainers I'd bought for the trip, wishing I'd worn something a bit more scruffy before entering so I didn't look like even more of a foreign tourist twat. Before I came here I only thought of it as an interesting place to see in my life, but naively hadn't really thought much about the real people living their lives amongst it all, and having met them I found myself wondering had I wound up on some sort of poverty safari. Rodrigo and Luiz insisted our entry ticket money didn't entirely go to the gangs, that some of it did go into the local economy to support the people. I alone had effectively paid for Rodrigo's wage for the day, enough to provide food for his family, which helped shift the poverty tourism feeling a bit if I thought about it like that. Rodrigo took us to his house as we passed one alleyway, effectively two small rooms stacked on top of each other. It was incredibly cramped once inside as he had managed to squeeze two beds in it amongst the TV, shelves and toilet. I could see the bottom of the toilet was left open and it led to a gutter, any bodily waste ran outside down the hill along the favela. It looked grim, and needless to say, without a proper plumbing system, diseases like cholera and dysentery are common in some favelas. A small fan tried its best to cool the room down, but the heat was trapped by the metal roof and walls. This was a guy with a regular job hosting people around the favela, he was probably quite well-off in relative terms, and yet his house was still small and basic inside. I moan about England's shortcomings a lot, our corrupt shithouse of a government and appalling public services, but visiting places like this really does put life in perspective and how good we have it back home.

When I was fourteen years old, school could be a rough place. I think other than a small handful of spoffs, my whole school year, both boys and girls, had bouts of being disruptive. Sure, me and my friends just enjoyed the innocent mischief, but I look back about it being a ruthless place at times; having to hold a shit in all day for fear of having the door kicked in by other pupils for using a cubicle, or kids pinning down others and beating them up. Heaven forbid you tried to forge your own individuality by wearing unbranded trainers or weren't into football like everyone else; not even worth considering for fear of being bullied. No wonder some teachers were suspected to drink so heavily — they were dealing with our classes. A memory springs to mind of an entire classroom cheering when a barrage of mind games from the pupils finally broke a teacher and they began to cry. This may sound like my public school was found in a rough area, but ours was actually one of the better ones around Cheshire. If this is what I remember the kids being like back home, then surely the ones in the favelas of Brazil would be even more unpleasant? This was my first thought as Rodrigo noticed a small school was open, nestled amongst the buildings, and led us in for an impromptu visit.

"Can we just walk into a school like this?" Mel asked. Could anyone off the street really just enter to say hello? People could do it at home if they wanted, thinking about it, but there's probably some sort of police register they'd end up on. Perhaps it was more the novelty of having the foreigners just wandering in like this, but we were welcomed in and led into a classroom by the teacher after a brief verbal exchange with Rodrigo. Much like the buildings outside, the school's walls had vibrant colours painted on them in bright red and purple, although there was little else beyond the hard concrete floor that was packed with twenty or so school kids sat down on it. They appeared to be midway through some sort of performing arts class, with the teenagers acting out scenes or doing songs together. Rodrigo invited us to sit down to watch, so both Mel and I awkwardly shuffled through to the corner of the room and quietly observed for five minutes or so before the lesson slowly broke down and the pupil's attention had fully turned to us. They were honestly the most friendly and polite kids I think I'd ever come across. Again, it could have been down to being in the presence of the foreigners being here, but they all still didn't have to be so pleasant, if perhaps a little on the shy side. One kid broke out a guitar and sung a tune for us, whilst his teacher rested his hand on his shoulder during the performance. They even knuckle bumped together after the song finished! Did I just witness mutual respect between teacher and pupil? That was a first. It was certainly a far cry from school back at home, and the time one of my classmates locked the French teacher in the stock room for a laugh. To this day I still think about how the entire class ignored her muffled pleas through the door to let her out for a full half-hour.

The time had come to descend the hillside, through the mish-mash of metal and concrete to re-enter the bowels of the favela (quite literally in fact, as some sewage run off rolled down in our direction). We were just in time to see a fight break out between two shirtless gents not too far from the exit. A small crowd had surrounded the men, shouting from the sidelines whilst the men exchanged punches; this was more aligned to what I remembered school being like. One of the men looked fucked up even before a concussion had kicked in. It was entering Friday evening so, much like people anywhere else in the world might, the residents were getting tanked up ready for the weekend. I was ready to leave for home — it had been an insightful way of life here, but having the sun edge away as evening approached and seeing this fight break out between two drunk meat-heads who could well be carrying firearms made both myself and Mel realise that, despite the nice people found higher up the hill and the promise of protection, there had been an underlying out-of-place feeling here that I assumed would only get worse at night. Brazil sits in stark contrast to some of the shanty towns in Asia I'd visited previously, which are usually quite safe to walk around, even at night, and especially without a guide (there are endless friendly faces in the slums of Jakarta, people who actively encourage you to sit down with them to socialise). It had certainly been an eye-opening experience to visit a place that had been so dangerous. Rodrigo stopped us just before crossing the barrier leading back to Rio and translated through Luiz that there was an offer to stay the night in his house as an extra package deal, where we'd get to experience more of the favela and what it is like when the sun goes down. Stood by the barrier, I pondered it with Mel and weighed up the pros and cons of staying an entire night. We already had a hotel back by the beach, but upon reflection of the offer, we were here to experience life in the dangerous shanty towns of South America and see how gritty it can be, here only once in my lifetime and that moment is now. To say I've braved it here for a full night, met and stayed with the locals, broke bread with them and slept where they slept! Then, I remembered I had air conditioning and a breakfast buffet waiting for me. I didn't give hopping over that barrier a second thought.

### Rio de Janeiro, Brazil — Saturday, 2nd November 2017

Brazil is one of those countries where the people that can afford it know how to live well, evident with the top-tier offerings of food and drink. There were many options of local beer, brewed with this hot climate in mind and all refreshing, or indeed paired with a juicy steak. Myself and Mel had recently been phasing meat out of our diet back home for various ethical and health reasons, but had completely binned all that vegetarian shite off in Rio as the meat was too good to be avoiding. There's something about the local stuff that makes it incredibly flavoursome — and as I only learned from coming out here — quality steak only really needs a bit of salt rubbing into it as a seasoning as the quality of the meat should generally be left to speak for itself. "Pay by weight" is a common restaurant setup found throughout the city, and I assumed the country, where an empty plate is filled with food from a buffet and the customer pays based on the weight of what's stacked on their plate. I usually find buffets in other places around the world are hit-and-miss affairs as the food has been sat under a heating lamp for some time, any moisture in the food evaporating along with the flavour. Perhaps I had been lucky, but I didn't eat one bad meal at any of these places in Brazil with a stack of meat that was very well priced. For desserts, we'd wander the streets looking for a currios stand, which only appear at night when people bring out deep fat fryers on wheels. Currios, for the uninitiated, are long sausage-shaped doughnuts commonly filled with chocolate or caramel and then rolled in sugar. They're the crack cocaine of street food; both sharing the qualities of having no nutritional value, rotting your teeth and being far too moreish, but it feels so good going into your body. Several times in Brazil I had experienced the feeling in my stomach which is only usually reserved for the afternoon on Christmas day whereupon I've eaten far too much food and my belt has to be loosened a notch. So, take note: the food in Brazil is bloody great.

It was Saturday night and after an evening of gluttony, the pair of us hopped along some of the bars found along Rio's coast and wound up sat at a little bar by Copacabana beach as the sun had begun to set. We'd been tempted by the lure of a renowned nightclub further into the city (clubbing usually being our favourite activity to get up to when away), but we were apprehensive not being fully familiar with the city's districts and worried whether we'd be safe once fully immersed in the nightlife and far from the safety of our hotel, so we decided a quiet bar by the beach was enough for the evening. The bar was mostly empty apart from a young Brazilian couple who sat on a table near to ours. They eventually struck up conversation in English, curious about us two tipsy foreigners with multiple empty currios wrappers on the table around them. For all the apparent tourists in the city, it seemed like the majority were from other parts of the country, or at least from Latin America, making us true far-flung foreigners less common, which I found unusual for such a famous destination. Many of the Brazilians we had interacted with were really friendly and interested in our backgrounds, but the language barrier was everywhere, like much of South America, so conversation wouldn't progress much beyond names and places of origin. English is widely used as a second language around a significant number of countries these days, so communicating is usually a breeze, but the dynamic changes when you're isolated linguistically visiting somewhere like Brazil. It was finally nice to meet a native couple on the continent who we could actually converse with, and after some time speaking across half the bar, we moved tables together and drank as a foursome. They were great company. The fella looked tough and told me he was security officer for an international firm, whilst his petite partner worked as a teacher; both were from a city in the south of country on vacation. As tourists to the city, they had been ticking off a similar activity list to ours, and showed us a video of their visit to Christ the Redeemer earlier in the day. The video was quite hard to make out, but it appeared to be of two human silhouettes in dense fog getting battered from wind and rain whilst attempting to pose together for a photo in front of the Redeemer. It then became obvious they were the silhouettes, struggling to keep their footing in an inadvertently comical video shot earlier in the day. It had been nice and toasty on the lower ground since daybreak with barely a breeze, so it was almost inconceivable that despite the Redeemer being only four miles away from the beach as the crow flies, the altitude makes the statue dramatically susceptible to low hanging clouds and the weather bought with them.

One thing that spoils drinking along Copacabana beach is that the bars don't usually have their own toilet facilities, and this doesn't leave many options to relieve a pressured bladder. Mel can go a whole night of drinking and make use of the toilet only once, whereas me, I tend to piss like a racehorse throughout the remainder of the night soon after finishing my first drink. Midnight was getting close and I was aware we were pushing our luck remaining out this late in the city, and although drinking with two Brazilians offered us a little protection in a well-lit bar, I really didn't like the idea of walking around the streets of Rio looking around for a public toilet. If they're anything like the public toilets at home, they tend to attract the worst sorts of people. Those in my hometown had to be locked up overnight because druggies and other such vagabonds used them as hangouts, so God only knows what sort of grim creatures would be lurking around the public latrines of Latin America. I wasn't too far from the hotel, five minutes away at most, but there's the whole walking there, then waiting for the elevator to the room that I couldn't be bothered with. I just wanted a leak now and to get back to my table so as to not waste precious drinking time.

"Just use the sea," my new Brazilian security buddy suggested. Although I couldn't quite see the water across the sand because it was dark, the waves could still be heard crashing. I agreed with him that a short stroll across to nature's toilet might be the preferable option. I noticed people still out on the beach even at these hours as I made my way to the water who I hadn't really noticed sat at the bar, murky figures sometimes with hoods up, just about visible, stood around in the darkness; a complete shift in the type of people that were found enjoying the beach in the day time. I quickly took my piss, doing a slight dance on the sand to avoid the lapping waves wetting my trainers, which also happened to dislodge the piss from some of the building stage fright I had from assuming I was being watched by the figures on the beach.

I gave my lad a quick shake dry, turned to make my way back up to the bar and was soon intercepted by two fellas in hoods who moved in front of my path. It's finally happened, after all my time abroad, this is it — I'm going to get mugged for the first time, and it's my own fault for going across a dark beach. My eyes took a second to focus on what they looked like in the dark; young, perhaps early twenties. Their clothes hung off their skinny frames. I thought I'd be more nervous in this situation when faced with it, but then again, I'd had about eight pints of beer, so I couldn't be bothered to process the severity of what was going on. Maybe they're alright lads deep down? Maybe I can talk them down and get them to join us for a beer? All my online self-training on travel sites about not looking them direct in the face or throwing my belongings at them straight away was instantly forgotten. I looked over to the bar to Mel and the couple sat down, hoping they'd noticed me in the predicament. They hadn't. One of the lads spoke a jumble of Portuguese which I didn't understand and the other one said "De Niro" after a short pause. Why are they saying an actor's name at me?

"Robert De Niro?" I replied back in absolute confusion. With my brain not fully functioning, I didn't think that the actual word of De Niro, or rather dinheiro as it is correctly spelled in Portuguese, is the native word for money, similar to that of Spanish. I'd left my wallet at the bar with Mel anyway, so the actor's name was the best they were getting out of me tonight. I think I had outright confused them with my reply, buying me enough time for my new Brazilian mate at the bar to pick up that something wasn't right. He stood up from his seat when he saw the two lads stood in my path, shouted from the bar and began running over across the sand. The two assailants weighed up the situation for a split second, realised he was quite a big lad, then decided they didn't want to deal with both him and the drunk English tourist spouting shite and ran off along the beach into the darkness. I thanked my new buddy for his help and let him escort me along the sand back to the safety of the well-lit bar, and as a group we decided that as we had made it this far into the night things may only get worse, so we'd better drink up and call an end to our session.

### Rio de Janeiro, Brazil — Sunday, 3rd November 2017

For a guy who usually finds the novelty of a beach wears off quickly after ten minutes of being there, mainly down to the inability to get comfy on the sand and quick onset of boredom, I was surprised that I couldn't help but find myself attracted to them in Rio. They're just a great place to spend free time. There's always something going on within its fantastic vibe; sports, barbecues, and stunning scenery to admire. Not long before our arrival to the country, there had been a horrific case of a woman getting raped and murdered on Ipanema beach late at night which had been horrendous even for the city's standards of violent crime. It had caused outrage in the news and was a striking reminder to all that Rio, even with its gorgeous beaches, great places to eat, nightclubs and well-dressed residents, it is constantly ranked amongst the most dangerous cities the world for violent crime. This itself is a tragedy, because as late afternoon hits the clock, the buzz in the city, particularly around the beaches, is honestly something to behold. The residents finish their business for the day and spill out onto the sand for food, football and drinks, and sat there watching it all; Mel and I, on our last night, sipping a mojito prepared by a guy on a beach with a small stall, agreed that this is honestly a special place. The atmosphere improves further with the haze from the sea air that rolls in with the early evening, along with the gorgeous orange of the sunset over people dancing and having fun. This is peak beach fun time and the ambience incredible. But then, as night falls, most people retreat along with the daylight. The fun atmosphere is gone well before 9PM, handing the beach over to only a few hardy souls, or those which are likely up to no good. The city is a place of duality wherever you look; the wealth, living accommodation, the people, all of which is exacerbated by the cycle of day and night. Keen to avoid a repeat of last night's De Niro beach idiots but pained we didn't want this evening to end, we finished our drinks as the sun set and headed back to the hotel. It left me with mixed emotions. I was pleasantly surprised with Brazil. Sure, there's a lot of dangerous parts within the country, but the nice spots within it truly shine. The city of Rio has the potential to be one of the best places on earth, if only it could make a clean break from the crime.

Our time for this trip was over. If I was a backpacker now, I'd likely be off elsewhere within the continent the next day, but was instead heading back to home to resume normal life. I had thoroughly enjoyed my time here though, and knew I'd be back one day in the future to see what else this exciting continent had in store for me.

# CHAPTER TWO
## EAST ASIA

# CHINA

**Beijing, China – Sunday, 4th March 2018**

China had been on my radar of places to visit for a while. Having spent a few years collectively in Asia, sometimes skirting near China's borders but never quite making it to the continent's second largest country for whatever reason, some time spent in the country was well overdue. A few months had passed since we had returned from our South America excursion and, due to meet Mel in a few days' time in Korea (who wasn't at all keen on going to China), I decided I still wanted to tick the country off my list — even if it meant going at it alone for the first time in years. Old concerns of travelling by myself resurfaced; what happens if I lose either my passport or my wallet without anyone to fall back on for money? Will I miss having a conversation with anyone throughout my whole time there, as apparently English speakers are rare in China? And what of China generally and its intimidatingly huge cultural differences to the West? Previous travellers I had met who had been there referred to it as The Deep East, basically meaning it's about as far removed from Western culture as you can find on mainland Asia, taking on very little influence than other Asian countries might have. I think on reflection it was probably the main reasoning behind not visiting before now, as I imagine it doesn't cater to foreign tourists well compared to, say, regional neighbours in the South East such as Thailand. Whether you approve of it or not; Western culture, through either diplomacy, television or tourists, permeates around a lot of the globe and can be felt subtly when travelling, making your time abroad a little easier to adapt to. This manifests as English being used by local people as a second language, so you can have a conversation with them — helpful if you need to visit a doctor or need directions. You may be able to buy food that you can find at home, which is good comfort when you've become sick of endless white rice and noodles for days. I knew China would be quite alien in this sense as it hasn't generally taken on much culture from abroad (well, unless they're copying products to make cheap imitations of, which is another story entirely!). There was an excessive £200 fee for a tourist visa to think about too, which I never fancied paying. I didn't really know much about the country either, I could name a few cities and landmarks, maybe a few dishes from my local takeaway, but not much beyond that — which is pretty poor considering it contains a seventh of the entire world's population, is the fourth largest country by size, and likely half the stuff I have in my house has been manufactured there. I had planned to do a bit of research before arrival, but as I ended up doing a tiring three-week work stint in Jakarta before my flight over, I didn't really have the time nor the inclination to do it. I was effectively going in blind, but with the right attitude; that can be part of the fun when visiting a new place.

To boost tourism, China now allows a 144-hour visit period with use of a transit visa, effectively acting as an extremely short tourist visa as long as specific rules are followed; this includes leaving from the same airport you arrived in and remaining in the same region the airport is. This also foregoes the large tourist visa cost and all the bureaucracy that goes with it, so I decided this transit visa was the way to go. The downside is, 144 hours isn't a great deal of time, so I was therefore keen to maximise my short time here! My connecting flight into the country was from Singapore, and there I found a heap of trouble convincing the onward airline staff that British passports don't need a Chinese tourist visa for a short stay. Transit visa travel was evidently not used very much, nor its rules widely known. At one point, with the way things were going with the Singaporean airport staff, I reckoned I wouldn't be getting on the flight at all as I was stuck in a side room of the airport with people from immigration control, getting dangerously close to departure time without a clue what was going on outside the walls. 'This is what you get when you don't just go on a "normal" holiday somewhere,' I thought to myself, doubting my choices to enter China this way, 'none of this turmoil happens if you go to Europe for two weeks, does it?' After close to an hour of back-and-froth chats between the airline and Chinese immigration that all was legitimate, I was finally allowed on the plane. It was an iffy start, and I had concerns that I was going to have trouble again once I had arrived into the country. Thankfully, as soon as I disembarked from the plane, I could see signposts in English for the 144-hour visa-free travel desk in the airport terminal.

Stood at the transit visa desk was a short, young Chinese woman in a sash which read 'Here to help' and, next to her, an old surly security guy. Her English was terrible. I don't mean to sound unappreciative as I'm sure learning English extremely difficult if you have been raised on Chinese, but as the first point of contact in a new country for many foreigners with the added responsibility of instructing them on how to enter the territory correctly, I would have expected her to speak English on some sort of decent level. Communication is the only key requirement of this job, and yet she struggled to convey what I needed.

"You... need permission," she said to me rather abruptly when it was my turn to speak to her. I started to panic... permission? I hadn't spoken to anyone about permission prior to coming here. Had I missed part of this entry process? Picking up my hesitation, she snatched my papers from me and pulled out my onward flight ticket to South Korea, which I guessed was the proof I was intending to leave China eventually. "Permission" was an unusual choice of words!

The queue was short, but it was moving painfully slowly. Behind me was an American woman in a wheelchair; she, too, was struggling to understand the Chinese woman in the sash. The sash woman took her papers for inspection, read through them and began pointing and laughing with the security guard at something she had found within it. The wheelchair woman looked utterly confused — if her immigration papers were anything like mine then there was nothing humorous about them. Then the guard sneezed without covering his mouth, and some of the air and mucus droplets hit the back of my neck. I had been in China for twenty minutes and already I could see a chasm of cultural differences here. I had heard about stuff like hacking up phlegm in public and laughing at things that, back home, we might consider impolite. These things are apparently typical for Chinese people – and here I am experiencing it for myself, looking at a confused woman in a wheelchair with a fresh sneeze spread across my neck. These are the airport staff, what the hell are the people in the street like?!

It was pushing midnight and I was getting cranky for some sleep. The queuing didn't stop after my transit visa token; immigration took an hour to clear after that. Then there was a queue for the train to baggage collection. Then I had to clear customs. The taxi rank had a big line. I will never complain about the long waits at Manchester airport ever again. Well, maybe. With all this free time to pass buried in the line of people, I inevitably pulled out my phone and started having a catch up with *Facebook* and other apps. Interestingly, I had read prior to coming that most Western social media outlets like *Facebook* and search engines like *Google* have their access restricted by the Chinese government, but I appeared to be able to use them without any issue using my roaming data. Well, that was the case for about ten minutes. Then my internet connection utterly died. I wondered if I had been caught using forbidden sites and they killed my internet. It was a weird moment to think my innocent internet activity, checking out cat memes and posts of people's dinners back home, might have been logged somewhere. The Chinese government does take the internet very seriously, particularly with regard to how its citizens use it, and the handful of native social media platforms which are allowed are heavily monitored and regulated. This is likely in place to stop the internet being used as a tool to organise a potential uprising against the one-party government, or any other activities the government doesn't approve of such as mocking of those in charge. For instance: the country's current serving president, Xi Jinping, has had internet memes shared for his likeness to *Winnie the Pooh* (yes, that's right, the big cartoon bear that loves honey). This mocking is seen as dissidence and is swiftly shot down by the government; these days, having images of Winnie the Pooh is outright forbidden in the country and, in extreme cases, authors of posts that reference the President looking like the honey-loving bear have been arrested. In my case of losing my internet connection, it probably wasn't government intervention so much as a coincidence, as any images of *Pooh* I usually share have nothing to do with bears and are more likely to involve my weird sense of humour with the lads back home. I was probably just being a bit paranoid, but it was still odd that my connection had totally dropped out.

I was finally handed all my complete paperwork from a man behind a desk and within the wad of paper received a note stating that if I was staying at a residence somewhere and not a hotel, which I was doing after tonight, I needed to register my stay with the police. It appeared they even wanted to keep tabs on the tourists, and it's all good and well telling people they have to register their stay, but the paper didn't really inform me on the process of how to do it. Do I now have to go to a police station at some point? Will there be translators available there? How long will this take, as I only have a couple of days in the country? All questions that weren't answered by the man behind the desk because, of course, he didn't speak English. I started to feel anxious about how I was going to meet this new requirement that had been dropped on me. Fortunately, the airport signs translated into piss-poor English lifted my mood a little, my favourite being the translation of 'train' which had become 'people mover' and was displayed on large signs around the airport, so that was something at least.

I usually find myself buzzing with excitement when I arrive in a new country, but for the first time ever I didn't really have it with my arrival to China. Getting to the airport front door had taken time and effort. I was a bit nervous arriving so late at night, meaning I'd have to navigate my way to the hotel in the dark. I was definitely a little grumpy from all the travel, plus the recent work stint in Jakarta had completely tired me out (sometimes I would be in Jakarta for weeks at a time, ironically leaving Mel in my hometown as I was in her home city, meeting by chance there all those years ago, and then events within life had us temporarily swap locations. I'd sometimes tease her by sending pictures of me and her family sat at a bar having drinks in the good weather whilst she was stuck at home during an English winter). I got to the hotel and, with the use of a translation app I downloaded onto my phone, I attempted to communicate with the hotel's two young reception staff that I had already pre-booked a night here. I'm sure you've seen these apps before and generally, although not perfect, they are quite smart, offering real time translations of any text you type into it to one of the many languages around the globe. I believe some languages are translated quite well, but the app was apparently no good with Chinese. Whatever the translation said just left them looking confused. They managed to eventually find my booking by looking at my passport. I then asked, using the app, if there was anywhere I could buy some food, but with the addition of hand gestures this time. Looking puzzled once again at what they had read, they typed something into a translation app on their phone, and it read the single word of 'length' in English, leaving me stumped as to what they were trying to tell me. It was interesting to see both our apps were fucking useless.

The language barrier was already beginning to frustrate. My grasp of Indonesian is passable now for the basics; I had been using it regularly over the past few weeks at work, sometimes going an entire day without using my own native language, but here in China I had reverted to the classic British method of communicating abroad: pointing to things and talking in English a bit louder. One of many things I enjoy with the Indonesian language along with its overall simplicity, is it uses the Latin alphabet, so even if I don't know what a word means, I can at least have a decent stab at trying to read and pronounce it. I wouldn't even know how to begin to try pronouncing anything written in Chinese, you might as well throw a handful of noodles at a wall and ask me to read that. Although the Chinese do have their own numerical characters, they appear to use the same as we do in English sometimes, but not always. Luckily in this instance I could understand when the hotel staff gave me my room number, *349* written on the key, and pointed for me to go to floor three. When I got to the right floor, the room numbers looked nothing like what was written on my key; they were five-digit numbers that all started with an eight. I went back to reception to tell them I had no idea what my room number was, but the reception shutters had been pulled down and the foyer was deserted. It took me ten minutes to try every door on the floor until I found the one that worked. My internet was still down so I couldn't speak to anyone at home to let them know I had arrived safely. I hadn't eaten all day. I sat in my cold, small hotel room with nothing to do. Fuck me, did I ever feel like a foreigner.

I tried to get the internet back on through Wi-Fi, as I wanted to know more about registering my stay with the authorities. My VPN wouldn't connect for me to use *Google*, but weirdly I did manage to get the poor man's version to work, *Yahoo*. The only information I could really find on online message boards was either "Don't bother registering your stay, they never check", or "Do it, you will be fined a lot if they catch you!". The second one worried me slightly. I managed only a few hours of sleep that night.

## Beijing, China – Monday, 5th March 2018

I had met a local fella called Wei through *AirBnB* before arrival to the country, and was staying in the spare bedroom of his flat in central Beijing for two nights. I needed to make my way there in the morning to drop my baggage off, then intended to spend the rest of the day sightseeing around the city. I had woken too early to be knocking on Wei's door just yet, so I took a quick walk around the immediate area around the hotel to see China for the first time in daylight. The temperature was pretty fresh, four or five Celsius above freezing, however *Yahoo* told me it was going to reach a whopping twenty-seven later in the day. Such a significant temperature leap like that couldn't be right, could it? I just put it down to *Yahoo* being a bit shit. I had imagined the streets of China to look like this I guess; huge wide roads with blocky, industrial soviet-style architecture along them, some covered in huge Chinese writing. There were many red lanterns hung above and along the adjacent alleyways, I thought it was cute seeing this outside of the Chinese restaurants we get back home. There was a strong sense of patriotism as there were many Chinese national flags around, draped along the faces of buildings or hanging from telephone wires. The trees, just emerging from the winter months (which I'm told can reach as low as -20°C here) had no leaves and all looked dead. The real treat for me, though, was the strange people that were considered 'normal' here. For example, there was this guy in a little home-made electric buggy thing – that absolutely would be forbidden on the roads back home – doing slower than walking speed in the middle of a busy highway, cars crawling behind him with raging drivers trying to overtake. It was brilliant. Another man walked down the street backwards, using a mirror strapped to his head to see where he was going. I'm guessing it might have had something to do with exercise, but it could just be the way he preferred to walk. To combat the fresh morning, people on mopeds had a little coat they put on the front of their bikes that they can also fit their arms in. It's kind of innovative really, but it just looks over the top. I could see already that China was full of all these strange people and their quirks. I should have felt right at home.

I made it to central Beijing via taxi later that morning. I'm pretty sure the taxi driver was gambling during the whole journey, using one of those massive phones that might as well be a tablet. He had it mounted high on his car's dashboard, taking up a significant portion of the visibility through the windscreen, and would frantically tap away at it throughout the journey. It was a bit hard to tell what was going on as it was all in Chinese, but some numbers would flash up with a picture of a laughing baby accompanied with a cheering sound effect, or sometimes there would be booing sound and no numbers. Even during the time on the motorway, his focus didn't really leave the screen, but to be fair, he got the baby picture lots of times so he must have been on a good winning streak.

The taxi dropped me off deep in the heart of the city, amongst many tall residential buildings, again in a very soviet-looking block style, like they had seen better days; in dire need of a clean and in some cases a bit of repair work. I was surprised to see these residential blocks looked so rough because they sat in stark contrast to the modern and clean highways next to them. I hoped I had been dropped off in the right area as the taxi driver had only looked at an address that had been written in Chinese, and again it meant absolutely nothing to me, so I could have been anywhere now. My phone's internet had thankfully come back, the Chinese government must have heard my cries in the night and switched it back on for me, meaning I was able to share my exact location through my phone with Wei for him to come and meet me (I know people generally do use their phones for too much in modern times, but I genuinely would have been lost without it today). I anxiously waited for Wei at the meeting point, gathering stares from the passing locals on their way to work who couldn't figure out why a rare white guy was stood around doing nothing, but to my relief I was in the right area when I recognised his face as her approached with his girlfriend in tow. They were both genuinely lovely people who spoke pretty good English. I asked Wei if he had registered my stay, and he told me, "No, but don't worry about it."

I was still worried. We exchanged some pleasantries, he showed me briefly around the small apartment and then after dumping most of my stuff, I was out ready to explore Beijing by myself.

My itinerary today focused on the city's highlights of Tiananmen Square and the Forbidden City. I didn't know how long a visit to these would take; I assumed most of the day, so if I had free time for anything else then it would be a bonus. Aided by a taxi booked by Wei, I'd made it to Tiananmen Square by ten in the morning having had such an early start to my day. The taxi driver pointed in the general direction of where I needed to go once I left the taxi, leaving me by a huge congested road that I didn't expect to come across. I could almost see the site, but wasn't really sure how to enter as I assumed it would be an open area for people to easily walk into, like a park or something. That wasn't the case. I spent a full twenty minutes walking around looking for the entrance, getting increasingly confused about how to get on the other side of the fences and multiple lanes of traffic, with no one around able to speak English to help me on my way. If there was an obvious way to enter the area I was missing it. Every time I thought I'd found an entrance, there'd be lots of security guys standing around that would gesture with their hands for me to go away. A few days later I would learn that North Korea's president Kim Jong-Un had come to Beijing, making his first visit outside of the country in six years on the very day that I was here. Kim had made his way from North Korea on a bulletproof train, presumably fearful of being shot out of the sky otherwise, however once safely in China he'd likely be using the roads to get around. I'd seen a few blacked-out limousines driving near Tiananmen so ol' Kim could well have been inside one of those, his window passing the lone white guy stood at the side of the road getting lost and upset. There is apparently an important government building near Tiananmen Square, so that could have explained the additional security presence around — especially if Kim was making a visit there too — and also may have explained why I had so much difficulty getting around this particular area today. Thanks for that, Kim!

Plodding around the outskirts of the Square attempting to find a route in, I saw another white person ahead of me walking in the same direction. I caught up and struck up a conversation with her, hoping to get an answer on the correct way to go. Thank God, she spoke English, and happened to be going to Tiananmen Square too, offering to walk me in the right direction. We talked on the way to the entrance and in the queue to Tiananmen, realising we pretty much had the same day planned, and ended up spending the day together sightseeing. Her name was Talia and she was from Israel. Similar to myself, she had a full day in Beijing to try and get as much tourist stuff covered as possible before moving on. Unlike myself though, she had just completed a six-week stint in the country prior, experiencing the true rural life of the countryside, as well as its freezing temperatures in the north at the back end of winter. As she was telling me about the snow and the cold from her adventures, it was hard to picture right now, as it appeared to be reaching the low twenties even before midday, and my nose and cheeks had already begun to burn slightly from the sun in the cloudless sky.

Beijing is the capital city of a country with 1.2 billion people in it, therefore it's reasonable to expect that the majority of the city's tourism actually comes from the Chinese themselves, making foreign tourists few and far between. It was positively bustling with native people today, groups of families or young couples snapping photos of themselves. I tower above most people, being nearly two metres tall, but coming to places that are crammed with Asian people seems to magnify my height and I become a big, noticeable white lurch, head and shoulders above a sea of black hair. I couldn't help but feel more of a foreigner at Tiananmen Square than usual. The Square has significant history attached to it since it was first built in 1417 and has featured prominently in Chinese culture and historical events since — I'm not going into great detail with it all here, but in modern times it wasn't offering much else in the immediate area other than it being crammed with people. It felt like I was in a big car park more than a particular tourist attraction. A huge picture of Chairman Mao was one of only a handful of things to see on the outskirts of the Square. Mao is credited with creating the communist Republic of China, starting it down the path that led to a "one-party" political system in the Forties, transforming it from a divided and poor country with particularly low living standards into the political and economic behemoth that we know today. With the implemented system being a relative success, certainly financially, it has pretty much set the country with only one political party in charge of affairs with no way to democratically remove them. In the 1980s, not keen with the idea of this one-party rule, a group of protests formed around the country hoping to inspire and enact political change, but gathered predominantly in Tiananmen Square. The Square today is mostly known for the government's mass slaughter of said protesters pushing for reform, the bulk of which were students. The reported numbers of those who lost their lives vary between the hundreds and the thousands, depending on which source you check. This was America's version of events, anyway, and there is evidence to suggest that some of it was fabricated by the Yanks to try and destabilise the country as a precursor to military intervention which was being considered at the time; hoping to win the hearts and minds of Americans before it entered the country by spreading misinformation stating how bad the Chinese government was acting. Or even stirring the pot, hoping the Chinese government would collapse and rebuild as a democratic society. What may have happened is there was some people killed, but it was actually the Chinese military who died, trying to protect themselves from rebels who were trying to overthrow the government – and the students there to protest left unscathed. I honestly don't know fully what to believe, there are so many lies peddled by both sides with their propaganda bullshit these days, and I'm not going to dive any deeper in a light-hearted travel book. Either way, the Chinese government doesn't help itself as it acts suspiciously on the subject; it still restricts online information published about the incident and quashes the annual gatherings to mark the event. It's still quite a touchy subject for *Winnie the Pooh* and gang.

Talia and I walked onward to The Forbidden City, which is directly accessible from Tiananmen Square. It is a place steeped in ancient history, yanking visitors right out of the twenty-first century and into walls built by a Dynasty six-hundred years ago. Despite the age, it has been kept in pristine condition making the market value an estimated seventy billion USD today — it's the most valuable piece of real estate anywhere on the planet. I was mildly amused to find the city was so-called because when this was an active political hub for the Chinese emperors, they made sure the general plebs from the street were 'forbidden' to enter. Beyond the initial wow-factor of the ancient Chinese architecture showcasing how a few people lived in opulence many years ago, it did start to feel a little samey afterwards, and then once our feet started aching from walking around and the realisation set in that we were not going to see all 178 acres on offer in a single day, it was a good indicator to move on. We managed an hour around there; walked around the alleyways of the city, poked our heads into the rooms, looked into a few of the gold plated-bedrooms, checked out a couple of elaborately decorated halls, and decided it was time to get back into the modern world amongst the skyscrapers of Beijing forever in the distance poking over the walls of the city.

When I was 23, I took public transport on the main island in Fiji and managed to get lost. Young, confident and sure of where I was going, I hopped on a bus from my apartment by myself in the hope of finding a pharmacy and the medication within for my sick ex-girlfriend. I am not sure where I ended up exactly, but I must have been in the outskirts of some iffy area near the city of Nadi. You might be surprised to learn Fiji isn't all sun-kissed beaches, tropical reefs and laid-back people; particularly on the main island, it can be run-down, fairly dangerous and a little rapey in parts. Multiple years have passed since then, but it was still a significant event in my life for me to refer to it, still, as The Incident. I can vividly recall the intimidating stares of the locals from the bus window, getting the feeling of unease and, even in my young naivety, knowing there was trouble inbound. The unease then developing into horror as this bus was at the end of the line, all passengers were to get off, and I had to somehow get back to the safety of my apartment as the sun was setting. I begged the driver to take me anywhere, even back to the depot with him would do. He told me to get my jogging shoes on as it wasn't his problem. At this point, getting home was the only focus; the pharmacy wasn't going to happen and the poor ex-girlfriend would just have to suffer with the shits for the night. I found on the smaller islands of the country that the people were great, but some of the mainlanders were unpleasant and looked pretty hard to boot; a significant number of native Fijians are naturally big and look hard as nails, even some of the women there are absolute units. The group of lads I encountered after I disembarked from the bus were huge, aggressive, and after the money that they assumed I had on me. Luckily, they weren't particularly fast and after a brief confrontation I got away by running roughly towards where I thought the sea was — my plan being to get to the coastline and follow it home. Wandering lost through streets and, later, expanses of tropical vegetation of a Pacific island, running through open fields with long grass, palm trees and probably hidden poisonous critters as the sun began to set, I managed to get back to my apartment in one piece. It was an hour of panic which I wished never to experience again. For the past ten years I had told myself that it was the bus driver's fault for putting me in this situation, not mine, and since then public transport abroad is something I have actively avoided. I realise taking it again might not leave me in a rough area somewhere, as Fiji was unfortunate, but I could still end up lost in the back end of nowhere with no way to get home. You could forget taking it in China too; it would be all written in Chinese, and there'd be no English speakers around to help me. Talia could not believe I hadn't taken public transport in Beijing yet, claiming the underground here is fast, efficient and above all, easy.

"No chance, how can you even read which stop you're supposed to get off at?" I asked her.

"There's written English there," she said. Her good point went straight in through my ear and pinged out the other. I'd rather walk the ten miles.

Talia took the lead on transport (which was fine by me) through the city's underground tunnels and metro networks leading us to the north-west of the city, and onto the next stop of her list for today. I will admit I was impressed with how easy the journey was, it was well-priced, along with English translations underneath the Chinese signposts. We were now at the Summer Palace, a huge park featuring gardens and lakes and, of course, a palace, built again in the photogenic traditional Chinese-style architecture. We enjoyed a walk around the park, then spotted a huge hill to climb, and once at the top we could see as far as central Beijing in the distance. The weather was perfect, clear, mid-twenties and sunny — *Yahoo* was right after all. We'd been lucky with the smog today as there didn't appear to be any. Usually the city suffers as one of the worst places in the world for pollution; the locals endure a condition known colloquially as the 'Beijing Cough', characterised by a persistent tickle at the back of the throat from breathing in excessive fumes whilst outside. A thoroughly booming manufacturing economy and twenty million inhabitants getting around with less restrictions on exhaust fumes compared to Europe evidently comes at an environmental cost. We sat on the hill overlooking the city for some time and I noted my internet, which had been connecting sporadically throughout the day, was currently offering me the whole five bars of signal so I was able to talk to Mel in England, whilst

Talia Skyped her parents in Tel Aviv. I waved to Talia's dad through the phone, a big old Jewish dude, who looked puzzled as to who I was and why I was sitting so close to his daughter all the way in Asia.

The Summer Palace area appeared to be shutting down and uniformed men ushered people out of the site by late afternoon, so we took our hint to leave and made our way back to central Beijing on public transport again. We finished our last hour together taking an aimless walk through small roads lined with shops. The city is quite pleasant to walk around in certain areas, particularly those where the roads have been pedestrianised amongst the more traditional style of Chinese architecture, away from the brutal Soviet-style buildings in some districts. We spent some time in the shops to see what weird and wacky stuff was available here. I noticed many shops sold shelf upon shelf of rice wine at the strength of 56% — at the cost of about eighty pence a litre. No wonder I saw a man walking backwards earlier in the day! I bought a small bottle of the clear spirit to give Talia a laugh. I cracked the seal in front of her and took a few swigs. The inner lining of my throat melted away. If I held a lighter to my breath, I reckon I could have filled a hot air balloon.

Talia's flight home was looming ever nearer and by early evening it was time for us to part ways. We hugged goodbye and thanked each other for the company for the day. It had been a completely random encounter but I had really enjoyed my day with her, she was fun to be around and her knowledge of China had improved the day considerably. I certainly wasn't ready to be back by myself again and her departure killed my mood for exploring the city more once she'd left. Probably for the best I headed home anyway, I had a big day tomorrow at the iconic Great Wall of China. The spot Talia left me at wasn't too far from where I started at Tiananmen Square this morning, and even I, with my limited knowledge of the city, knew it would certainly still be a few miles away from home. I tried to flag down a taxi walking in the direction of Wei's along the massive multi-lane roads, many passed but none would stop for me. I realised unless I wanted to spend over an hour walking, the only way back would be the use of public transport. At first, I shuddered, but encouraged by the no-nonsense approach I'd seen with Talia earlier in the day I took the plunge. There was instant confusion with the station I needed once at the platform even in English, reading Guangqumenwai, which looked incredibly similar to the neighbouring station of Guangqumennei, almost putting me off stepping foot on the 'people mover' right away. I managed it though, got to the right stop without incident. Foreign public transport all by myself, in somewhere as foreign as China too. Well done me, and fuck you Fiji.

The sun had nearly set by the time I'd left the station and after exiting the platform I made my way through the alleyways between the towering apartment blocks heading back to Wei's. The evening's low light was exacerbated by the complete lack of street lighting. In fact, along with the lack of basic lighting, most of the roads through the residential areas were not the modern tarmacked ones from the nearby main streets just a minute away, but rather small dirt tracks with corrugated metal walls alongside them. The underdeveloped surroundings were quite peculiar considering I was practically central to a capital city with a booming economy. Local men sat playing card games on the floor with dim battery-powered lights, meanwhile some had made little makeshift stalls, essentially nothing more than a plastic sheet on the ground and a small bulb in the middle with clothes and fake watches spread out. Walking through this setting – dark alleyways with strangers around – even twelve hours ago at the start of the day would have had me nervous, but with my head giddy with confidence after successfully taking foreign public transport by myself for the first time in a decade, it was actually an interesting little stroll which I highly enjoyed. Plus, I'd had a buzz off just smelling the vapours of the rice wine, never mind the quarter bottle of it I'd drunk so far. There was a Chinese restaurant near by Wei's place (it's probably just called a restaurant here, thinking about it) that caught my eye earlier in the day. Not having a chance to eat a solid meal since arriving in the country, I was now ready to stuff my face. Inside, I could see patrons munching on what looked like huge bowls of noodle soup and I really wanted to try it too. I approached the counter of the restaurant, encountering two women who couldn't shift their visible surprise that a foreigner had entered the building. Even with the aid of the translation app, alongside me pointing to what other customers were having and making the gesture of eating with my hands, they didn't have a clue what I wanted, or likely what I was even doing in here. I had to settle for some small duck sandwich with a fried flat vegetable pancake thing, which looked and tasted like it had been sat on display at the counter most of the day. It was so disappointing compared to the noodle soup I wanted, and was annoyed that the translation app had let me down once again.

I had walked just under twenty-five kilometres by the end of the day – if my walk monitoring app wasn't letting me down too — and, having not eaten much, I was out like a light when my head hit the pillow.

### Beijing, China – Tuesday, 6th March 2018

I was up early the next day for the Great Wall tour I had already pre-booked, woken by cramp in my legs from all the walking yesterday. My poor old legs had an even longer day ahead of them today. There are two main sections of the wall close to Beijing; Badaling, which I read online was closest to Beijing and usually packed with tourists, or Mutianyu, which appeared to be a longer drive, but there were reportedly stretches of the wall you could have to yourself. I opted for that because, whilst I don't mind individual people, I fucking hate them when they form into crowds. It's a shame this isn't a *TripAdvisor* review because I feel I need to vent somewhere about the four hours it took the coach to get there — it wasn't the distance that was an issue, it was due to the badly organised tour that had us jumping around on several coaches, getting people on different tours mixed up in the process. I wanted to like our guide Mr. Chang more too; a man in his late twenties, but his mix of over-enthusiasm and speaking too fast in poor English just wound me up. I couldn't tell what was supposed to be a joke and what was serious.

"My wife not good looking," he started one sentence, stood at the front of the coach with a microphone in hand, and I'm thinking to myself 'He's building up to a joke here'. "But I am lucky to have a wife because there not many women in China due to one child policy."

Either it was an attempt at a joke, or just a comment on a cruel fact of reality here. China began a population control programme in the 1980s due to concerns of overpopulation and it was a policy that lasted for several decades, enforced by penalising couples who had more than one child with fine that often exceeded several years' wages. Most couples adhered to the rule but wanted to carry the family name on with a male, so females were sometimes aborted, or left to die once born.

"Anyway, we visit piece of wall that Donald The Trump go to."

Again, not sure if adding a 'the' into the name was a joke, but it certainly generated a laugh from the simpletons sat on the back seat of the coach, which annoyed me as hearing this was probably egging him on to tell more poor jokes if indeed he was trying to be funny.

"Be careful," he went on, "Many Mongolian prostitute live on this wall. If you want lady, meet in nightclub, not on wall. Also, do not expect their tea to be cheap."

Mongolian prostitutes?! That sell tea? Throughout the bits of waffle I could understand, he mentioned that there were two options once we got there. Either walk uphill and see the rebuilt part of the wall or take a cable car up, making easier access to the original wall that hadn't been renovated — with a stunning view of a lake to go with it. That sounded great. I looked out of the coach window, and despite *Yahoo* promising another roasting hot day, at this time of the morning it still looked cold outside. I don't know what it is with the locals, but many of them were wearing many layers, jumpers under thick bubble jackets and hats with ear flaps. This, combined with the trees still being completely bare of any leaves, the grass looking yellow and dead, and there was even ice hanging off some of the small rocky formations in the countryside – you could be forgiven for thinking we were still in the middle of winter.

The coach took a rest stop in a town somewhere on the route to the wall. Whilst technically still part of Beijing, it had likely once been an independent town which had since been engulfed by the ever-expanding capital. It was interesting to see Beijing out of the heavily built up districts, in a relatively quiet long road with the familiar block-style architecture along both sides, and masses of electrical wires. It doesn't matter where you are in Asia, or how developed the country is; a thick nest of telephone and electrical wire tangled together up a wooden pole are an absolute guarantee. Groups disembarked the coach for a break to enter a small shop, and I noticed I was the only guy here by himself as the rest of the tour group were either together as couples or other small groups. It had been fun to rekindle my solo travelling days but honestly, I'd rather have had Mel here with me. An experience like this almost feels wasted doing it by yourself, not being able to share it with someone else.

After a full morning listening to Mr. Chang dribble on for the whole journey, the coach eventually left Beijing and shortly after pulled up at the bottom of some hills in the countryside. Mr. Chang handed out entry tickets as we disembarked, instructing us that we had three hours free before we had to meet back up at the car park. I bolted off from the group as soon as I could and went straight for the uphill cable car ride to the top of the wall. Walking to the wall was an option, but it was a huge uphill trek, and my logic was, if there was lots of walking to be done today, it might as well be done on the wall itself rather than tiring myself out on some random hill before I even got to the thing. The wall soon appeared above me through the cable car's windows, comprised of large, chunky grey bricks that ran along the top of the rolling hillside with occasional outposts built into the wall. I don't think seeing a wall had ever stirred such excitement in me before. There was an immediate crowd once I disembarked the cable car, clusters of old people struggling with the multiple steps, whilst the rest of the tourists were posing for photos using selfie-sticks, eager to capture photos of their time here. Across the point of arrival and past the bulk of tourists to the other side of the wall, little one-man stalls had been set up on the floor, selling tat and drinks like beer and cans of coffee, ranging from one to two years out of date (I checked after nearly buying one!). I had a choice to follow the wall either east or west from the entrance; I picked west as it went straight up a big hill and appeared to put the majority of the people off heading in that direction. Credit here to the poor lads who were originally tasked to build something like this 2,300 years ago without the technology we have today, the effort it must have taken to create and haul the large bricks and form it into a towering wall that averages eight metres off the ground and is reportedly 21,000 kilometres long (it varies slightly depending on the source) is an impressive feat of raw manpower — in either direction, you could see the wall carrying on for miles. I am led to believe it was built with the purpose of keeping the neighbouring Mongolians out, although it was obviously not working as intended in modern times if Mr. Chang's Mongolian prostitutes were lurking about somewhere. Just walking the wall, up and down the steep inclines where it followed the hills had me out of breath, and I spared a thought for the poor sods that struggled with lots of stone on their back to build this thing millennia ago.

The atmosphere became increasingly quiet the further I got away from the entrance, where areas of the wall had been left to fall into disrepair with entire sections of brick collapsed to the ground, leaving fascinating little stretches to navigate and explore. The only thing that was missing from this adventure was my tunes, so I reached into my backpack for my earphones and, as I did, a little bottle brushed against my hand. It was the rice wine from yesterday! Perfect. It was building up to be another beautifully hot, sunny day. I was in my own little bubble, walking along an ancient wonder appreciating the epic scenery, with drum and bass blasting in my ears, getting slowly drunk on paint thinner. I couldn't have had it any better. I climbed to the highest point I could see for a quick photo and I wondered if I was pushing my available time and had to make my return. Mr. Chang had been chatting shit once again though; to my disappointment, there was neither Mongolian prostitutes nor a good view of a lake. Just arid yellow grass with a strip of the wall across the countryside as far as the eye could see. Prostitutes or not, it was still a brilliant day.

I'd fallen asleep on the coach home and, to my joy, Mr. Chang and got off before I woke up. It was great because I didn't have to give him a tip.

I took the subway home from the coach drop-off point without any trouble, confident as anything. I walked into the same restaurant as last night, although this time I was armed with a picture on my phone of some soup and noodles, determined to eat a proper meal for the first time in two days. They say a picture paints a thousand words, and I guess it applies to words of any language as the staff recognised what I wanted and actually brought me a bowl of noodles over. I was so excited, all that build-up for a proper Chinese meal... and once I got to taste it, it wasn't actually that good. Whilst the texture of the noodles was decent, they had a faint bleach aroma about them. I'm vaguely aware that bleaching of pasta and noodles goes on in some parts of the world (it's banned at home in Britain) — so, unless I was using a bowl that hadn't been rinsed properly, I could definitely taste it faintly in my food. I half expected the beer I'd ordered with my food to taste of *Dettol*, but was actually impressed by the excellent Chinese lager which improved the otherwise poor meal considerably — I will say this, they know how to brew a tasty beer in China!

Slurping away at my noodles, I noticed in the corner of my eye that I was being watched for some time by the restaurant cleaner who took the usual curiosity of looking at Westerners who are far from home and turned up it to maximum. After circling around me for some time, he eventually settled at just over an arm's length away and stared at me for entire minutes, mouth slightly ajar. I waved, he smiled back. I was hoping this small interaction would be enough for him to carry on doing his job, but it wasn't and he just carried on staring at me. His eyes started to dry as he didn't seem to even blink. It became a little unsettling after several minutes of continuous watching. I don't think I've ever spent so long watching animals in zoo exhibits as this guy was watching me, so I started to try and make a conversation with him just to break the awkwardness that apparently only I was feeling. The interaction became a confusing mess, I would point to myself and say "Steve" and then gesture my hand towards him, and he would only smile and nod. Out came the translation app again, which to be honest hadn't been much help on the whole trip and wasn't really much help now either as the words I typed into it generated a string of Chinese that he didn't appear to understand. The cultural differences and language barrier meant we weren't even able to get to the basics such as each other's name. I mostly felt the locals here were not bad people but interacting with them on any meaningful level was usually impossible. The restaurant manager shouted over to him after noticing the build-up of dirty plates on other tables and he quickly scampered off, leaving me to finish my bleachy string in peace.

I noticed I'd had a strange sensation at the back of my throat earlier in the day and had put it down to drinking the paint thinner rice wine, but by evening it had spread to my right ear and I felt a little tired and feverish. I had a stroll around some of the local night markets in the area that evening, trying to walk it off but also wanting to make the most of my last few hours in the country. It was nice to see how much the back streets that were quiet in the day came to a vibrant life of their own at night. I could have spent all night wandering around and seeing the rest of what Beijing had to offer. Unfortunately though, I had an early morning flight looming and really didn't feel a hundred percent, so I made the call to head home.

Wei and his partner were still up watching TV by the time I entered his apartment, so we had a chat together before retiring to bed. He asked what I thought about China, and I was honest with him. I said that I was apprehensive about the country at first, but I ended up really having a good time. I didn't expect Beijing to be so modern, safe and clean (well, in parts — although I think I had some luck with the good air quality of the past few days!), but then curiously found parts of the city that were like stepping back in time being so underdeveloped. We touched on the subject of politics; he openly told me he really doesn't give much thought to the government monitoring and censoring aspects of life as he was just used to it, whereas, although it doesn't affect me a great deal as a tourist for a few days, I do take issue with the practice of it. I am not saying we in the West are much better (the governments of the UK, US and their European allies definitely monitor online activity of their own people in one way or another), but at least we still have the freedom to vocalise our criticism of those in charge. I don't like this whole idea that those in charge can lead unchallenged, where they stamp out resistance by increasingly authoritarian methods. Don't get me started on China with Taiwan either. Having visited Taiwan in the past, it is a highly developed, picturesque island of high living standards that broke away from mainland China in the 1940s during a civil war. At this point it is pretty much its own country; crucially, it is a thriving democracy that wants to be recognised globally as independent, and you'd hope after eighty years China would just leave it be. Instead, it regularly threatens Taiwan that it will take back control there one day — if not by diplomatic means, then by force if necessary. From my conversations with the people of Taiwan, they just want to be left to decide their own futures away from the bully next door. Some were particularly wary of its attempts to gain control by installing a puppet leader (if this does happen, the least China could do is choose a puppet leader that looks like *Piglet*). Again, the US, and to a lesser extent the UK aren't a lot better, and have poor reputations with global interference over the years. We're not currently trying to take over an area like China is with Taiwan, but for years we meddled in the Middle East or other places that haven't warranted it. China is like our Western countries in that aspect; the people and the country are generally great, but it is just run by wankers. I imagine the global superpowers will become even bigger arseholes when resources become scarcer as global warming continues to boil the planet, or as technology evolves into new and scary ways of monitoring the people and censoring what they can watch or think. Even registering my stay with the authorities is, I think, just a way to set the tone for tourists for when they arrive — "We are monitoring you". I didn't end up registering over my stay, and there was a moment of increased heart rate as I wondered whether there was going to be an issue at the counter to clear immigration for my flight out of the country. But there wasn't, I'd worried over nothing. The effort to monitor everyone, residents and tourists alike, must take considerable resources to enforce, and I guessed in the grand scheme of things my short stay wasn't interesting enough for the inhabitants of *The Hundred Acre Wood.*

NB – *I posted a short version of this online not long after my trip, and one of my Chinese friends commented on it. Firstly, they said why didn't I tell them I was going, so they could offer support and advice! But they took issue with me making a fuss about having to register my stay. They said that people from Asian countries have to register their stay all the time when coming to Western countries, along with additional requirements like bank statements, proof of employment and planned itinerary to get a visa. I had never really thought about it that way before, so I thought it was a fair comment and worth a mention. It comes from the genuine privileges of travelling with a British passport that I don't usually have to deal with this sort of thing whilst visiting most places, and only a handful of countries put British travellers under such a level of scrutiny.*

# SOUTH KOREA

### Beijing, China – Wednesday, 7th March 2018

I woke up at Wei's small spare bedroom in Beijing feeling rough, the sore throat and ear ache from yesterday were followed by a raised temperature and shit night's sleep. My last hour in Beijing wasn't spent appreciating the scenery for the last time through the taxi window to the airport, but with my eyes closed lying along the back seat trying not to groan out loud and unsettle the taxi driver. I then had the plane ride to deal with. I don't usually like flying at the best of times, but luckily Beijing to South Korea's capital, Seoul, is less than a two-hour flight east, and today's flight thankfully avoided any turbulence so it wasn't the worst flight I'd ever suffered through. Possibly pre-empting the rise of something like Covid-19 before it smashed around the globe, even back in 2018 South Korea's international airports had stringent entry requirements for flights coming in from a handful of countries, China being one, and passengers were subjected to on-the-spot health checks. A big red notice on the immigration declaration form stated that the sick could be launched into quarantine or denied entry, and I didn't like the headache this might cause, leaving poor old Mel stuck in Korea by herself, whose flight from England had come in a couple of hours before mine. Korean immigration had a mandatory high-tech temperature scanner which I had to stand in and allow it to read my body temperature. I honestly have no idea how it didn't flag me because I felt completely off by the time I'd got to this point. A green tick appeared on the machine's digital display and I was ushered on through to arrivals, leaving me ready to spread whatever I'd picked up around Korea.

Like the weather had been back in Beijing over the past few days, it was a perfect 22°C, pleasantly warm and it felt nice to step outside into the sun from the terminal. I could see Mel waiting for me at a coffee shop by arrivals with a small latte in her hand and ran over to hug her. We'd managed nearly a month apart with my work stint in Indonesia before China, and I had honestly missed her a lot. She wasted no time in reminding me that I had promised to take her out for a fancy dinner on our first night in Seoul as a treat because I'd been away so long. I had secretly booked a restaurant ready for the night with some of the best reviews in the entire city. We were also looking to go clubbing over the weekend (the capital is renowned for a good night out) and were even attempting to enter North Korea — both on the same day! In the meantime though, we'd be spending a couple of nights centrally in the country in a traditional village called Jeonju, an absolute tourist trap that manages to retain the look and feel of a Korean town from hundreds of years ago. There are so many options to consider when visiting South Korea beyond the capital; coastal villages, cities, numerous islands off the coast of the mainland; that whatever we'd picked, we would be missing something else equally as cool. Jeonju was easy to get to from Seoul on public transport, looked cute on the pictures, not to mention it was highly rated amongst travel websites — so it was as good as anywhere for a couple of days.

One of the stereotypes that you might associate with South Korea (similarly to neighbouring Japan) is that it's often at the forefront of developing new technologies and unleashing them to the public well before it inevitably makes its way over to our shores. Unbelievably, there were small robots that moved around the airport on wheels, acting as information points on-the-go, interacting with lost or confused passengers and aiding them — it really was like stepping ten years into the future (whereas, at my local airport, Manchester, time goes backwards; the queues through immigration get longer each year and instead of robots they'll probably start using horses and carts for luggage transport). Even the coach we embarked on to our destination was high-tech; modern, comfy, individual TVs like on a plane, lots of leg room — spacious even for a long creature like me — topped off with a space to plug a phone charger in. It was fantastic. Mel and I sat near the front of the coach and caught up properly on our past few weeks. She'd had a pretty boring time stuck in England with our notoriously bad weather at this time of year. I got to tell her about bleached noodles, Mongolian prostitutes and people walking backwards in the street — and that was just in the past two days! We were having such a laugh at the front of the coach that even before we had departed, the coach driver turned around, faced us and made a loud "shh" noise with his finger over his lips. That might have been a cultural faux pas on our behalf there, being loud and obnoxious on public transport. I mean we weren't being offensive or anything, just laughing loudly, but only after the driver had done this had I noticed everyone else on the coach had been practically sat in silence like well-behaved children. This made us feel like the naughty kids on a school trip, trying not make each other laugh for the rest of the journey in fear of getting another telling off from the grumpy driver.

Time spent in transit seems to batter my energy levels even though I'm sat on my arse the majority of the time, and the journey to Jeonju took another couple of hours which had us arriving just as the sun was setting. Although tired and groggy, I couldn't help but appreciate the beautiful surroundings. The Hanok village is a district of Jeonju made entirely of quaint, traditional Korean bungalows which is part of an otherwise modern Korean city. The style in the Hanok village isn't all that different from traditional Chinese-style buildings I'd recently seen, at least to my untrained English eye. Neat brickwork and tiles with intricate patterns on them formed the base of the buildings and above that, highly polished, carved wooden roof supports that seem to flick the roof up at its corners. The locations of these buildings have supposedly had land and seasonal considerations for optimal sunlight, and a correctly-built Hanok has a mountain at the rear and a river at the front. Traditionally, the decor and furniture is of a very minimal style. I had imagined our Hanok looked cute and traditional on the outside but would still cater for tourists with modern amenities within, but from the onset, sliding a thin wooden door to enter (a burglar could have easily put his foot through the fucker if he wanted) should have really been an indicator to me of what laid within. Shoes are forbidden beyond the door and had to be left outside — fair enough, this is Asia and standard practice across most of the continent. I can deal with a burglar-approved door and no shoes, but then things started to get tricky; the table in the centre of the room was no more than a foot high off the ground, with pillows around it on the hard, wooden ground. I could hear my back already creaking in anticipation of a sit-down meal there. Then, the beds were "mattresses" of foam, not deeper than a single centimetre laid out on the wooden floor, with a tiny pillow made giving a further generous offering of about twenty centimetres. Of course, the toilet would be a squatting one, and the shower head only reached half way up my body.

That night, I'd have been a little more up for embracing the traditional lifestyle had my head not been ringing from my illness, and I found that my back just couldn't hack sleeping on hard ground; it ached after only a couple of hours on the foam. A thin mattress is actually supposed to be quite good for posture, but my spine is too used to having a big comfy mattress for over thirty years now, so I'm never going to settle into a thin strip of foam wrapped in a bedsheet. I asked for another mattress the following day as I just couldn't hack another night on it, and whilst the hotel owners did provide me one, they weren't used to such an unusual request and charged me the cost of two beds for the remainder of my stay. Needless to say, it didn't improve the comfort much.

### Jeonju, South Korea – Thursday, 8th March 2018

I woke up feeling ill, dizzy and with one of my ears completely blocked. Even with two whole mattresses, my fever dominated the night — giving me the worst sleep I'd ever had in my life. The room spun as I stood up. The symptoms were not improving and, worse still, I was wasting quality time on my holiday. I decided it was time to haul myself to the doctor. Just before storming through the door to try and get myself fixed, Mel insisted I had breakfast first before we set off anywhere.

In a small neighbouring room outside from our entrance was where the hotel served breakfast. Inside, I was thoroughly saddened to see yet another table no more than a foot off the ground with no seats like back in our room, although it was my own fault for getting my hopes up that there might have been something comfy to sit at. I should have also been mentally prepared for food that wouldn't look like "breakfast" to my Western point of view, but I wasn't. Breakfast to me doesn't need to be a big English fry up (although you can't ever beat it); simple stuff like toast or porridge will do. But no, it has to be all weird stuff in Asia doesn't it? Mel was loving it, sat comfortably at the small table being presented interesting Asian food. Out came little pots of beans and fermented vegetables. Mashed unidentifiable green stuff that tasted like shit. White rice boiled into a sticky blob. Some sort of fried squid balls. Kimchi, which is fermented cabbage added to every meal, usually quite nice, but again not a breakfast food as far as I'm concerned. I sat awkwardly, like a big lanky crane leaning over the table picking at tiny bits I could stomach, but I just wasn't feeling this hardcore Asian breakfast. I'm not actually a fussy eater usually, as I mentioned in the Peru chapter, but when it comes to breakfast, it's just one meal where I don't appear to have much wiggle-room for any weird foreign stuff. I've even been tricked by the word "porridge" in the past: in Jakarta, Mel's mum had asked if I'd like some not long after I'd woken up. Totally expecting oats, I was presented with handful of mung beans swimming around in a sweet watery green solution. Straight in the bin when she wasn't looking. The world is becoming a more connected place these days; culture is shared and sometimes adopted elsewhere across the globe, but from my perspective, breakfast is just something that the East and West don't ever seem to align on.

Let me just quickly tell you that dinner is thankfully a different ball game in Korea. Bulgogi is a delicious type of Korean barbecue meat enjoyed across the country, but for me the signature dish of the South Korea is Bibimpab, a large ceramic bowl often served too hot to touch, filled with warm rice, lots of sautéed or boiled veggies on top, followed by soy sauce, kimchi again, meat and a fried egg. It doesn't sound particularly exciting when looking at the ingredients list, but when it's all stirred up before eating it's honestly one of those delicious hearty meals that is thoroughly enjoyable. The thought of that for my dinner gave me the motivation I needed for the day and, having picked at my breakfast for five minutes, I set off to look for a doctor.

I couldn't see many other foreign tourists out on the streets. Korea was very much like China in that respect, most of the tourism appeared to be native. There was no historic European colonialism here, nor a high number of Western tourists flooding the streets. The knock-on effect from this is that English isn't understood much within the local population. Sure, there'd likely be a few speakers around Seoul, but out in the rest of the country there wasn't anyone I found I could properly communicate with and this was proving problematic when trying to get help from a doctor. I didn't trust the translation app for a second, and there was no way I'd be using it to relay what was wrong with me. "Suspected ear infection" could have read to the doctor as "I want a vasectomy". Korean is a tonal language, much like many languages in east Asia, meaning it's a bit difficult so I immediately gave up on trying to learn any. A Thai friend explaining the Thai language to me once said that tonal languages can use a word that sounds almost identical to the untrained ear, but a slight change in pitch of how the word is pronounced can completely change its meaning or context. I generally try to learn a few phrases before arriving to a country, even if it's just please and thank you, but attempting a crash course in Korean whilst ill in bed to later convey to a doctor what was wrong was a task that was currently beyond my mental capacity. Regardless, I persisted and visited several separate doctors and pharmacies in the city and tried my best to explain in loud English what was wrong, but I didn't get anywhere with them. I returned to my thin foam bed, absolutely defeated from a morning wasted walking around, and then begun with a bout of diarrhoea. The time here was beginning to turn into a nightmare. I'd hardly seen any of the area during my time there, and certainly hadn't spent enough time around it to appreciate it all. The Hanok village genuinely looked gorgeous to walk around, and at least Mel got to enjoy herself for the day without me. I guess you have to take the highs with the lows when on the road. Hopefully I'd have more luck getting fixed in the capital.

## Seoul, South Korea – Friday, 9th March 2018

Seoul is a monster of a city. With ten million people across its 25 distinct districts (each of which reportedly with its own feel to it), we went in knowing we'd barely scratch the surface during our limited stay of an extended weekend. It's easy to get lost amidst rows of signs, adverts, neon lights, LEDs crammed onto the side walls of the towering buildings; every direction had something for the eye. Occasionally there'd be small decorated parks and cute traditional buildings like those found back in Jeonju, but mostly it was just a modern city with either huge main roads or small alleyways adjacent to them, bars and small restaurants squeezed in below the skyscrapers. It was pleasantly clean too, which is a rarity for a city in Asia, although like anywhere on the continent it was a little busy on the traffic side of things. We had purposely booked our hotel in the Gangnam area (yes — that same Gangnam from the song) as it was renowned for some of the best nightclubs in the city. The fever was bogging me down and I really needed to get it shifted before I tried to hit any of the clubs otherwise I risked more wasted days, and worse, a wasted weekend.

Mel and I are pretty fortunate that our combined experiences abroad over our lifetimes that has led us to know people from places all around world, more often than not, knowing a person or two that we can rely on when a crisis arises in foreign lands. In this case, Mel had kept in touch with a native South Korean who she'd met as a child, and this friend had managed to organise an appointment for me with a doctor in the city. I was lucky because I honestly didn't know where to start, even aided by the internet. I have been to the doctors a few times abroad after accidents or illnesses, and I always fear how much it will end up costing me. Only a fool travels without insurance, but there's the whole excess which can often be up to a couple of hundred pounds before the insurance itself kicks in. Plus, hospitals and doctors' surgeries aren't exactly the nicest places even back home, so mixing in a foreign setting, often with lower hygiene standards and doctors that are hard to communicate with, can make it quite an unpleasant experience. I needn't have worried though as the surgery in Seoul was far superior, above anything I'd experienced back home in England. The doctor — a charming Korean man who spoke English better than most English people, aided by his state-of-the-art gadgetry, soon had me feeling confident I was in good hands. He placed my head in a fancy headrest at the edge of a high-tech but slightly intimidating machine. A metal tube came out and horrifically went up my nose a bit to take a swab, and the arm retreated back into itself to process the swab that was now wet and green. It was honestly all so sophisticated there, I was surprised I wasn't been seen to by a robot. The doctor was able to diagnose that I'd picked up a sinus infection which had blocked something called a Eustachian tube (a little pipe that normally drains ear fluid to the back of the throat). I was in and out of the place within fifteen minutes, given the medication that I needed and sent on my way. It was perhaps a little on the pricey side, but definitely worth it, and I'm sure the placebo effect kicked in because I started to feel better only minutes after taking the prescription. Right — it was finally time to really start enjoying South Korea!

Mel loves two things above all else: eating out at posh restaurants, and not paying for it. If I ever need to make things right if I've fucked up, then taking her out for a meal is my get-out-of-jail-free card — well, not exactly free, but you know what I mean. I'm more of a cheap pub grub sort of guy, but with my long work trip having kept us apart from each other for the best part of a month, I really wanted to give her a good restaurant experience to make up for it. I had a look around on *TripAdvisor* for highly reviewed restaurants and found one not too far away, still in Gangnam. Both dressed up, me in my best shirt and Mel looking stunning in a figure-hugging black dress, we took an evening stroll through Gangnam to the restaurant and entered into what, in hindsight, may well have been one of the most expensive restaurants in the whole of the city. I'd expected to pay a fair bit for my compensation meal tonight, but I was about to get bent over and shafted. All the clues were there; the foyer had photos of previous clientele with the restaurant owner, boasting the A-list Western celebrities who had come in before me (Arnold Schwarzenegger and Lady Gaga to name a few). If this is where millionaires go to eat then I'm sure the food will be great, but it's a far cry from a *Wetherspoons'* pint and a burger for £4.59. It was fancy once inside the restaurant seating area, black marble flooring and a dimly lit interior with rich couples quietly dining at candle-lit tables. Thank God there were proper tables and chairs at least, none of this child's play-set table shit like back in Jeonju. We sat down and were presented the menu.

I've never before paid a day's wage for a single steak and it honestly brought a tear to my eye once I saw the whole bill. Let's just say the steak was one of the cheaper things on the menu. The nausea I experienced likely wasn't from the medication I'd taken in the afternoon, but rather seeing a long number I was due to pay. I managed to convince Mel to go for the cheapest bottle of wine on the menu, which was still more than any bottle of alcohol I've ever purchased. The rest of the meal was fine, again very similar to the breakfast; little pots of fermented cabbage and bits of weird unidentifiable veg and sauces to go along with the expensive main course. I was a little underwhelmed by it even without factoring in the price tag, but Mel was happy which was the main thing, and tomorrow was another day where I could try and claw back on spends. More importantly, I was going on a day trip to North Korea in the morning so I'd be doing something cool, and tonight will just be left as an expensive memory.

## Seoul, South Korea – Saturday, 10th March 2018

Our trip to North Korea had been cancelled. I was absolutely gutted, only noticing the cancellation as I checked my inbox over breakfast and seeing an email from the tour company with the subject "URGENT". To find the reason why our day's travel plans had been ruined, we have to start at the beginning, many decades ago. Korea was once a culturally unified peninsula existing for over five hundred years, then that pesky World War Two happened, and around the globe many countries drew up new borders in the aftermath. Korea arguably had one of the most dramatic post-war changes of any country and was split into two, the North taken by the Soviets, while the South was taken by the Allied Forces. Both sides, over time, imprinted their ways on how to rule a country, resulting in two incredibly disparate Koreas, each with vastly different levels of freedom, technology, population and quality of life. In 1950, the North attempted to unify Korea again by invading the South, resulting in a three-year war which only cemented the newly divided peninsula. Even to this day, the two Koreas don't like each other, viewing each other with extreme suspicion through the heavily fortified border, separated by rows of large fencing that runs the whole peninsula from east to west, with the occasional watch tower stationed along it. The whole length of where the two borders meet is called the Demilitarised Zone, or DMZ for short. There's a special point along the wall named Panmunjom, or Truce Village, which is a series of simple but small blue buildings, sat between a small gap in the fences where officials from both North and South can physically cross to meet each other. It's still a highly militarised area with many guards from both countries stationed there (if you ever see North Korean defectors running into South Korea on the news, its usually here) and this area is the only legal option to set foot onto North Korean soil without having to enter via a visit visa and getting a stamp in a passport. Mel and I had hoped to visit here today, seeing the North Korean border guards up close and personal, but Kim Jong-Un had struck again — not content with disrupting my travel in Beijing last week, he had now decided to meet the South Korean president, the first time in nearly eleven years for such a meeting between the two sides. As this is the only site they can practically meet at without travelling to a third country — and Kim only travels by bulletproof train don't forget — they closed it down to tourists weeks before the meeting was due, ruining our travel plans for the day. It was big news internationally, and left our plans in the bin. Cheers again, Kim.

The travel company we booked the tour with offered an alternative tour, which still involved going into the DMZ to get right up to view the North. We reluctantly accepted the new plans. It was still worth doing, but honestly, it just wasn't as exciting. I wanted to boast next time I'm in the pub with the lads that I've actually had my feet on North Korean soil. Whilst I'm not completely ruling out visiting there one day and travelling in the country properly with a stamp in my passport, I'm honestly a bit scared of visiting. Some stories trickle out of the country of Westerners detained arbitrarily for things we wouldn't even consider a crime back home. I know instances like these are rare, but with the number of near misses I've had abroad over the years, it's only a matter of time before it all catches up with me. There was the case a few years back of poor Otto Warmbier, the American lad on a group tour to the capital who stole a propaganda poster from his hotel as a dare. You might think "idiot", and sure, why risk it, but then his punishment was completely over the top; he was detained in prison and may have been tortured — the details from the story are murky — and was eventually released, effectively brain-dead, on "compassionate grounds". He died upon returning to the States a few months after the initial incident. Whilst it's likely the above is true, the problem is, similar to our information on China, all of it comes from our Western-biased media outlets and it does make me wonder how much of that story is the truth, or has it been reported in a way that paints North Korea negatively, without any objectivity to it? Did he only steal a poster? Did he fall sick in custody? Still, I get it isn't a country you want to fuck around in, but the potential of doing something wrong, intentional or not, and receiving entirely disproportionate penalties really puts me off visiting. I'm hardly a responsible drinker either, and beer is available there — once I get a beer in me, I'm up for anything. Take a poster down from a hotel?! Fuck that, I'll take two!

I was surprised to learn that the trip from Seoul is worryingly close to the DMZ and therefore the North Korean border, at around forty miles. Considering the two countries don't like each other, having your capital city so close to the enemy and its ballistic missile capabilities must be quite sobering for the inhabitants, or then again perhaps not. Perhaps the severity of having a threat looming over you every day wears off after a while. So close is the city to the border in fact, that multiple tunnels have been found popping up around Seoul's districts over the years where the North has allegedly attempted to dig into the South, possibly in preparation for an invasion. Our Korean guide stated that while it had been twenty years since the last tunnel was found, eighty had been located over the years and there were likely some that still hadn't been found today. I'm sure the South probably has a few secret ones going the other way, too! Our tour was taking us into one of these tunnels as a consolation for the original plans being cancelled. I can go into a tunnel at home though, what I wanted to do was go to North Korea. I mentioned this to Mel and she told me to stop sulking about it.

The journey to the tunnel once entering the DMZ was thoroughly bleak. Natural vibrant colour hadn't returned to the landscape yet as it was still early spring, so the fields and trees were a palette of brown and beige colours, and amongst the fields. I actually found myself missing my last tour guide, Mr. Chang; although most of the information he said wasn't accurate, with his mythical Mongolian prostitutes, he was at least upbeat compared to our current Korean guide who'd just state grim facts in a monotonous voice. One fact was that he had family on the North side somewhere, but the two sides of the family haven't talked in two generations because the divide between the two countries prevents communication. He also instructed us not to stray too far when we left the coach, as there were buried landmines everywhere and we could be blown into pieces with a misplaced foot.

The DMZ went on and on. A no-man's-land that simultaneously felt huge because of the ongoing miles of it, yet oppressive due to the relentless man-made structures designed to restrict movement throughout the whole thing. Parallel to the road through the Zone ran tall chain link fencing with barbed wire at the top, and occasional watch towers stationed in the empty fields some distance away. I couldn't quite figure out if they'd be manned by men from either the North or the South. Large, spiked metal barriers lay in the wide road which forced our coach to chicane around them — I wondered if they were stationed there to halt invading tanks. It was all a bit grim and the thought of it going along the whole border of the two countries, dividing two neighbours who share more culture, language and people than anyone else in the world was a bit sad to think about. The coach's first stop within the DMZ involved having the South's military enter the coach to check our passports, a moment which set a serious tone for the next few hours. The first stop on which we were actually allowed to disembark was a visit to the Dorasan train station, a single large, authoritarian, grey concrete platform that led straight to the North's capital, Pyongyang. I'm not quite sure why we'd stopped here as there wasn't really a lot to do once we got to the platform, maybe the guide had just been bulking up the time with other things to do because of the loss of the main attraction that had been cancelled. The station was huge, a modern facility which was kept clean, but I suppose with no transport allowed between the two countries it was probably quite easy to keep that way. Our small coach group wandered off to the little visitor's centre, leaving Mel and I alone on the platform. We both stood as if waiting for a train that would never come, peering down the eerily quiet tracks leading North. Alas, no trains were due now, or likely ever; despite having been built as a symbolic hope of the two Koreas once again reuniting, there was fat chance of it happening any time soon.

The second stop was a little more interesting, the bus had weaved uphill to a vantage point allowing us to look into the North Proper, further along the DMZ. The thing I found most strange about it all was that this was clearly a military zone with large numbers of the South Korean army stationed there, occasionally performing drills, but the area doubled up as a tourist attraction complete with a gift shop and food stand. I might be wrong, but surely there are no other military-fortified borders in the world that treat the zone like a tourist attraction too? I highly doubt the Gaza Strip has its own gift shop! Tourists disembarked in their dozens from multiple coaches in a car park shared with military vehicles, the army walking amongst the tourists. I found it peculiar. We took a moment at the vantage point with the other tourists to look out to the North. The view was unexpectedly higher than I imagined it would be as the rest of the DMZ we'd seen had been quite flat, but this gave us a view that spanned miles into North Korea. It was mostly fields, and again, the same dried vegetation as before at the lower levels, which left a lifeless light-brown colour everywhere. Most of it was unremarkable, other than a small industrial town that I could just about see through the morning haze. Music began playing from the town faintly — the North's national anthem could just about be heard — I assumed they were using large speakers somewhere in the town facing towards our direction. As it started, countering the faint patriotic sounds of a nation's anthem, the South's anthem began blasting out too, possibly from underneath the very tourist platform we were on. For several minutes the music overlapped, the countries trying to out-patriot each other. Absolutely crazy these Koreans are, the both of them.

The final part of the tour brought us to a tunnel the North had dug many years ago, but had been discovered well before it was able to be used. These days it sits, still a tunnel between the two countries as it hasn't been filled it in, but this particular tunnel out of all those found over years had been designated for tourists to come and stand around in. It took quite a while to gradually descend the slope on foot from the ground level, as the tunnel was about twenty metres underground and once at the entrance it was a cold, dark, narrow hole bored through the rock. I had to crouch slightly to get inside as there had obviously been no consideration for tall foreign tourists of the future when it was dug out — some tourist attraction this was! It was claustrophobic too as there wasn't much width to the tunnel either, perhaps a metre across. Tourists are allowed to walk a bit into it, but you will soon reach obstructions and signposts instructing not to pass any further in both Korean and English, I assume you'd be greeted by the North's army at the other end. I wouldn't have been surprised to have seen another gift shop squeezed down here somewhere, but in reality there was nothing more than a long tunnel leading off into the darkness. I suppose seeing it and what it represented was interesting. Hell, it's probably the most interesting hole I've ever seen in my life, but ultimately it wasn't the trip into the North that I had spent months waiting in excitement for. The day had left me a little disappointed if I'm being honest. I hoped sampling Seoul's legendary nightlife tonight would make up for it all.

We got back to the hotel late afternoon and showered up in preparation for our big night. Advanced technology has permeated all aspects of life in South Korea and therefore I shouldn't have been surprised to see that the toilet in our hotel room wasn't just your standard shit collector but rather a bit of high-tech kit offering a total of ten option buttons on a panel next to the bowl. I sat down on it, playing with the control panel, passing time as Mel spent the usual age getting ready. The buttons weren't in Korean but rather had basic images as symbols on them, symbols that were supposed to be universally understood, but figuring out what each symbol represented had become a mystery which I intended to get to the bottom of. The buttons did a whole manner of things — the ultimate aim was to effectively clean a bum-hole without ever having to reach down into the toilet bowl using a hand. A light spraying of water with temperature controls, a little heater blowing warm air to dry it afterwards. It was great, I didn't really need to take a shit, but pressed a little one out anyway just to see how clean the toilet could get my arse. One button puzzled me a little though, it looked like a pair of bum-cheeks with water spraying between them. I'd already pressed the button that sprayed water onto my crevice, and had no idea how this one would differ, so I gave it a go. What I couldn't see at the time was a little plastic tube slide out from under the bowl, stopping just below my anus which then shot a jet of pressurised water past it, a sort of colonic irrigation mode if you will, causing me to scream in surprise and fly off the toilet. Shitty warm water dribbled out onto the toilet floor, a trial following me and my shame of being penetrated by a futuristic toilet. I've been with Mel long enough now for her to not even bother asking why I was screaming in the toilet while she was getting ready in the bedroom.

Me, Mel and my incredibly clean arse were ready to hit the town and see what one of the best party cities in the world had in store for us. Mel's Korean friend, who had sorted my appointment yesterday, was helping us out further by kindly meeting up with us and taking us out for a night on the town. Her name was Sook, a friendly lady in her mid-twenties and only the second Korean I had met that was fluent in English. She and Mel had studied in at an International school together in Vietnam when they were in their early teens, and now as adults hugged in the street upon seeing each other for the first time in fourteen years. I said hello and introduced myself. Sook led the way on the night's plans through the streets of Seoul (God, how much better places are when you're with someone local!) and eventually brought us to an incredible semi-outdoor restaurant on a busy side street. Each table had a small barbecue at the centre, enabling patrons to cook all-you-could-eat slices of meat on the grill. The atmosphere was great; the place was packed with people enjoying the start of their evening, the smell of barbecued meats filled the air as each table cooked their food, whilst neon light from the outdoor street signs poured into the edge of the restaurant where we sat. I was slightly annoyed that I had spent all that money yesterday on fine dining — which was pretty average if I'm being honest — when there was something like this at about £12 per head which tasted much better, all without a cap on the quantity of food I could eat and a bustling atmosphere to go with it. It was great. I'd be lying if I said a cheaper price doesn't improve the enjoyment of something, but it also shows that paying over the odds doesn't guarantee a good experience either.

We began a mini pub crawl around Seoul after the food, hopping around to different places hand-picked by Sook. I was in my element with countless streets of good bars on offer, they were trendy and all had a great atmosphere, although pretty generic I suppose, but such are bars around the world — it's hard to put too much of a unique spin on a place where the ultimate goal is just to sit and get drunk. Where Korean bars did offer something different was the alcohol, a wide selection of locally brewed beers, pale ales and later shots of the native fruit spirit, Soju, that were all fun to try. There hadn't been any awkwardness with only recently meeting Sook as she was amicable anyway but even so, with an evening of alcohol thrown into the mix, our table of three spent most of the early evening laughing at each other's terrible jokes. On one table sat next to us was a large middle-aged white guy playing with his beer mat by himself. I could see him occasionally looking in our direction and laughing at some of our jokes, and could tell that it was all a precursor to eventually introducing himself. Bert was an American guy out here on a week's business trip, with his wife and kids at home back in California; here by himself, drinking alone without anything else better to do on a Saturday night. He asked if he could join our table. We said sure, the more the merrier. Bert was evidently a wealthy man due to his job as a particle physicist and was keen to quickly jump up the friendship ladder a few rungs by getting multiple rounds in straight away (all this was making up for the costs incurred last night as far as I was concerned!). He seemed like a nice fella and did go into detail a bit about his reasons for being out here and his job (particle accelerometers or something), but when you've had eight pints of Korean wheat beer it's hard to focus on subjects that require your brain functioning at full capacity. Once he had his claws in, Bert tried to coerce the group to go bowling after learning that our intention was to ultimately end up in a nightclub. This guy was a forty-year-old scientist who looked like he had never seen a strobe light before, never mind the inside of a nightclub, and the idea of going for the first time tonight didn't appeal to him, instead offering a few more rounds of beer as an incentive if we went bowling. I had to stop him there; I've not come all the way to South Korea, overcome both a fever and being raped by a toilet just to go bowling. Sorry Bert — you're coming to a nightclub with us.

1AM. Sook led the way through the streets of the city which looked even better at night, as the many neon signs and adverts stationed in vertical rows along the buildings reflected off the floor from a recent rainfall, giving the whole area an artificial glow. I had found an affinity with the drinking culture and the scenery, as a fan of the cyberpunk aesthetic which takes inspiration from big neon Asian cities like Seoul, a polar opposite to rural England where I grew up, I find it fascinating to just be immersed in it all, even if my time is merely spent walking through the streets. The endless bars filled with people having a good time is the cherry on top. I was happy to see people were walking with drinks in the streets too, as we'll be damned if we're going to spend three and a half minutes sobering up whilst walking between places. Amusingly, some people looked like they might have headed straight to the bars direct from work, some were as old as Bert, still in their office shirts and ties. One wasted guy even had the foresight to handcuff his briefcase to his arm; clearly, he'd be free to get blind drunk without fear of losing it. Statistically, South Koreans are the biggest consumers of alcohol in Asia — and sure, the majority of the crowd out tonight were certainly younger, but the older people were still out getting wasted. I can't speak for North Korea, but in the South alcohol plays a huge part in their culture, used to build relationships and relied on to remedy stress, people are almost obligated to drink for a social occasion or after work with colleagues — I could have been writing about the UK there, and it resonates with the heavy drinking culture I grew up in. Whilst this does indeed make it a fun place to spend a weekend partying, there are some dark numbers behind the scenes. An estimated 1.7 million Koreans out of a population of 51 million are alcoholics, bringing with it problems for the health service and increased levels of crime (up to 50% of violent crime is alcohol related, which again sounds like I could be writing about home). Where we differ though is getting blackout drunk; passing out in the street, sleeping against cars or shop windows, an activity usually for the hardcore dedicated piss-heads back home (often the young male yob types), whereas its normalised in Korea for respected individuals from all walks of life; office workers, engineers, accountants, all sleeping in alleyways sometimes with dried vomit on them. I wondered what the Korean peninsula would be like if all the bloody foreigners had just left it alone after World War Two. The States, bringing their capitalism and abusing alcohol as a crutch for the stresses capitalism inflicts, meanwhile up North, sure, they don't have office workers handcuffing themselves to briefcases, but are instead subjugated to a rotund dictator who restricts their freedoms. Between both Koreas, they truly are one of the most interesting areas on Earth.

As I'd noted when entering the country, South Korea was a step ahead of the rest of the world regarding disease transmission in public, and it was curious that roughly a quarter of the youth who were on a night out were wearing the face masks which the rest of the world would be using in a few years' time when Covid struck. I doubted most of the masks were for germ prevention though, quite obviously some individuals were making fashion statements, huge teeth or logos printed on them. One guy even had a small plastic hole in his mask, enabling him to drink using a straw without him having to take it off. Whilst the girls caught up from their years apart, a few steps behind them Bert and I spoke and got to know each other a bit more. He was quite modest and certainly not a show off, he was just an interesting guy. He name-checked some of his friends which I'd heard of, surprisingly enough; impressive connections to renowned people in technology from Silicon Valley and such. Ultimately though, he was himself a geek. Admittedly, I am a geek too; don't get me started on gaming, computers or especially GPUs, but I'm one of the geeks that enjoys getting wasted in nightclubs as a pastime, whereas Bert had made it clear that a usual Saturday night for him was making his way through a Star Trek boxset. To his credit, he'd gone out in a foreign city on his lonesome and pushed himself to meet a group of people, but, already getting himself out of his comfort zone, he was being dragged further away from it by meeting us lot. I have a slightly naughty side to me, some might say perverse, where I enjoy seeing people who have led good, wholesome lives getting pissed up and twisted, showing them what a proper good night out looks like. Bert wasn't getting out of this now.

We descended a staircase off a side street guarded by two bouncers, and entered what I can only say was one of the greatest nightclubs I've ever been in. It wasn't the biggest, but it was still packed with several DJs with huge screens playing vibrant 3D video effects behind them, with rucks of lasers and confetti blasted from the ceiling. Staff handed out free battery-powered glow sticks for people to dance with (even the free glow sticks here are high-tech). Mel made a beeline for the dancing pole to show off some of her moves in front of the crowd. We'd certainly chucked Bert in at the deep end; he looked completely lost wandering around with his drink in his hand, being one of only a handful of Westerners and certainly the only guy over forty.

"Does this bass need to be so loud?!" He shouted at me. The bass was loud enough to rumble my insides deeply (lucky I'd had my colonic irrigation before coming out so there was zero chance of shitting myself) and I would argue it did indeed need to be that loud. I made my way to the bar shortly after to buy him several shots of the local Soju to get him into the swing of things. I saw a smile begin to crack at the side of his mouth some time later and I daresay he was beginning to enjoy himself.

At 5AM we spilled outside onto the wet side streets of Seoul, the whole area just as busy as it had been in the early evening. People sat along the kerbs in rows underneath sheltered areas where the rain hadn't reached, eating hotdogs from the street food vendors. One or two people slept hunched up on the street, presumably wasted punters due to their trendy clothes as opposed to stylish homeless people. To our surprise, one of the sleeping people included Bert who had left for home an hour before us citing excessive intoxication. Evidently, he hadn't made it far out of the door and had crashed out in a heap outside, face down alongside a kerb. It was almost karma that Americans had brought the ways of excessive alcohol consumption over to Korea, only for it to take down an American — I suppose the situation had been helped along by a mischievous English person though. I propped him up and fed him a hotdog I had bought. Through mouthfuls of chewed food, he begged me not to put any photos of him on *Facebook* in case his wife found out about what he had been up to tonight (don't worry Bert — I've only written about it in great detail and published it in a book instead).

The night, and our time in Korea, wound down on the streets outside the club; we were mingling with locals who spoke English, and then wandered home at dawn via a detour that put Bert to bed in his hotel. Both myself and Mel had enjoyed our time here, and with good reason — it offers everything you could want in a destination. Exotic food, a rich culture with traditional architecture like back in Jeonju, or the complete opposite of futuristic technology. Great nightlife, multiple cities and towns and apparently nice countryside and beaches for the summer months. I was aware we'd hardly scratched the surface of the country with the two stops we'd done, especially having hardly seen one of them being stuck in bed for most of the time there. From what I saw though, I wholeheartedly recommend spending some time in the country. I knew I'd be back again one day, and would even consider a proper trip into the North too, not just dip my toes in from the South — although that's providing Kim doesn't plan on giving me any more hassle.

We had a hungover flight to Vietnam the following day; I would have loved to have written about some adventure there but the ear infection came back with vengeance and you've already read enough of me moaning about it.

# CHAPTER THREE
# EAST AFRICA

# KENYA

**Nairobi, Kenya – Friday, 14th December 2018**

I had been to Africa before for short breaks; Morocco, Tunisia, but I don't consider them proper Africa, and by that, I really mean Sub-Sahara — safaris, massive angry cats, the deadliest tropical diseases, tribes, and those weird flat-branched trees sat by themselves in the savanna. 'Proper Africa' was next to be crossed off the list of places I hadn't been to yet, and the first stop on the continent was Nairobi in Kenya. Following four nights here would be both the countries of Uganda and Ghana. Having just flown back to England from Indonesia a few hours earlier (once again, for work), I had a mad rush to get everything washed and packed again before heading straight back to the airport with Mel. It's not often you can say you have been to Asia, Europe and Africa in a single day!

During the application to get our *East Africa Tourist Visa* via the Kenyan embassy in London (which gives the holder entry to both Kenya and Uganda on the same visa), I had begun to notice how awkward Kenyan bureaucracy could be. The Kenyan Embassy's website gave conflicting information on how to go about getting the visa, taking several attempts to read in an effort to try and interpret the information on the site and leaving me guessing on parts of the process. Keep in mind: this is the official website. The visa form was a scanned photocopy which wasn't put on the scanner straight, and then uploaded to their website, so I had to fill out a form printed on angle. The processing time on the website clearly said two to three days, but after not

87

receiving my passport during this time — which I needed for work for the aforementioned Indonesia work trip — I learned on a phone call to the embassy that it was probably going to be more towards two weeks. It wasn't the most difficult visa I had applied for, but it was definitely more hassle than it needed to be, and there was certainly an underlying sense of disorganisation throughout the whole process. As all four-hundred people disembarked from the plane to the Kenyan border control, it was clearly more than immigration could cope with and the messiness I had dealt with on the visa application had spilt over trying to enter the country. There were multiple queues, no one was quite sure which one to get into. People were shouting and getting upset. Some poor people had to queue to get their visa on arrival, then queue again to enter the country, each queue taking the best part of an hour. Even with our visas ready, we were stood for ages in a slow-moving queue, frustrated. Once at baggage claim the carousel screens didn't have any flight information on, so no one knew where to look for their bags. For the first time I can recall across the many airports I've been to around the world, bags had been taken off the carousel to make more room for new oncoming bags and were littered across the floor at baggage claim; hundreds of them, without any apparent order to where they'd been placed. Needless to say, it took ages to find ours. I'll admit that seeing the chaos; both with the visa and here at the airport, had me a little worried about what lay in store beyond the airport doors.

Anticipating our late arrival to the country, we had organised a night at a homestay close to the airport and for the owners to pick us up upon arrival. It was a relief to see my name scrawled on a bit of cardboard, held by a local called Anthony; a short but incredibly friendly native who, like all of our taxi-based first-encounters, filled us in on the basics of Kenya on the ride.

"We have forty-two indigenous languages here!" he boasted proudly.

"Well, you lose," said Mel, who has to make a competition out of everything. "We have over three hundred in Indonesia!"

Anthony contradicted the other travellers I knew that had previously had warned me that the Kenyan capital of Nairobi "was unsightly and dangerous in parts". Whilst I suspected this might be true, certainly the latter, I was surprised to see the roads in the good condition that they were, with freshly-painted markings, and the surrounding buildings looked fairly new and well-developed. The city had a handful of skyscrapers in the distant downtown region which looked as nice as any other city's. Anthony said the nightlife downtown was banging and worth a visit whilst we were here, even offering to take us out for a couple of hours. We didn't really have the time to do it, but for a moment Mel and I wondered whether we could clear a bit of our schedule and go clubbing. I asked if it was safe at this time of night as I'd heard stories of the city suffering from a high crime rate. Anthony said of course, provided you knew where to go but insisted the stories I had heard were likely exaggerated. It was a bit hard to properly gauge the safety with it being night time, but it didn't feel like it would be dangerous if I got out of the car and walked the streets. The people I could see out and about from the car window didn't appear like they'd be trouble — compared to, say, the cities of South America, and some of the people there that had a certain look about them. A large amount of people were hanging around on the streets though, even in areas without many buildings, lying around by the side of the main roads which seemed a bit odd given it was well past 1AM. The only real worry I had for our safety was malaria; we had bought the best anti-malarial tablets money could buy, but the advice on the packaging was stressed that no medication is 100% effective and that the best preventative measure against malaria is to not get bitten at all. I had passed through risky malaria areas before, but for no more than a few days at a time. This was deep in a high-risk zone, one I'd be staying at for weeks, too.

### Masai Mara National Park, Kenya – Saturday, 15th December 2018

We woke up early at our bedsit, brushed our teeth and gave our skin a liberal running-over with mosquito repellent, all in anticipation of being picked up by our safari guides. We had organised a three-night stay in the Masai Mara National Park south-west of the capital, which is almost on the border of Tanzania. We'd hopefully see *The Big Five* (which is safari geek-lingo for elephant, rhino, leopard, buffalo & lion), plus a whole host of other animals. During our time here we'd also be paying a visit to a traditional tribe for an afternoon to experience village life. Sat around outside the homestay anxiously waiting as a full hour had gone past the pickup time, I decided to call the safari company to see where they were, only to learn our guide had already been parked up around the corner since the crack of dawn and hadn't made any effort to find us, instead just sitting in his van asleep. Finally meeting Paul, a middle-aged native, he was instantly likeable, so the initial annoyance of him wasting the past hour quickly dissipated. Explaining why he hadn't bothered looking for us for the past hour, he told us about the notion of *'Africa Time'* — which basically means, no rush, take your time, no problem; *Hakuna Matata*. The Indonesians have the same concept, called *'Jam Karet'* (rubber time, indicating flexibility), which I've experienced for myself; people can be two hours late for meetings and such, and when they finally arrive just say *Jam Karet* like you've not wasted two hours of your life waiting for them. People in hot countries seem to have a loose grasp of time-keeping, and it's really fucking annoying being a punctual white man.

Paul was soft-spoken, calmly informing us that he would be our guide for the next few days, staying away from his family in the process by sleeping at the same campsite we were staying at. He said the location of the site was a whole six-hour drive away through the Kenyan countryside, so obviously it wasn't practical for him to drive back home to Nairobi every evening. I had expected a bit of a drive but was a bit disappointed half the day would be wasted in his van (and was even more saddened when it ended up being more like eleven hours! *Africa Time* there again, wobbling my head). The van was fairly spacious inside at least; a proper safari one with and an open interior and a central section of the roof that lifted up vertically. It was also designed to seat eight people behind the driver, which was great as Mel and I had the whole thing to ourselves. It wasn't a solid drive either; we did get a couple of breaks on the route to stretch our legs. These rest stops involved spending time at corrugated metal shacks along the side of the road, often nothing remarkable other than being high-tourist-traffic shops with their owners pressuring punters into buying some of the local tat or bottled drinks. Inside they were crammed with handcrafted stuff from nearby villages, the contents arguably worth more than the shoddy building that housed it all. Some items were admittedly impressive — one was a six-foot wooden carving of a tribal guy, towering above the many carved ashtrays and printed tea towels. The store seller clocked I was impressed and was then locked-on to sell it to me. I tried joking it off, saying "It won't fit in my backpack mate," but then when he offered to post it to England, I flatly said "No."

There must be some realisation for the fellas here, having spent weeks crafting a two-metre mahogany man, that as impressive as it is, it weighs more than a real person. Who in their right mind would want it? Shipping around the world would be next to impossible from here. It would take three hours just to drive it to a post office in Nairobi, and four postal workers to carry it. I could probably buy one at home for a fraction of the postage costs. To be fair to him, I admired the audacity of trying to sell it. Sadly, he would have had more luck making money if he carved it down and bulked up the numbers of the wooden ashtrays.

Our van trundled along wide open roads cut through dry savannah countryside, and a large reddish-brown dirt path ran parallel for pedestrians who had to walk huge distances to get anywhere. The same landscape repeated for miles, all mostly flat with dry grass, although an occasional scattering of trees or bushes would appear for something to look at. There was an obscene amount of litter lying around, even in the long stretches between villages. Money appeared not to travel far from the capital and the further into the country we travelled, the poorer the region became. Sometimes our journey would run through what I presumed were villages, but they were so small that I wouldn't be surprised if they didn't register on a map. In these villages, there would be a couple of shabby-looking stand-alone buildings or shacks with people sat around outside looking fairly bored, as there didn't appear to be any sort of entertainment venues available. Some people would be asleep in the street, finding all sorts of crazy places to rest like on large discarded lorry tyres that were frequently scattered around. Kenyans love a hand-painted sign, everything from *'butchery'* to *'mechanic'* in big hand-painted letters above the doors of buildings in the larger villages. Donkeys and carts often replaced cars. An occasional fire would burn next to the road. Cattle freely wandered the streets. A couple of times I saw kids playing with rubbish; kicking a bottle about or messing around with a plastic bag and I suppose, with that mindset of utilising the extreme amount of trash around, they would never be short of toys. Despite the lack of wealth, the people here (especially the kids) would often wave and smile, sometimes running over to the van when we slowed down for one of the many potholes. I've thought this before when visiting poorer countries: these people don't have much, but they still seem happy enough. The fact they bothered to wave and smile at passing strangers said a lot. There are the cliché travel comparisons people draw against the ungrateful Western world in situations like this, but I'm not going to make them today because you already know you're a miserable unappreciative shit, despite having a quality of life far superior to these people. At the final rest break before we entered the national park, I went to wash my hands and a tiny dribble of water came out. A cleaner happened to be in the toilet at the time, watching me waiting for water to come out of the tap. He laughed and said it had not rained for a while. I remember people complaining about the lengthy hot summer we had in England in 2018 and the subsequent prospect of a mere hosepipe ban. In Kenya, not having things here is just part of life, and people seem okay about it.

The last three hours of the drive we left the main road and turned onto, well, not your standard definition of a road, but more like a track made by the squashed yellow grass from the tyres of previous vehicles. We were now in the Masai Mara National Park. Paul had promised several times during the journey that we'd be receiving an African massage when we arrived at the park, but I was suspicious as *Africa Time* had turned out to be shit. It was as bad as suspected; the van bumped along the road and threw us around inside, enough to jolt me out of my seat on occasion.

"You like the massage?" joked Paul.

'Good one mate,' I thought, 'keep your eyes on the grass'. This far out into the country, houses stopped being made out of standard building materials such as metal, concrete or wood and had turned completely to dried mud. There were a lot of individuals, usually very skinny, wearing traditional robes (which was a sort of sari with embroidery on it) and herding large amounts of cattle with a stick. It's one of those moments that you get from time to time whilst travelling that makes you realise just how far away from home you are.

After a further hour of massaging, the human settlements ended leading us to an area that had completely opened up to wildlife. It started with a couple of birds, to suddenly a herd of giraffe, then minutes later baboons, meerkats, warthog, impala. At one point I could see ten species in a single view, numbering around a hundred animals in total. I knew I'd see some wildlife here, obviously, but the landscape was positively teeming with life. Paul lifted the van's roof up, which allowed Mel and I to stand up whilst the vehicle was driving. This improved the experience massively, feeling the wind on our faces, and removed any physical barrier when cool animals like hyena and lions started showing up deeper into the reserve. It would have been a perfect afternoon had the roof not become unhinged whilst hitting a bump, crashing 30kg of metal down on our heads. Mel was left unscathed; luckily for her, my height took most of the impact, squashing my neck like a marshmallow and forcing me back into my seat. Paul apologised profusely and, to remedy the roof's precarious mounts, fixed a couple of shoelaces around the hinge to stop it happening again (in all honesty though, fully enjoy the rest of the day's safari with the fear of having my neck broken if the shoelace gave way). The several compressed neck bones from the roof's impact were not helped by another hour of African massaging and my neck creaked when I moved my head, but at least the wildlife we spotted definitely made up for it.

As dusk rolled in, we had made it to the camp in one piece after what now had become a full day of driving. I knew the camp that was going to be our place of residence for several nights was inside the nature reserve somewhere, but this was deeper than I had anticipated; miles away from any major civilisation. The van finished the final stretch down an embankment and parked up in a clearing through some bushes, where a cobbled pathway led us down to a large river. It looked welcoming as much of it had been illuminated by large bamboo torches in the dim evening light, the fire giving off a nice orange tint to the surrounding bush. Alongside the river was a campfire and a large tent, with smaller ones scattered beside it. The large tent was a sort of communal area adjacent to a kitchen with — to my absolute glee — a bit of a bar inside, whereas the smaller tents were bedrooms for the guests. These tents were more in line with what Mel would repeatedly call *glamping* (for the uninitiated: an amalgamation of the words *glamorous* and *camping*). As entry-level camping can be pretty rough-going from my experience (I'm thinking three days being sat in an inch of water as torrential rain comes down at *Leeds Festival* here), 'glamorous' to me meant anything that didn't involve living in perpetual damp. I was therefore chuffed to find we had a pretty comfy bed inside, a toilet in a separate room within the tent and hot running water. The water had a slight smell of sulphur about it, but a hot shower was available a hundred miles into a nature reserve; who's complaining? There was some basic plumbing run around the campsite, and most of the electricity and hot water was generated by solar power. It was probably one of the most carbon-neutral stays I've ever had. Better still, this was a week before Christmas — all the guests were due next week. Mel and I had the place to ourselves — well, in terms of humans. Our neighbours were hippos and crocodiles sat in the river less down an embankment less than ten metres away from our tent. We could see them from our porch most of the time, letting out angry grunts when they got too close to each other. I was assured by the camp's security guard — a man with a large stick — that the hippos rarely leave the water and wander around the camp. All sorts of creatures do wander around though, in from the reserve and into the barrier-free campsite at night. We would lie there in bed in complete darkness, hearing animals ranging from crickets to carnivores. When I heard a patter of feet around the tent, I was hoping for some sort of gazelle, as the thought of a lion sniffing around put me on edge a little. Electricity was turned off at night to conserve power, leaving us with nothing but a little torch in our room. Lying in bed in total darkness, it sent my mind into overdrive listening to the amazing sounds of nature all around us that easily permeated through the thin material of the tent. As potentially dangerous as it sounds, the campsite owners reassured us that the set-up here was completely safe and whilst we had to stay within our tent during the dark hours, we had been provided with an emergency whistle that hung over our door, "just in case". When Mel asked the guard what circumstances would require a whistle, she was met with a vague, "No one has had to use a whistle yet!"

## Masai Mara National Park, Kenya – Sunday, 16th December 2018

I woke to the sound of someone outside the tent asking if we were both awake. Waking up to an unfamiliar voice like that, it took a few moments to remember where we were. The sun wasn't quite putting out enough light for us to see around the tent properly and the only bright thing was the spooky movement of someone with a torch outside. I unzipped the tent door with my torch and whistle ready in hand to see Paul with his gentle smile through the zip. He asked us to meet him by the van after we'd had breakfast. He was obviously keen for an early start today, it must have been only 5.30AM, perhaps a little too early for us both for the first day here. What happened to *Africa Time*, mate?

Before this trip, buffalo to me were a bit of a background animal, certainly not impressive compared to the likes of your lions and cheetahs. The first stop Paul made in the early morning had us entering a clearing in some bush, on an apparently random scout-around for animals, where we found a single male buffalo stood in a small muddy puddle. He noticed us the moment we arrived. We settled nearby as Paul turned the engine off while the buffalo watched us for a few seconds, sussing out whether we were a threat. Happy we weren't, he continued on with his mud bath. Many animals like buffalo use mud as a means to keep themselves clean, whilst also acting as a natural barrier from the sun and biting insects. Paul told us that older buffalo like these had spent most of their lives as the prime males of a herd, but once they reach a certain age, they are fought off by the youngsters and are forced to spend their last days wandering in solitude. Learning this poor buffalo's backstory, we spent nearly half an hour in the orange glow of the sunrise once it reached above the horizon, in the middle of nowhere, just watching the single buffalo having his morning clean. It was one of the most peaceful things I can ever recall doing in my thirty-three years on the planet. I suppose it was really a non-event compared to what else we were to see in the reserve, but to me, it struck a chord, for whatever reason, and I had a new respect for these often-overlooked animals. The next morning, we were close to the same clearing and could see vultures circling; indicating to Paul that some action was going on. Sure enough, as we arrived, a male lion (who looked very full with his huge gut and blood-soaked face) was sleeping next to his kill, guarding it against the onlooking vultures and hyenas. The kill was a huge buffalo which had most of its face and belly ripped apart — apparently the softer meat is eaten first. When Paul told us it could well be the buffalo we watched in the mud bath yesterday, I was devastated. We'd had a wonderful moment with that creature, and there it was now in pieces – in part, being pushed through a lion's digestive tract. Nature is indeed brutal.

Other highlights on the savanna included rare sightings like a serval cat (I'd never heard of it either) which looked like a cross between a house cat and a leopard — luckily, we saw their rarer (and bigger!) cousins; the awe-inspiring cheetahs and leopards. A leopard had managed to kill a small gazelle and, with sheer strength, drag it up into a tree to consume. We crossed a river in our van (the water nearly covered the wheels) which was just cool to do; it was even better that we made it across without incident, whereas a van behind containing a load of French tourists managed to get stuck in the water. It was funny watching them struggling to get unstuck. We later paid a visit to a traditional village which was a real culture shock. These guys live in mud huts, use cattle as currency and place dried animal shit as fuel for fire – and yet they still knew about *Manchester United!* The village was excited when they heard I was from near Manchester. I've written several times in the past about the difficulties of travelling as an Englishman who has absolutely no interest in football and the awkward conversations with foreigners that it generates. The great thing about travelling with Mel these days is she's the football fan out of the two of us, so once the subject is inevitably raised, she does all the talking to locals about the performance of Teddy Sheringham and how Alex Ferguson shouldn't have sold Keegan to *Spurs*, or whatever the fuck they all talk about — so I can go off and do my own thing which is far more interesting, like in this case watch the village chickens peck at cow shit for a bit. As genuine as the village seemed, and how definitely poor some of the residents were, I still had a feeling that some of it might have been for show and I bet the 'village experience' is actually a good money-maker for a select few people. It was fairly expensive for the privilege to visit; our money had clearly gone into *someone's* pocket. Our hosts spoke excellent English, so they'd had a decent education from somewhere — although that said, as far as I could tell, everyone I had encountered in Kenya seemed to speak English well. And they were somehow keeping up to date with the latest football fixtures as well, there was no way they were relying on tourists like Mel to keep them abreast of the latest football stats.

The villagers assembled and performed a traditional dance to showcase parts of their culture for us; this mostly involved chanting and jumping up and down on the spot as high as possible. We jumped up and down with them after a bit of encouragement from Paul to join. The villagers were impressed with how high I could jump, although I did have an advantage starting off as the tallest person around. My height made entering their mud huts difficult, effectively folding myself in half to squeeze in, leaving me incredibly uncomfortable factoring in the stuffy trapped heat inside too. As night rolled in, the villagers brought the surrounding cows into the settlement, meanwhile the women and children retired to the huts for protection. The men took it in shifts to watch over the herd ready and alert to fight off any carnivores such as lions or hyenas that may attempt an attack on the cows at night. I had no cause to doubt the authenticity of what I was seeing, it just seemed a little odd that one of the villagers knew the football fixtures, appeared to have something as modern as a mobile phone (albeit an old one) and yet would be expected to fight lions at night with a stick. It really is a weird mix of the old and new for these people.

Our guide, Paul, had really rubbed off on me during the days we'd spent on the reserve. As I said, he was a likeable guy anyway, but he had a real passion for the animals and the area here. He trained as an electrician but fifteen years ago decided he wanted a job that nurtured his love of wildlife, so did a huge career change and never looked back. It was good to hear him say that the importance of wildlife and conservation is taught in Kenyan schools, and how anyone caught poaching gets life imprisonment. Notably, there was military base style beefed-up security to get into this reserve on the first day; patrolled security barriers, men with guns, that required us to show our passports to allow passage. The tour guides took being on the reserve seriously too, at all times ensuring not to drive their vehicles away from the main routes through the reserve so the wildlife had some space away from people. I know wildlife numbers are taking a hit around the world, but in this small part of Africa, I genuinely got the impression that they value what they have here and are doing what they can to protect it. Ideally, humans would leave the area alone completely, but we know that's never going to happen. At least now, with the aid of tourism, it has minimal impact on the area and the money generated gives the locals an incentive to protect what they have. It's a good set up.

### Masai Mara National Park, Kenya – Wednesday, 19th December 2018

*Africa Time* apparently doesn't just mean everyone on the ground is a bit late, it also appeared to mean that organised times with airlines can change around at random as well. Our internal flights within the African continent had changed twice over the past few months. I happened to check my emails by chance on the camp's Wi-Fi and had received a third email about our upcoming flights to Uganda being moved; to three hours earlier this time around. This meant a big change for our route back to Nairobi — we would have to get up at 3AM and drive through the reserve at night. This isn't normally allowed as it disturbs the animals, and of course isn't the safest time to travel either, as most of the big carnivores are nocturnal and on the prowl for a feed. We didn't have any other option though; we had to leave this early otherwise we'd miss our flight out of the country. Paul had to get special permission from the park rangers for us to travel over walkie-talkie, which was thankfully granted. For safety, the camp owners said they would escort us up to the river crossing where the French were stuck the other day, but after that we were on our own. I happened to wake up naturally around half two in the morning, just before our alarm was due, and lay in bed a few minutes listening intently for anything other than the sound of the heavy rain. I was positive I heard something that must have weighed a quarter tonne, something on four legs, wandering around near our tent — soft yet still fairly striking footsteps moving in between the tents. I unzipped the tent, making a small hole and putting my face through just to see if I could see something. I couldn't even see the immediate rain tipping down in front of my face, there was nothing. I didn't dare use my torch in case it attracted whatever was walking around, but it was thoroughly freaky looking outside at total darkness.

'This is certainly going to be a memorable ride out of the park,' I thought as I watched a sleepy Mel eat an apple for breakfast under a canopy as the rain came down, waiting for the campsite staff to do the final checks before our journey. They radioed someone on a VHF mounted to a desk, likely those gatekeepers with guns, informing them that we were now making the journey out into the darkness. The savanna was a different world at night. I think I'd fancy my chances if I had to walk across the park during daylight hours, but now it was pitch black and optimal for the meat-eaters to sneak up for a feed. I reckon I could easily take on a pack of jackals and probably win one on one with an adolescent hyena. A lion, though? No chance. Our van massaged us through the bumpy roads of the park, with a small convoy of two other vans containing a guard and various other people who worked at the camp. The headlights of the vans would often reflect the eyes of creatures hiding in the long grass, little round balls that glowed like fire, vanishing when they blinked or turned away. For the most part, we could just about make out that it was a gazelle or some other grass chewer, but a couple of times they were huge spooky eyes that wouldn't be startled by our presence and simply watched us travel by. It had started to rain pretty heavily by the time we reached the river crossing, increasing the water level quite noticeably. A few hippos were in the water that I'm pretty sure weren't there last time we'd crossed, a couple of metres away from the van at most. Mel had returned to sleep the moment we had entered the van and happened to wake up to see a hippo nearby from out of the window, startling the shit out of her.

"What is that doing there!?" she screamed as she rose from her slumber. Paul tried to reassure her we were fine; I was more worried about having laughed at the French, as karma could have gotten me right there and then. I guess Paul, being such a nice guy, carried us all with his karma points. After several minutes of being watched by the hippos, slowly edging the van across the river as rocks slipped away under the tyres, we made it across and up the muddy embankment on the other side in one piece. The camp owners had kindly made sure we passed the river safely, once we were across they shook our hands and wished us a good onward journey. We were now on our own, with miles to go through the reserve — just me, Mel and Paul in our little van.

I had started to become conscious of time. Ideally, we needed to be at the airport no later than midday, we had not left the reserve yet it was already edging towards 4AM, and there were still many miles to Nairobi. The tracks we had previously taken with relative ease during the daytime had become muddied trenches in the rain. Paul had to focus on operating the van. Mel had fallen asleep again, which was probably for the best because there were several times the van skidded on an angle out of control, and there may have been expletives heard should she have been awake to witness it. Of course, out of all the days we'd spent out here, this would be the worst day for a tyre to blow. Even Paul, who had been easy-going so far, looked a little concerned when we heard a loud thud on the front left of the van and skidded to a halt. It was obvious there was now a flat tyre and someone had to go outside to fix it, and it wasn't lost on me that there were packs of roaming carnivores in the grass.

Paul turned to me and said, "Okay, Mr. Steve, we have two options: we do what we are supposed to and wait until sunrise and get help from the park rangers when they come through. Or, I can attempt to change the tyre myself, right now."

There was no way we could afford to miss this flight, I said, so changing the tyre was the only option. He opened the door of the van and stepped out into the rain. I could see he was prepared to try and fix it himself, but I couldn't let him. It would be nearly impossible in the dark conditions, and I couldn't be bothered attempting to drive on these roads to Nairobi if he got eaten by a lion. I stepped outside with him straight into a thick pile of mud. Maybe it was the rain, but outside of the van was cold and there was a noticeable temperature change from day to night. The day is relentlessly hot, but at this time of night and with my clothes soaking in the rain, it almost felt cold enough to see my breath. Paul opened the boot and rummaged around, bringing out a car jack which, after some messing about, we realised would not fit underneath the van. We then had to wander around the immediate area in complete darkness (other than the thin bar of light given off by my phone torch) looking for huge rocks to drive the flat wheel up upon; only then would the van be high enough to fit the jack under. We found the rocks half-buried in the mud, Paul had a good eye for spotting them with minimal light — he had obviously done this before! Placing them directly in front of the flat wheel, he drove slightly forward whilst I held the rocks to stop them from falling to the side. Sure enough, it worked! We had the van raised just enough for the jack to squeeze under. To get to this stage had eaten into our precious time and we still hadn't got the tyre off yet. Had Mel been awake, I'm sure she would have been worried.

It was a surreal moment in which I found myself; using the torch on my phone to provide light to aid Paul for the tyre change but swinging it around every couple of moments to the long grass just to check we weren't being eyed-up by any predators. I had been wearing suitable safari clothing for the entire time since leaving Nairobi but, sod's law, on the day I decide I don't need them as "I'm only going to the airport", I ended up caking my normal clothes in mud.

The tyre finally changed, we washed off in a nearby puddle as best we could, and were on the road again. The road just kept getting more treacherous — we would frequently encounter strange barricades made out of mud, and I couldn't work out what they were for. I assumed it was to make it more difficult for poacher vans to pass, but this was an absolute guess. Either way, it made our journey a nightmare. Sometimes, they would be impassable, and Paul had to take the van down an embankment to the side of the road, sliding down and often getting the van stuck for a minute or two. It was a little hairy at times, but after some persistence, we managed to get back onto the main roads towards Nairobi which were thankfully made out of tarmac. The rain subsided with the dawn, and a nice day began to form from out of the clouds.

Paul looked like the ordeal had taken it out of him a little bit, so he pulled up at a petrol station on the road to Nairobi and had a much-needed break and a coffee. I had given up getting anxious about making it to the airport and agreed we needed the break, so enjoyed the downtime we had at the petrol station. Sat looking out of the window waiting for Paul to fuel the van whilst picking dried mud out of my clothes, I noticed fifteen middle-aged women who looked like they were waiting for a bus by the side of the road. A small hatchback turned up moments later and they all squeezed into in like a clown car at the circus. Paul nonchalantly informed me through the window that they were "going to work". I was impressed that somehow the Kenyans had discovered how to bend physics, because the total mass of the fifteen women was without a doubt bigger than the available space in the car. My worry was that it must have been a fair old drive cramped in that car, because if it was a short distance they'd have just made two trips. Poor buggers.

It looked like we were going to make it to the airport with some time to spare, so we took it a bit easier on the last hour or so of the journey. Paul drove through a new part of Nairobi which we hadn't seen, close to huge sprawling shanty towns on the outskirts which somehow managed to look even more deprived than the shanty counterparts in Jakarta I'd passed through last week; endless cramped housing in a mishmash of shapes clinging to the side of hills or sprawling along the roads. I'd rather have been out in those little villages in the countryside rather than the crammed conditions here, but I understand there was probably more work opportunities closer to the city.

We had made it to Arrivals and thanked Paul for his time, and he thanked us for ours. What a genuinely nice guy. And Kenya too, what a place! It had been an incredible time. The locals were friendly, had excellent proficiency in English, and the wildlife was out of this world. It's just a shame we missed the nightlife. There was rumoured to be some decent partying waiting for us at our next stop, at least. We boarded our flight to Uganda, and I couldn't wait to see more of the continent.

# UGANDA

## Entebbe, Uganda – Wednesday, 19th December 2018

The pair of us had decided to approach the next few days a little differently compared to our usual style of frenetic travelling. At some point last year in Peru I had caught our visages in a mirror by chance between destinations and noticed how tired we both looked; that had really stuck with me, so we thought it might be an idea to dial things back a notch for Uganda. But dialling it back wasn't all intentional — part of the reason was we felt priced out of most activities on offer for tourists, or they took too long to travel to. There's plenty to see in Uganda, don't get me wrong. Want to see the source of the Nile? Some do. It was a lot of travel from where we were though, anywhere outside of central Uganda takes over a day to get to. How about seeing some gorillas on a jungle trek? I'd absolutely love to. Sadly, we didn't have the two grand – per person! – spare. There was a cheaper alternative to this; a monkey sanctuary on an island in the nearby Lake Victoria, but even that cost hundreds of pounds for us both to visit. We decided we'd do our own thing and make our own fun exploring the country, whilst saving a few quid. What could go wrong?

Our first two nights were to be spent in the town of Entebbe, less than an hour's drive south of the capital of Kampala which we'd be making our way to afterwards. Although Entebbe is not the true capital, it certainly acts and feels like one as it's the main hub for the country's politics, hosting many of the Ugandan elite, and also has the country's only international airport. Armoured guards with huge guns wandered the streets along with numerous police officers as a means of keeping anyone from trying to overthrow the government. With this in mind, Entebbe is probably the safest part of the country (out in the sticks, miles from here, there are still tribal skirmishes that are active today, plus there's regular trouble and political unrest in both the neighbouring countries of South Sudan and Congo; this often spills over the border into Uganda — these remote regions are best avoided as tourists). Several international organisations operated from Entebbe, meaning there was usually a few foreigners around (so I was told, anyway), although most had gone home for the Christmas period. The *United Nations* base for East Africa was right across from our *AirBnB*, located in a leafy suburb to the east of the town. There was clearly a bit of wealth around Entebbe, certainly compared to what I had seen in Kenya. There were a couple three or four-storey residential buildings, but mostly there were nice houses hidden behind huge fencing with large gardens. Here in the town too was a massive botanical garden and even a golfing resort, all set alongside Lake Victoria which is as big as a country in and of itself. Kenya had been dry and dusty, but in this part of Uganda it appeared green and lush with many trees, gardens and lawns. The roads were in fairly good condition, which can often be a sign of there being some money around, but they still had those big brownish-red dirt ditches either side which I had grown accustomed to in Kenya; offering the locals a dumping place for trash and a channel for the occasional open sewers pumping streams of shite out.

We dumped our bags in our room (scaring several monkeys off the porch in the process), gave our mud-encrusted dirty laundry to the maid, sprayed mosquito repellent, and headed out for an aimless wander around the town. I enjoyed using my legs properly for the first time in days, having spent most of the last week sat in Paul's van. Whilst there were supposedly a few foreigners around usually, we still clearly weren't from these parts so we garnered a lot of interest from the locals who were going about their business. There are notable height differences between Mel and I, plus we're each both from different parts of the world, so we sometimes get stares when we go outside of Europe. I'm unsure how many Indonesians have ever made it to Uganda too, as a lot of the locals we encountered were inquisitive about her origins and strangers would come up for a friendly chat; leaving me, the boring plain old white guy sometimes stood at the sidelines.

Part of Entebbe's coast along Lake Victoria has a holiday resort vibe going for it, with a smattering of restaurants, bars and hotels along the beach. An internet search uncovered the names of a couple of bars, but like many of these places that are less travelled by tourists, there isn't a huge amount of information available online about what's there — certainly not enough to paint a clear picture. We're in Africa now; it could have been nothing more than a couple of shacks selling unrefrigerated drinks, but to find a lovely cul-de-sac next to a beach with a few nice bars and even a Thai restaurant was a pleasant discovery. The vibe was relaxed; house music played from the speakers out onto the beach but many of the Ugandans were sat chilling inside bars sipping beers or cocktails. Attracted like flies to shit by the presence of alcohol, Mel and I ordered a drink and joined them. It was strange to think that we were currently hundreds of miles away from the ocean, and yet Lake Victoria had its own actual sandy beach with small waves lapping up to the shore. Maybe there's lots of fresh water lakes around the world that feel like you're by the sea with cool stuff like bars around, I've just never been to one before. I'm just used to the lakes of England — freezing cold water with thick mud around it, usually in a remote wet field somewhere with no one around other than a few nosey cows. I think I'd choose cows over the Ugandan nature however; in equal parts intriguing and bothersome, a species of tiny lake fly goes into a breeding frenzy at sunset. Their lifespan is only 45 minutes long, so it's already a freak, but for some reason, once it has completed breeding, it flies to the nearest light it can find. The nearest light around these parts used to be the moon before man came along, but these days it's the beach bars of Entebbe. It doesn't have to even be a direct light source, they were attracted to the light reflected from my sweaty forehead. Hundreds of thousands, maybe more – who knows – swarmed all around us to the point where visibility became foggy. They were going in my ears, my eyes. Mel screamed as they got stuck in her hair. Hundreds would fly directly into our table and some would fall into the wax from the candle. Only then did I notice there were layers of them trapped in the wax as it had set once the flame was blown out on previous nights, encased in wax like some sort of miniature geological excavation site. Some of the bars had signs up telling us not to worry about them as they're harmless, but it's still a bit difficult to ignore as you're swallowing three with a glug of beer whilst one wriggles to death under your eyelid.

### Entebbe, Uganda – Thursday, 20th December 2018

A whole day in Entebbe lay ahead of us. We checked the weather over breakfast and, based on the forecast stating there was zero chance of rain, we decided it would be perfect to go for a long walk around the town, maybe get some food somewhere, make a stop at the renowned local botanical gardens, and of course, make time for a few beers in between. Well, the forecast lied. The heavens opened shortly after stepping outside and the rain came down hard like it always does in tropical countries. There wasn't anywhere to shelter properly as trees only work to a certain level of rain; when it comes down too hard one might as well stand out in the open street. We ran through the streets of the town with rain bouncing off the ground, after some minutes fortunately coming alongside a pavilion on a kid's park offering a proper roof with a place to shelter. It appeared everyone else was caught off guard with the weather forecast today, as many locals (some businesses men, women with shopping, kids, all sorts of people) had put a halt to their day's activities and were waiting it out at our spot, desperate to keep dry. One thing that is hard to miss about some African fellas, particularly in Uganda, is that they love an ugly suit. I'd seen many over my short time here, making them worth a comment on how frequently they're worn by the blokes here. And it doesn't matter if it looks old and tatty, massively oversized or, in the case of the guy stood under the pavilion with us, neon green with a purple shirt underneath along with bright red shoes. They just love wearing bad suits. Yesterday, I'd seen a guy with an oversized suit and flip-flops at the airport. I say good luck to them, fuck what everyone else thinks or writes about in their poxy travel books.

A break formed in the clouds. It looked like we'd be getting a few minutes pause from the rain, so taking our chance, we ran to a nearby shopping mall further along the road. There are two small shopping malls in Entebbe, and both were weirdly empty inside — only a third of the shop spaces appeared utilised, like they had been built and then struggled to get the businesses in. There's a place near where I live back in Cheshire, and it's pretty much the same thing; an expensive, trendy-looking mall having been built, and in this case even revitalising the old land it was built on, but it costs too much rent for most businesses to operate from so the units never get filled. Although a few big chains did set up shop there, these days it's mostly empty, quiet to walk around, and an overall waste of effort. It's interesting to see the exact same thing being mirrored around the world, although the main difference here is they have more open sewers in the car park and men walking around inside wearing bright green suits. Maybe now that Uganda has become more politically stable in recent years, industry is slowly growing with it. Maybe I could come back to these malls in a couple of years and see them brimmed with shops and people — which I still doubt will be the case for the place in Cheshire.

Festive Christmas music filled the mall along with tinsel and a decorated Christmas tree positioned by the main entrance. The mall also led to the entrance of a supermarket, featuring a tall Ugandan man in a Santa costume wishing everyone a "Merry Christmas!". It had been a little jilting seeing Christmas stuff, I'd almost forgot the big day was a mere five days away because being in the heat and tropical vegetation tends to yank me out of anything associated with the festive time of year. I'd once spent Christmas in Australia and seeing all the knobs wearing Santa hats on the beach in 30°C just looked wrong. Unless I can see my breath outside, it doesn't feel like Christmas to me, and people trying to celebrate it in the tropics look strange. Frank Sinatra's *Let It Snow* filled the supermarket from the speakers, which didn't seem appropriate with its lyrics about a phenomenon completely alien to Uganda. Sure, it's nice to see the Ugandans embracing the festivities, but surely they don't have to strictly follow the West's way of doing things this time of year? Perhaps they could put their own spin on it? How about recording their own tropical Christmas songs, ones that wish not for snowfall, but rather a lack of lake fly swarms? They could create an African version of Santa who wears red shorts and a t-shirt or some sort of festive over-sized neon suit? I thought the Ugandan mall Santa would have appreciated wearing something more suitable as I watched him wipe sweat off his head as we passed him to leave. He must have been boiling with the humidity in his traditional Santa outfit. He was probably excited for Christmas, but only because it meant he could get back to working behind the tills in normal clothes at the supermarket once it was over.

Fortunately, the weather had improved considerably by lunchtime which allowed our outdoor exploration to continue onwards to the botanical gardens. The botanical gardens of Entebbe are a huge forty-five acres running between Lake Victoria and the town. Like any botanical garden in the world, this was a serene expanse of pristine lawns, showcasing well-trimmed plants and bushes, labelled with their common and Latin names. Usually, within any botanical grounds, there's a cute little café where you can partake in a scone and tea. Not so in the case of Entebbe's; it is quite easy to stroll off the manicured gardens and enter dense jungle, with trees and vines towering over you enough to block out some of the sunlight. I could see some little creature scuttle off but couldn't quite make out what I'd seen. It was strange to think we were only a short walk from Santa stood in a mall, and we could have easily imagined ourselves in a remote jungle in the countryside as the tall trees created a canopy above us. The faint sound of a repetitive dance beat in the distance reminded us that we were actually not far from civilization, and my guess was there might be some sort of beach party nearby at Lake Victoria. An inland beach rave in Uganda, how cool would that be to go and see and get drunk at? There's a problem here: we've followed this sort of party noise before; the incident on the Brazilian / Paraguayan border was still quite fresh in our minds. I hadn't felt unsafe once here on this Africa trip though, plus this is a botanical garden in the wealthiest part of the country, not out in the sticks somewhere with all the insurgents. Has anyone ever been mugged in a flowery garden before? Probably not, no! With this presumption driving us on, we followed the noise through the miniature jungle to find an opening in the trees that led down to Lake Victoria. Atop the embankment was a grassy mound with a large group of children and adults having a picnic; it seemed odd to think that this group were responsible for the source of the loud trance music. It wasn't until we peered over the mound that we could see a large group of Ugandans were partying away down at a small beach alongside the lake, amongst a small wall-less bamboo shack with a bar and DJ inside. The picnic group were merely looking on at what was quite an eventful party whilst eating their sandwiches. The beach crowd consisted mostly of young adults, but a few teenagers too, perhaps around a hundred people. Some were dancing, others sat around tables drinking. Most notably of all, it didn't seem like we'd be under any threat by walking down to join in for a beverage.

We caught the eyes of almost everyone as we proceeded down big concrete steps that cut through the long grass of the embankment down to the beach, feeling pretty awkward having gathered so much attention straight away, but we needn't have felt like that. The locals soon smiled at us and gestured with their hands to invite us to sit down with them on their individual tables. We politely declined and found an empty spot by ourselves just to get a feel for where we were. The beach was only small, the entire length was walkable within a minute. To one side of the beach away from the partying stood a lone man in a tatty old suit, stood up to his knees in the lake fishing, which was another first I'd seen for a suit. It was a hot day and some brave souls had decided on cooling down by venturing even further than the fisherman into Lake Victoria. I'd have been tempted to join as I was sweating more than most here with my un-acclimatised body, but luckily I'd checked first about any hazards that come with entering a large body of water somewhere with weird wildlife like Africa. One of the things I kept coming across in articles about the lake was waterborne parasites. Bilharzia (or *snail fever* as it's also known) is a parasite that lives in freshwater lakes around parts of Africa and Asia. Different stages of its life cycle has it switching between preying on mammals and snails. In mammals, it burrows in through the skin whilst they're in the water, making their way into the intestine, and then growing over the years into huge parasitic worms, slowly releasing its own offspring in the form of microscopic eggs that leave the body through faeces. In the snails stage of the process, they are usually caused by wild animals that defecate by or in the water, releasing the eggs that eventually end up in the snails to begin the next part of the whole disgusting process. A couple of drunks in the water continually tried to tempt us in for a dip. When I declined and shouted over to them the word "Bilharzia!" (wondering if I pronounced it correctly and probably sounding like a wanker shouting out a word like that even if I had), a person on a nearby table told me there were treatments available after a swim to kill any parasites that may have entered the body. I assumed the people here would be having these done once they got out. We have our own treatments available in the West too, so even if I fancied a dip and happened to pick up a parasite, I could probably have it cleared out safely without any issue. But you know what, as refreshing as it did look to have a quick dip in this heat, I simply don't like the idea of horrible snail worms anywhere near my body, and you can forget them having a few days holiday inside me before the medication kicked in!

I believe the legacy of the British empire has left some of the Brits in modern times a bit arrogant. Let me explain; I once invited my Malaysian friend over to my hometown (who speaks English along with several other languages), and for a tease we both decided to tell my local friends when introduced that he only spoke Malay. It became a bit of a running joke to introduce him like this throughout the night whenever somebody new showed up, and it was particularly funny watching him play up to my friends trying their best to interact with him without being able to rely on verbal communication. The fun continued until we wandered into a working men's club in town for a pint — I hate to stereotype but the older people that drink in these sorts of places in small English towns tend to have a narrower view on the world, and a group of individuals in there picked up on what was going on. One man couldn't wrap his head around the situation and actually came over to tell us that it was unbelievable that someone from Asia had "come 'ere for a 'ollyday wivvout bein' able to speak Engerlish".

I asked the man where he last went on holiday. He replied, "Spain" and, when grilled on how good his Spanish was, he said he didn't speak any. He of course didn't see the great irony of his comments, nor did he realise that the world does have people who don't speak English in it, who may want to come and visit here for all sorts of reasons. I don't think the man necessarily meant it in a malicious way, just that, mentally, he was thick as a Boxing Day turd. My Malaysian friend introduced himself in perfect English after the comment and the man laughed about it, and there was no harm done. The whole situation has since stuck with me though, and I think on reflection this mindset does come from how big the British empire was at its peak, covering a quarter of the world's landmass at one point. Even with most places achieving independence since, it has left them with locals using English in their day-to-day lives. It's just a given that, chances are, you'll be able to get by on your travels just using the one language if you only speak English. And, of course, the language has since spread beyond the original boundary of the empire; it amazes me when I see Mel speaking to Thais on holiday, two regional neighbours using a language from the other side of the world to communicate. The difference between me and the old bloke back in the working men's club is that I don't take the global use of English for granted and genuinely appreciate that I don't have to learn a new language to meet and enjoy the company of local people. Even here in a developing country deep on the African continent, it struck me that I was here using my native tongue to ingratiate myself with a large group of people at a beach party. The legacy of the empire was mostly poor and exploitative for the countries we took over (modern times aren't much better; if there is a disaster we might send Oxfam over to shag the locals like the scandal in Haiti 2018), but one of the few positives is that it has made it possible for locals and foreigners to communicate easily in many places worldwide. We'd have likely had a quiet time there had we not been able to speak with these people, but were instead coaxed from our table to eventually mix with everyone partying on the beach. One of the lads there introduced himself as Stevie, a scruffy fisherman in his early twenties who fished regularly on the lake with his dad as a source of income. I enjoyed a deep conversation with him about life in the area and his perspective on how the country was run. Stevie handed me a plastic cup filled with an unnamed orange spirit that everyone was drinking, encouraging me to drink up. The sun was shining, the music was good and people were dancing, swimming and having fun, and Mel and I had somehow managed to slot right in with a group of local people. This was awesome — did we miss something this epic in Brazil by not trying to find the source of that music?

Two huge Ugandan guys swaggered on to the beach later on in the afternoon. Stevie spoke quietly to me, clearly fearful they'd hear him say that they were "gangster types", pointing them out so there was no ambiguity. They wore clothes like they were in a gangsta-rap music video, wearing big gold chains, but also donning knuckledusters and gold teeth, with shirt buttons that were undone all the way down. Stevie didn't really need to directly point them out to me to be fair, he could have just described them as the guys who were dressed like twats. Their presence spoiled the atmosphere for everyone on the beach — I can't quite put my finger on it, but people just didn't seem to be enjoying themselves quite like they were before they had arrived. If the average Ugandan was keen to talk to us two foreigners in the numbers they had done, then I knew it would only be a matter of time before these two new guys would start trying to interact with us too. It started off relatively tame, asking for photos of themselves with Mel. Then one of them attempted to put their arm around her. Mel said no chance and they both began to get a little cocky when she declined.

"Are you brother and sister?" one asked me, interrupting a conversation with Stevie, moving to get into my face a bit and spilling beer on Mel in the process. It worried me that the other Ugandans seemed wary of them and would move out of the way if they got too close.

The trick whilst boozing abroad in places like these is to enjoy yourself, but never get to the state where you can't think straight so you can react should a situation arise (admittedly, it's advice I don't always follow myself, as evidenced by the situation I had got myself into on that beach in Rio). When I lived in Koh Phangan, Thailand back in 2013, having met backpackers in the hostels in their early twenties (often younger and sometimes female), I would on occasion end up carrying them back to their hostel, away from the island's infamous nightlife, to make sure they got home safe. To my amazement, they would get in paralytic states from the notoriously cheap and abundant alcohol and drugs, then, having passed out on the edge of dance floors surrounded by strangers, be left completely unguarded. I would often require the help of the other backpackers I'd met to get them home okay. I could have been anyone, or rather they could have been left alone to anyone. I still find it unbelievable that people get themselves in these sorts of states, but particularly abroad. Even though I'd been drinking at a steady pace most of the afternoon today, I'd sobered up all of a sudden having these new guys arrive on the scene. We assumed a botanical garden *should* have been fine to visit, but we could have stumbled across some sort of private party there and just let ourselves in, as in hindsight it did seem weird to have a party going in full swing on a Thursday afternoon. These weren't gangsters (probably), but certainly a couple of drunk pricks who were huge and looked like they were up for trouble. Picking up on each other's unease, Mel and I hastily said to the group we had become friendly with that we had to leave. One of the gangster guys realised we were making a break for it and tried to grab Mel as she passed. She swerved out of the way, only for him to attempt to grab her again. Leaving our drinks and new friends, we quickly ran up the embankment into the protection of the dense vegetation offered by the botanical garden. I glanced back momentarily; Stevie looked sad as we left without really saying goodbye, as did a few others, but no one had stepped in to help the situation, so I think our prompt goodbye was justified. It had been getting a little dark outside due to the evening rolling in, but re-entering the trees of the botanical garden again made it practically night-time. We kept up a fast pace through the gardens, looking back to make sure we weren't being followed.

After several minutes of quickly walking through a dimly lit path through the towering trees, we eventually found a clearing leading to a large black gate at the top of a hill. Adding to the excitement of getting out of here, there was also a main road in the distance we recognised as being nearby our hotel. We followed the path, only to find the gate padlocked once we got there. The gate was huge, but we thought 'fuck this': there was no chance we were going back through the botanical garden to find an exit, so we climbed over the eight-foot gate and dropped down onto the main street, in view of several curious pedestrians who watched us make the climb. We had both looked at each other whilst at the top of the gate, and making eye contact we could tell what each other was thinking: why have we got ourselves into a situation again that had required an exit like this? We later agreed that was the last time we'd ever follow distant dance music in developing countries. What an unusual botanical garden it had been, too. I made a mental note to my ever-nebulous *Things to avoid abroad* list to include botanical gardens that sell beer, and stick with the ones that just do the tea and scones in the future.

### Kampala, Uganda — Friday, 21st December 2018

Now done with Entebbe, our plan was to head an hour's drive north to the country's true capital of Kampala for a weekend of partying. We had heard good things from multiple sources that the nightlife there is legendary and a weekend of bar hopping on the piss was all we really had planned. We were both still a little rattled from the weird beach gang yesterday though, and the unsettled feeling rode with us in the taxi as we reached downtown Kampala early morning. It was largely a dump, large dirt lanes rammed with cars and bikes, carving through multi-storey buildings caked in soot and other crap kicked up from the roads. Some buildings were painted in vibrant colours but were all greyed out due to the smog in the air. Piles of litter cluttered the alleyways. It sat in stark contrast to the quiet leafy streets of Entebbe. The taxi driver warned us to put our phones away whilst travelling through parts of the city as the crime rate is high — having a local taxi driver warning you about how bad a new city can be is always a great way to lower your confidence.

The name Kampala originated from the local language, meaning "Land of the Impala", the native African creature that looks a bit like a deer. The impala were long gone these days, and in their place there was a busy, polluted expanse of concrete. We found ourselves overwhelmed and lost in the downtown district for a couple of hours late morning, trying to enjoy the surroundings, but the inescapable pollution from the thick traffic remained heavy on our chests throughout the time we spent outside. We'd dip inside to take a break from the heavy air, but the shops we entered were endless repetitions of touristy clothing or cheap electronics, nothing particularly worthy of our time. Little struck us on the traditional tourist to-do list and Kampala didn't really impress beyond the lure of the supposed nightlife. I couldn't imagine this city being some sort of party hub for East Africa. There were stalls at the side of the road selling alcohol, but no bouncing nightclubs or bars I'd heard so much about, just streets packed with shops and small businesses. It's not all gloom depending what you're into; there's no doubt the city's economy is booming and it's one of the fastest growing places in the world, relatively speaking, now currently hosting two million people and counting. Those are of course rookie numbers for a capital city, but it still felt like there should be more people with the lack of infrastructure. It was clearly a victim of rapid development like so many countries around the world; little thought had been given to urban planning and future growth. As we stood in the middle of a busy street crammed with people barging past, without a clear plan forward, I wondered whether it was really a good idea to come here for a full weekend? We were to find out it was, later learning our hotel was in central Kampala, a part of the city usually avoided by tourists. The place we needed to be was the district of Kololo — more of an affluent area in the north of the city with a vibe slightly more on par with Entebbe; wealth, greenery, and a lot less traffic. There was a hell of a lot of bars there as well.

Although *Facebook* gets on my tits, I still use it, often catching myself mindlessly scrolling through that infernal feed. It does have its uses though, and one is the hidden wealth of knowledge about a given destination which can be found within *Facebook's* expatriate groups. You can often find a large group of English-speaking Westerners in the group, or even locals that speak English, ready to impart their advice having lived in the area for many years. Been away from home for a while? Fancy somewhere that sells a traditional

English roast dinner in Denmark? Struggling to find new shoes your size in the Philippines? Get yourself onto the expats group of the country or area — it might take a bit longer than a *Google* search for an answer but you'll usually find exactly what you need. A Kampala expat group duly pointed me to an Irish bar called *Bubbles* as the best place to check out in Kololo, so it became our first port of call for our Friday night. It was a surprisingly big venue; a good size indoor bar area and huge outdoor dancefloor decorated with neon lights and surrounded by tropical trees. One thing we should have checked with the expat group was what time the nightlife really began — arriving at 8PM we found it absolutely dead. Uganda is one of those countries where people come out towards midnight for drinks. I say "one of those countries" like its less common; from my experience, most places in the world opt to go out later at night. It's only the Brits and the Irish that wouldn't dream of going out that late for a big session, sometimes choosing to start not long after lunch time if they can! Not that it was any sort of problem for Mel and I, we made the most of it just enjoying each other's company to pass the time. There were many bar staff who were idle, but due to their high number, it looked like they anticipated a busy night. I took this time to get friendly with some of the bar staff.

Mel was a little anxious about what to wear before leaving, worrying that her originally planned figure-hugging dress would be too raunchy for a night out in this conservative country, and instead opted for something a little more dressed-down. I say this because the country holds strict conservative values like being incredibly pro-bible and criminalising homosexuality along with street mobs beating shit out of homosexuals. I could well have imagined dressing racily (or anything sex-related really) would have infringed on this way of thinking, but Mel needn't have worried. As the place slowly filled up we'd notice a few of the local girls wandering in wearing next to nothing, but then realised they weren't alone and many women opted for this dress style. In some instances, they're somehow fine with wearing less material than you'd find on a reel of dental floss. Whilst the majority of patrons were local, there were some foreigners dotted about. Some Westerners and a few Arabs, tourists and expats alike from what I could gather. A small group of Arab lads sat next to our table and were nuisances, making no attempt to cover up their outright gawping at Mel or the dental floss girls, occasionally reaching for a touch when they passed to go to the toilet. They eventually began to make Mel feel uncomfortable. I have a standard response of staring back to stop them looking if it becomes a problem for her, and I'm not beyond pinching a man's arse in retaliation if he's had a go at pinching Mel's first. It always clears them off with sheer confusion. I've pinched at least five men's arses as payback in nightclubs over the years, which is a bit of a weird quantity now I think about it. There was also a fair few Ugandan *mosquitoes* around —

the local euphemism for prostitute. They would often grab my hand as I walked past to try and pull me in. A "gedoff!" and pulling my hand back would be enough to get them away. I know I've not really portrayed the place in good light there in the past few sentences, but don't let that fool you; there are lechy guys and prostitutes in bars all around the world. The main thing was that the atmosphere was fantastic on the whole, complemented by great music, cheap beer, and I guess it was pretty safe too (if you didn't mind the nearby buzz of a *mosquito* or the occasional flesh of an Arab's arse between your finger and thumb) and that's what Mel and I had come here for. The mingling with strangers had begun after meeting the other punters at the bar; dancing and taking shots together, and trying to focus on their attempts to shout over loud dance music, sharing instantly forgettable information when you're drunk like what they do for a living or even their names. Several had recommended a venture further into Kololo to a new nightclub in town. We were having fun in *Bubbles,* but with several hours under our belt already we were overdue a change of scene so agreed to move onwards.

Pushing midnight and stepping back onto the main road again from the exit had been a little disorientating, there had been a little bit of daylight left when we'd entered *Bubbles* but as night had set in and without any streetlights, it had rendered the surroundings hard to see — particularly the tripping hazards waiting for us in the disjointed footpath and grids. The only real light source was the headlights of the traffic on the road; taxis and motorbikes slowly moving in a traffic jam, carrying punters off around Kololo's bars. Numerous people were also trying their luck with us on the wonky pavement, whilst shouting and laughter filled the air along with the distant music from the numerous bars. All this wasn't here earlier in the evening, the nightlife was positively thriving. I wondered if we'd be at risk walking around so late at night, but I'd say in retrospect that the city in general did seem to feel safe, even when we were downtown earlier in the day. We weren't once hassled, and anyone who did come up to talk to us appeared friendly and genuinely interested about why we were in Uganda. I don't have much basis on which to compare Kampala against the nightlife of other East African cities — I'd heard Nairobi was unsafe, but then I'd heard that about Kololo before coming here, too. Perhaps the excessive amount of people around at this time of night was actually providing the protection, or it could well be that the worst stories tend to be the ones that circulate, but in reality, the city is probably as no worse as somewhere like London to visit as a tourist. The whole night had gone without incident anyway, and it is thoroughly enjoyable when you can get yourself lost in an exotic place like Uganda without the feeling like you're at risk.

The change of scene from *Bubbles* didn't really pay off; I can't say it was a particularly good club in all honesty. It was pretty small, and I struggle to dance to entire DJ sets of R'n'B as I prefer something a little bit more fast-paced. There was absolutely a real novelty to being in a Ugandan nightclub though, particularly being the only white person in a building filled with hundreds of people; a tick off the bucket list that I never knew I wanted.

### Entebbe, Uganda — Saturday, 22nd December 2018

Saturday was even better. Topping up from the night before after a few hours' sleep, we just wandered around Kololo bar hopping, occasionally trying new food. Rolled eggs, effectively a savoury pancake with veg and meat fillings (lovingly known around the country as *Rolex* as it sounds similar to rolled eggs), are a Ugandan staple and great to try with different fillings. We ate barbecued meats prepared by the street food vendors. I drank ten pints of the local ale. Mel had exotic cocktails. I know it's nothing much to just be wandering around, effectively eating and drinking your way through a new city, but just doing it with my wife, meeting new people and having great fun in the process — it was probably my favourite day of our time in Africa, and up there with one of the best days I've had abroad. I'm a man of simple pleasures. We went back to *Bubbles* once the sun had set and, despite it being only our second time there, it felt like we were regulars with the reception we had from some of the bar staff. Some of the punters we had met the night before were back again, so we'd formed into a small crowd of friends, meanwhile the bar staff I befriended last night gave me great VIP queue jumping privileges when the place became busy.

You may have noticed by this point that nightlife is an integral part of our travel excursions. I like it for two reasons: one, meeting people. I genuinely like to meet and chat with local people, and what better place to do it than in a bar or nightclub, with alcohol acting like a friendship catalyst and its ability to break walls down between strangers. You meet strangers abroad all the time in the street, brushing shoulders but rarely ever getting into a conversation with someone; whereas, in a club, it's easy to get chatting with people — stood at a bar waiting for drinks or even in those couple of minutes stood next to someone in a urinal, you might strike up a conversation. These people are usually fascinating to talk to and offer a good insight into the way of life of their country. I still keep in touch with one the *Bubbles* bars staff and others I met that weekend, even all these years! Two, I love to dance; no matter where I am, I will actively seek out dance music and party the night away. Mel loves dancing and nightclubs too, and this helped our relationship develop in the early days after meeting each other back when we both lived in Jakarta, getting into drunk adventures before we became a couple. One of the things that I found attractive beyond our nights out was her daft sense of humour. We'd play 'the accent game', where we'd both pick an accent to affect during the taxi ride on the way up to a nightclub and try to convince people we'd meet on the night that we were from these places. Mel sometimes managed to convince people that she was Venezuelan and affected an accent for the entire night, complete with a few Spanish phrases, which was impressive considering she looks entirely Indonesian and other Indonesians apparently bought it. I went with Scottish as I can do the accent reasonably well, but what I didn't anticipate was pulling a girl in a nightclub later in the night after ten pints (don't panic: this was during the time before Mel and I had hooked up) and going back to this girl's apartment in the early hours of the morning once the club had shut its doors. I had to keep pretending to be Scottish as I couldn't just revert to my English accent at this point; even during sex I gave it a committed "Och, thon's the spot thare, lass!"

Then, the morning after waking up next to each other when the alcohol had worn off, having to keep the accent going — at this point finding it had become plain weird. You don't get the sort of times like these that you'll look back on fondly when you're old by sitting at home on a weekend; nightlife and alcohol is where the excitement is at.

I know people go to Uganda for bucket list stuff, see a great ape tuggin' in the jungle, visit remote tribal areas or see the source of the river Nile or whatever. If you've got the time, money and inclination to do those things, then good luck to you. But for me, a weekend of enjoying myself in far-flung bars, meeting people and trying local food, is where the real fun is at. Credit to the Ugandans too, they throw a decent party and were incredibly nice and genuine to boot. If you want to try somewhere a bit different to let your hair down, this is the place. Just be wary of any party invitations to the botanical gardens.

# CHAPTER FOUR
## WEST AFRICA

## GHANA

**Monday, 24th December 2018**

There was a lot of travelling to do today, which wasn't ideal after a full weekend spent on the pop. Our multi-flight, multi-country, cross-continent route had us travelling from Uganda in East Africa, through Rwanda, Nigeria, and then finally to Accra, the capital of Ghana in West Africa. The first flight was due to be a short one to warm us up for the day, no more than 45 minutes between Entebbe and Rwanda's capital city, Kigali.

I could have happily gone the whole morning without talking to anyone, only letting Mel know what I wanted through a series of grunts and sighs. The day had other plans for me. Firstly, I was stopped at airport security for carrying a toothpick in my bag as it was deemed a risk to fly with. As far as I'm concerned, anyone who manages to hijack a plane with a toothpick deserves the plane. This took almost an hour to resolve as the airport staff took their time with me, making sure I wasn't a security threat nor carrying more toothpicks about my person. Then, I got to my seat on the plane by the window to find an obese African man already sat in it. Feeling as rough as a dog's arse and pushed on by Mel to just hurry up and sit down somewhere. I couldn't be bothered to engage with this big man, expecting a huge upheaval for him to get up to move, so just sat in the middle seat next to him instead. Mel took the aisle seat. I tried to sleep but I couldn't get comfy, so opted to looking around idly to pass time before take-off. I realised this plane must have had a full life in Germany before making its way over to Africa, noting

German text on the seat in front indicating where the inflatable life jackets were, "Lifevesten unda de seatzen" or whatever it was (I don't speak German). There was a line of a marker pen across the German language, leaving only the English version below it. It seemed like the owners had made a half-arsed attempt to remove the history of the plane's early life, either that or there had been a very neat spout of anti-German vandalism across all of the seats on board. The plane itself did feel old; the seats felt like they'd come straight off an old coach, a whack of the hand on them would kick up plumes of thick dust.

Have I mentioned yet that I'm not a good flyer? Well, I'm not. I tend to get anxious more easily if I'm tired and hungover, or if the plane in the sky rocks at all. Today's new take on a classic fear is that I started getting upset that this budget airline's charter plane might be really old and possibly not well-maintained, imagining wings held together with duct tape. It pushed me over the edge when the air stewardesses began handing out peanuts that weren't even pre-packaged, just a single tissue placed on the tray table with a spoon of loose nuts on it. Surely if they can't afford packaging for a few nuts, then there's no chance the plane is going to be properly maintained is there? I closed my eyes when my heart started fluttering during take-off, hoping with my fingers crossed I could just ride out the flight in sleep. The fat man wasn't keen on just taking my seat, he apparently wanted his own back too and, struggling to keep both of his fat legs within his given leg allowance, he slowly encroached into my space. Flab enveloped my knee. Flying outside of Europe, rarely enough space is factored into tall Westerners' legroom. Sure, we get the best views at concerts, but budget airlines worldwide are a nightmare in limb cramping and as legroom is at a premium, it's certainly not something to be shared with a stranger. He eyed up the armrest next, and that was slowly consumed like something off *The Blob*. I sometimes wonder about the etiquette of two strangers sharing arm rests on planes as there is only ever space to accommodate one arm, similarly at the cinema. Normally I'm on the polite side to start off, and if someone wants to take the whole thing up I'll let them without pushing against them for it — but — be warned; if you move that arm away for a second then I will be taking and claiming it.

Rocking in my seat startled me, with the peculiar sight of salted nuts suddenly falling onto my lap. I realised I must have managed a little bit of sleep, having been woken by the turbulence and jets kicking in fully. For the first time in all my years of air travel the plane was taking off twice within the same flight; Mel confirmed the plane had botched a landing attempt whilst I was asleep and so was going to try again. I looked past the fat man's tits to the window and there was nothing but bright white light pouring through, reflected by the thick white clouds we were enshrouded in. The Rwandan capital of Kigali and its airport sits 1,500 metres into the African mountains and is often susceptible to low hanging clouds, which was evidently the case today. When the cloud is too thick it can prevent successful landings from happening, so a pilot might have a stab at a landing and if he's not feeling confident he'll head back up into the air, then swing around and attempt the landing again. It's apparently common practice, but obviously information like that doesn't matter to me at the time. The pilot piped up on the tannoy as we hit another bumpy pocket of turbulence and said the conditions were particularly bad today. After half an hour of circling the airport we attempted a second, bumpier descent that also didn't work, so we retreated back into the skies yet again. By this point I was a wreck, over-thinking the possibilities here, genuinely thinking this was how I was going out; on a cloudy day in an old African plane, into the side of a mountain with nuts scattered across my lap. Mel didn't seem phased — her resistance to hangovers and love of flying are two of the rare areas where we don't share any common ground. I've seen Mel drink so much she has almost required hospital treatment, but she'll be bouncy and lively the next day after a few hours' sleep.

We made the landing after four frightening attempts after the cloud had partially cleared. The time spent circling around Kigali airport took longer than the actual flight over! I made the effort to give the pilot a big thank you after disembarking. Fuck of a day this was turning out to be, and this flight was only 7% of the entire journey! Fortunately, the day became significantly more pleasant after departing from Rwanda, making our way to West Africa and into the Ghanaian capital Accra without further incident.

Accra International Airport appeared to have either recently opened up a new terminal or had been heavily renovated, and I will say it was up there with the best airports I'd ever used; absolutely modern and efficient. There were multiple entry points for immigration, meaning there wasn't much time wasted in queues to enter the country. The staff were amiable (I even knuckle-bumped the lady at border control), and a man played a piano by baggage claim which was thoroughly impressive to watch. I think it was the only time I've wanted my bags to take their time coming out, so I could continue to watch this guy. It's not often I will give full marks to an airport but fair play to the Ghanaians, they received a glowing review from me. I hoped this would be reflected in the rest of the country because Kenya and Uganda's airports were rubbish, yet the actual countries themselves were brilliant, so on that logic things were looking good for the next week. Like the airport, considerable money had been spent on renovating the surrounding infrastructure, giving our taxi driver (a quiet, elderly man) newly tarmacked roads with multiple lanes to glide down. It had been refreshing to see something a little more modern on the continent, but it didn't take long for this to completely break down. First, the occasional pothole appeared, then the usual sights of Africa filled the road; loose barnyard animals digging around in the copious amounts of litter; little corrugated metal huts alongside the road, some shops and others houses, often painted in multiple bright colours. Outside the buildings, people sat around idly along the busy road. Our taxi eventually ground down and moved no quicker than walking speed, at times encountering complete traffic gridlock – though to be fair, it was Christmas Eve, and I'm sure the Ghanaians all had places to be and people to see, much like folks back at home. The roads were further congested by people weaving in and out of the traffic, selling things like toys or bottled water. One guy had a ruck of puppies under his arm and was knocking on the windows of cars trying to sell them off. I could understand people selling water, I could almost see the point of toys, in case you had forgotten your kid's Christmas present or something. But puppies!? Who the hell decides they want a puppy on the middle of a motorway? The poor buggers looked hot and bedraggled out in the midday sun. There was a lot more activity than I had seen in Kenya and Uganda, certainly more people wandering between traffic looking to sell things. I had also noticed something early on that would be a feature of my entire stay here – I could constantly hear music from at least one source, sometimes loud enough to vibrate the glass on the taxi's windows. It seemed a regular occurrence — along the road were huge, monstrously-sized speakers used to blast out Ghanaian music; mostly it was shite R'n'B but there was the occasional bit of reggae as well, which I don't usually mind. Along with the reggae, there was a large quantity of Rastafarians wandering the streets, huge dreadlocks swinging behind their backs. It explained the smell of ganja I would occasionally pick up too.

After around an hour of crawling along the roads, the heat had begun to take its toll on us. I hadn't yet been inside a car in Africa that had working air-conditioning, and today's taxi was no exception. The difference of being 10°C hotter than we had been used to in East Africa was very noticeable, pushing the temperature outside into the mid-thirties. As the car left the main road and onto side roads to get closer to our final destination, the last bits of tarmac gave way to uneven dirt and any sort of structure broke down into total chaos; people, bikes, goats — all on a mad mission to get somewhere at the same time. I'd had my first African massage since leaving Kenya and hated it. Our taxi driver began to change his temperament from the friendly old man we met at the airport and started to become angered by the difficult driving conditions. Whilst his frustrated shouting out of the window at the obstacles may have had some effect on some of the people, it was wasted breath on the goats and rocks.

The air by the sea has a certain feel about it; maybe it's the salt in the air I can sense, I'm not sure, but the familiarity hit me the second I stepped out into the fresh air without even yet seeing the ocean. God, did it ever feel good to get out of that car. We were staying at *Big Milly's Backyard* in a small town called Kokrobite, a couple of hours' drive west of the capital called Kokrobite. We had five nights here, arriving today on Christmas Eve. Our plan was to enjoy Christmas Day somewhere markedly different than at home, mainly spending it unwinding and doing little light activities like mooching about and exploring. Christmas Day on a tropical beach for something different than usual, then having Christmas dinner at *Big Milly's* which had a simplistic beach resort energy going for it that I kind of liked. Mel wasn't convinced upon arrival; the small brick buildings with thatched roofs contained nothing more than a single room inside for guests, with just about enough space inside for a bed on a hard floor and a simple outside toilet. This was all little too basic for her — Mel's a girl more used to luxury resorts than this "no-frills" vibe. I'll admit the rooms were a touch stuffy and the ceiling fan didn't really do much to cool us down. There were big gaping holes in the mosquito nets that were admittedly pretty poor quality overall. There was nowhere to unpack our backpacks, so we had to leave all our clothes in them crammed in the corner. All this I could happily overlook, for one simple reason: the neighbouring building to us was a bar which led on to a tropical beach.

Endless sand had blown in from the beach over the years, meaning wearing shoes around the resort wasn't necessary, and I love to go barefoot when I can. Between the guestrooms lay a well-maintained garden with cobblestone paths and palm trees. Music played from the speakers, but only gentle reggae. The staff seemed laid-back and greeted you with a smile. We were in a new tropical country, completely free to explore, with many new and interesting people to meet within it. I tried to reiterate these positives to Mel, but she wasn't having any of it. She thought the room was hot, small and shit and wanted to look for something better, but it was unlikely we'd find any viable alternatives this late on Christmas Eve. I told her we'd be better off just heading to the beach, forget the room and try to make the most of the time here. Along the perimeter of the resort was a huge concrete wall with broken glass cemented firmly onto the top of it as a cheap alternative to barbed wire, presumably to keep the surrounding rabble out.

"Can't be a good sign if this is needed," Mel commented. A small doorway had been cut out of the wall which led onwards to the beach. Prior to stepping through this to start an afternoon chilling on the sand, a member of staff intercepted us and warned us not to follow the beach to the left of the doorway as it wasn't safe for tourists, saying we had to stay on the short stretch of beach to the right. I was surprised by this information, as reading up before our arrival had not prepared me for any higher level of danger in the area, but if potential muggers respected the invisible barrier of the passageway from *Big Milly's*, then fine. Like we had done when venturing out to the beaches of Rio, we left our phones and anything of value back in the room anyway (take note: that's a fundamental travel tip if you're still sussing somewhere new whilst abroad!), so the only thing anyone would currently be able to take from my person right now would be my stinking swim-shorts that hadn't been washed since we got to Africa (of course, I assumed no one would want them, but I was proven wrong when they ended up being stolen on the last day whilst being left out to dry). Along the beach were palm trees leaning over towards the white sand, the blue sea glistened under the sunshine and small wooden huts lined the sand with shops inside. All of this felt quite scenic and ticked all the boxes on the checklist for what you would expect a tropical beach. It was also very busy; hundreds of people were out enjoying themselves. There were some families, but the vast majority were young men playing football or swimming. Having walked the length of the safe area and back in a little over five minutes and left with nothing else to do, we stopped at one of the bars nestled between some palm trees a short walk from *Big Milly's* and, having carried no cash out with us, they allowed us to run up a small tab there. Like Uganda, the local ale was well over 5% alcohol, and it only took a couple to remove my hangover from the weekend.

We happened to catch a couple of foreigners leave the beach as we initially walked out onto it, leaving us two right now amidst hundreds of the dark-skinned natives. When I took my shirt off, I was absolutely the whitest thing on the beach, my pasty white skin seemingly acting as a beacon for unwanted attention. We were hounded by a constant stream of passing local lads after money, cigarettes or asking if Mel was single. It was manageable until two of them walked over, made only the briefest of efforts to talk to us and then reached for Mel's cigarettes in a brazen effort to steal them. In hindsight, shouting at some pushy locals over a mere four cancer sticks might not have been the greatest idea, but I had lost my cool having to deal with it all day and became annoyed by the rudeness. Strangers started sitting too close to us on the beach (all men) and whilst it may have been innocent in most cases, as I'm sure we are both a novelty here, it began to get a little unnerving. Even if groups of guys hadn't been sat so close to us, I wouldn't be able to settle — other young lads would tear past on quad-bikes or motorbikes. Along the beach, one lad managed to crash his quad-bike and completely topple it over, which was some feat on a largely flat beach; fortunately, no one happened to be sunbathing in the crash zone. The main terrorisers of sunbathers weren't actually motorised, but rather people doing acrobatics, using the sunbathers as something stationary to backflip over. One guy did an impressive backflip over a woman sat with her back to him, and once she realised what was going on she understandably went apeshit. If this lunacy was the 'safe' side of the beach, I couldn't imagine what the dodgy side past *Big Milly's* doorway was like.

The Christmas party atmosphere really started to kick off as the sun started to set. In the middle of the safe side of the beach was a sort of shack on stilts blasting out loud (but not very good) dance music. As the day went on the volume picked up, along with the number of people dancing outside of it — with a slight haze above it growing larger, most likely a massive ganja cloud judging by the smell. Whilst we hadn't been hugely impressed with the country so far, I must admit I quite enjoyed the atmosphere there and had a few hours' fun by dancing once the alcohol had loosened us up a bit. I even noted the frown on Mel's face cracking into a smile once or twice. We met a few people too; a girl from London who was out backpacking around the country, plus a few local guys who didn't pester us constantly for cigarettes. Most notable of these was a friendly Rasta called Rice who looked much younger than me, despite being 54. I honestly didn't intend to drink so much on Christmas Eve, rather intending to save myself for Christmas day, but at one point I found myself dancing with a traditional Ghanaian tribal show that *Big Milly's* had put on for everyone. Twenty natives in traditional dress with bongos and a lanky white guy in a Hawaiian shirt jumping around in front of a couple of hundred people. It's amazing how much of a twat you can make yourself look and still enjoy the night under the right circumstances.

### Kokrobite, Ghana – Christmas Day, Tuesday, 25th December 2018

The big day was here. I woke up at dawn on Christmas Day with the mother of all hangovers to Christmas music playing loudly over the resort's speakers, desperately needing to sort my life out. The use of a toilet would be a good start to the process. My urine was that deep amber colour, a classic indicator that too much alcohol has been consumed without keeping hydrated throughout the session. This process is enhanced in the tropics as the amount of fluid that is lost naturally through sweat is much higher; getting seriously dehydrated, even without the assistance of alcohol, can be easily done. I should have been physically lighter after unloading the piss, but as I got back into bed, it started to creak, followed by a loud snap as the whole thing broke in two. Mel was not in a good way with a possible touch of food poisoning from the night before, and so was severely unimpressed as she found herself crashing to the floor on a bed of splinters.

"Go and find a new bed!" she demanded. I begrudgingly got dressed, left the room and located one of the early morning staff sweeping up leaves outside. He looked highly confused when I began to explain myself. "Yes, that's right, we've ruined an entire bed. No, we weren't having sex. No, I'm not paying for it. Can you turn the Christmas music down too? It's 6AM!"

Having moved Mel and our luggage to a new room I was unable to get back to sleep again, so I took an early but aimless wander around the beach to see what was going on. I didn't realise this at the time of booking, but Kokrobite is a hugely popular area for locals to come and spend Christmas Day. Whilst not a problem on the face of it, I didn't realise that this meant there would be excessive crowds of people around. I don't think I'd have been bothered as much had the people kept to themselves, but similarly to yesterday, the young males would drop whatever they were doing to come over to talk to me, and I just wanted a quiet morning walk by myself. I was getting surrounded by up to ten people at a time, asking weird questions like could they have my shoes, or would I like to buy a shell from them — despite their abundance on the floor around us. I wasn't in the mood for it. I found a quiet area that had Wi-Fi and upon loading up my phone saw my mum had sent me some photos of everyone back home enjoying themselves starting their Christmas Day in England. I love Christmas Day. For me, it's usually a full-on family event. By this point I had been away from home for a couple of months, including the work stint in Indonesia just before this trip. I started to get homesick, seeing the pictures of everyone having a traditional English Christmas, galvanising my feelings of wanting to be there with them. It just didn't feel like Christmas here in West Africa as I sat here in 34°C heat, suffering that same number in mosquito bites, sweating, watching people crash quad-bikes on the beach, with my wife ill in bed to top it all off. The only two things to do in Kokrobite were to either sit on a dodgy beach or get drunk (well, surfing was an option, but I can't surf). I couldn't explore the area either, because the staff at Big Millie's had warned me it wasn't the safest thing to do even in the daylight. I felt stuck in this small area with little to do.

It was more of the same that evening, a couple of bars and *Big Milly's* pumping out excessively loud thumping dance music, but we'd seen all this last night and wanted something new. Ironically, we'd come to relax here, not to partake in our usually sought-after bars and nightlife; if we had come for a raucous time, we might have enjoyed ourselves. That's the thing about dance music and nightlife — it's top fun when you're in the mood for it, but it can be equally irritating when you're in earshot of it all whilst tired and just wanting a bit of peace and quiet. When Mel finally left the bedroom for Christmas dinner served at *Big Milly's* (a rather disappointing two boiled potatoes and steak with a popcorn starter) and after realising we weren't going to get the type of Christmas Day we had anticipated, we made two decisions over a mouthful of popcorn: one, to move onwards, absolutely anywhere in the country tomorrow, and two, for an early night so we could hit the road as early as possible. That was the plan. Our room may have been next to the bar, but it was also next to the main stage area with speakers big enough to fit a person inside. Christmas Night 2018 was spent feeling hot and sweaty in a bed that definitely wanted to snap with our weight again, listening to thumping music loud enough to shake the room, interspersed only with the occasional buzz of a mosquito around my ear; right through until dawn. What kept us both going through that particularly difficult night was focusing on the better times that were ahead, properly relaxing somewhere in a new town. Hopefully in silence too. We had heard music endlessly and everywhere since getting off the plane — I can now see why a constant stream of noise is a method deployed to break spies when interrogating them.

### Kokrobite, Ghana – Wednesday, 26th December 2018

The girl from London that we happened to meet on Christmas Eve was backpacking further around the country and planned to travel west to the city of Cape Coast today. We picked up on her plans over breakfast and, with no particular plan to go anywhere else, Mel and I decided to tag along — hoping to save money all travelling together by taxi. The vast majority of tourists in Ghana, quite few in overall numbers, were backpackers. All were living out of backpacks and staying no more than a couple of nights in each place, moving around the country in the process. Like backpackers anywhere else in the world, they became friends through chance encounters and travelled together, sometimes adjusting their own travel plans to stay with their new friends in the process. I could see it happening with the handful of tourists leaving *Big Milly's* and it seemed like it would be the case here for us with this London girl. She was alright as a person I suppose, but I didn't really click with her entirely. Things she would do would bug me massively. Proudly claiming to be part of the *Green Party* back home (the ones that care about the environment), but then during the ride to Cape Coast she wound the window down and threw a plastic bag and bottle out. Look, I know there's shitloads of litter around here, and one plastic bag isn't going to make a difference — but — you should be leading by example. *Especially* if you are supposed to be representing the *Green Party!* On Christmas Eve there had been kids — that we would definitely consider too young to be working in the West — walking around with flat-weaved baskets on their heads with things to sell, ranging from food to small bags of drinking water. These kids looked so poor they were borderline beggars, and I wouldn't be surprised if this was their only source of income. London Girl began arguing with one of these kids over the equivalent of ten pence in local money for the price of some of the water. I'm sure there was a little bit of price inflation going on as she's a foreigner but come on mate; it's ten pence going to desperately poor little kid. She started shouting in earshot of many strangers, sounding very much like an entitled foreign gobshite some might say, and for me stood next to her it was frankly embarrassing. Thinking about it now, she was an absolute twat actually, but she was here with us now and was making our taxi cheaper, so she was worth putting up with. She had a *Lonely Planet* guidebook on Ghana, which I read on the journey. Leafing through the pages, I happened to note it said Kokrobite was one of the rougher places in the entire country. A relief, finally, as it meant we must be going to somewhere safer. Then as I read about Cape Coast, it said parts of that weren't safe as well.

Money was beginning to get a little tight (visiting Africa isn't as cheap as you might think — certainly when doing a big pub crawl across the continent) so our choice of hotel in Cape Coast had been heavily influenced by cost. London Girl found a place in her travel guide south of the city that claimed to be a budget two-star hotel. I say city; Cape Coast was in reality no bigger than a mid-sized town in the UK but being such a notable place on a map of the country, in my own naivety, I was a little surprised by how small it actually was once there. I had the thought in my head that it's a beautiful city from somewhere, possibly picking it up from the internet or word of mouth, but it wasn't particularly nice at all — especially the area around our apartment. Dilapidated buildings made of breezeblock and corrugated steel were crammed together either side of the pothole-laden roads. Huge piles of litter and discarded building materials lay strewn about everywhere. Open sewers ran alongside footpaths with wobbly concrete slabs across parts of them for pedestrians to cross over, the stench of hot shit festering in the sun. To my dismay, that familiar thudding background music throughout Ghana was here as well, because why wouldn't it be; although this time louder and from several sources, all overlapping each other and creating a horrible racket. We had to walk over a huge mound of litter to get to the hotel to book a night there, as London Girl took the opportunity to empty some more shite from out of her pockets onto the floor. I didn't have the energy to confront her. I could tell Mel was disappointed to come to somewhere that was even worse than where we left. I felt her pain. The room was grim: the towels were smelly, the bed wasn't level and only one light in the room worked. Turning it on scared a cockroach that scarpered under the bed.

Desperate to get out of the rooms, the three of us went for a walk around town to see what the place had on offer. Like back in Kokrobite, groups of lads where everywhere, although this time usually sat idle at the side of the street, staring at us walking past. More kids with trays of water on their head approached us and asked if we wanted to buy any. I quickly stepped in before London Girl could speak to prevent any confrontation, which backfired, as politely declining the offer had one of the kids shouting "I'll smack you" quite aggressively at me as he made eye contact. I had just been verbally bitch-slapped by an eight-year-old child, but the three of us were a bit wary of the area in general and in no mood to talk back so we kept our heads down and carried on through the streets. After a whole fourteen minutes of walking Cape Coast we realised we'd seen enough for the day and decided finding somewhere that sold a beer would be preferable to dealing with the ongoing feeling that getting mugged was an imminent likelihood Mostly, I didn't want to risk encountering those aggressive water children again. There was a restaurant at the far end of the main beach that sold beer, so we settled there for a few hours. Sometimes I do worry about my draw to the pub and whether I really do maximise my time enough out in these countries, but the fact that London Girl (who was backpacking around "to see the country") deemed this restaurant preferable to walking around Cape Coast justified the choice of sitting down for a beer this time. It was a great choice too, almost relaxing even; the sound of waves crashing on the beach as the evening drew in, which could almost mask the standard thudding dance music I could hear from the main street behind us.

The bar was empty aside from a small group of female Europeans on a neighbouring table who we struck up conversation with. They had been in Cape Coast a couple of days already and warned us from experience that now it was dark it wasn't safe to walk around the streets, with the only realistic option to get home being by taxi. We said that our hotel was only a ten-minute walk from here, but they countered our point by outright stating the main road from here back to our hotel was notorious for tourist muggings. What they failed to factor in was that by this point I had consumed seven beers; I was feeling confident for the walk. Mel wasn't as keen, but she's nothing if not thrifty and saving a bit of cash by not taking a taxi was worth investigating. The second we left through the back of the restaurant and stepped onto the unlit street, it snapped me back to reality and the confidence evaporated. It was virtually pitch black other than small fires the locals had going along the road. Groups of youths sat around them drinking and shouting at each other. We attempted to walk for a few seconds or so, but there were too many people instantly interested in our presence and it halted us in our tracks. The groups of young lads got up from their fires alongside the road and came striding over.

"Hey, you! Mister! Where you go?!"

It may have been innocent, but why couldn't they stay sat down and be friendly from the floor? One lad grabbed my arm.

"Right," said Mel, "fuck this!"

We quickly retreated back to the safety of the restaurant, nearly falling over due to the broken pathways in the darkness, and waited there for a taxi. We both really resented having to get a lift for a ten-minute walk entirely because it was so risky to be out at night. Back at the hotel, the background music being played in various residential apartments had picked up and was nearly as loud as the main stage at *Big Milly's*. Lying in bed, my skin stuck to the bedsheets that stunk of blue cheese, I just couldn't wait to get back to my own bed in England. I didn't dare ask Mel how she was in fear of opening Pandora's box.

## Cape Coast, Ghana – Thursday, 27th December 2018

You know in old cartoons like *Tom & Jerry,* when one of the characters dies, and their ghost grows a big pair of wings and gains a halo? And as they float up to heaven there's a sound effect of a choir singing? Well, imagine waking to that choir sound at 3:30AM on full volume, being played by your neighbour's 8-foot speakers. I didn't know at the time, but we were sleeping near to a church that enjoyed waking up people within a two-mile radius with prayer songs. For a moment I thought that was it, Ghana had been that mental it had finished me off and I was currently floating off to the pearly gates. When I woke up properly and grasped that I wasn't experiencing the sweet release of death and did, in fact, remain in a hot, dirty room in West Africa, I was hugely disappointed. In the dim light I sat on the edge of the bed and put my head in hands, with nothing else to do at this time of the morning other than listen to Ghana's number one God Squad celebrate. I suppose background music is just part of Ghanaian life, but I just can't work out how the local people around here can tolerate it 24 hours a day, especially more so at 3:30 in the fucking morning. How is anyone else asleep through this racket? How do even religious people, who I'm sure enjoy all this choir noise, bypass the genuine human requirement of a good night's sleep to wake up three hours before dawn to stick this in the record player?

I was banking on getting a bit of quiet in a few hours when we were due for today's trip to Kakum National Park, basically situated in a jungle away from the city. I mean, from what I've experienced so far, I couldn't completely rule out some sort of festival-style sound system in a nature reserve — but surely this was unlikely. We'd had a leaf through London Girl's *Lonely Planet* book yesterday while sat in the restaurant and the highlight of the area was the park. It was something that Mel and I had been considering as a day trip from Kokrobite anyway but now, only an hour's drive away, it was something well worth doing. We had somehow decided to travel even longer with ever-annoying London Girl in the process though, so the three of us met in the lobby before dawn, crunched over the litter mound and made our way onto the quiet street. Relatively quiet, I should say; there was still music, of course, but no people. Ash still smoked a bit from last night's small fires at the side of the street. A couple of rats spotted us and darted away.

To get to the park, we were using what the Ghanaian locals call a Tro-Tro — a public bus of sorts, but more like a crazy little van crammed with people. As well as the driver, there was a young lad who would open the rusty sliding side door for passengers while collecting their money, jumping out onto the street with enthusiasm whenever the van stopped and encouraging people to get on board. A wide variety of passengers got on and off during our route to Kakum that I found rather interesting to observe from the back seat; these included a really smelly goat herder who I was unfortunate enough to sit downwind from (I assumed he was a goat herder because the bus picked him up stood next to twenty goats), a woman incredibly wearing two pairs of shoes (one inside the other on each foot, if you're struggling to picture it), a businessman wearing an oversized suit (which I was happy about as I hadn't seen many since Uganda), and a girl travelling by herself who looked no older than six years old. The girl struggled to get into the cramped van with two huge containers that she could barely carry — I assumed for fetching water — and Mel couldn't get over it, sending such a young kid by herself fetch commodities. That moment said a lot about both Ghana and Indonesia to me, as the latter is also considered a developing country and yet someone from there was still shocked to see such a young kid struggling on a long, difficult errand without her parents around. I find kids in poorer countries are usually pushed into work at an early age; unfortunately, the trend is that the poorer the country, the earlier the work starts for the child. I have seen kids working in Indonesia before, but they were not quite as young nor in such abundance as I'd seen in Ghana. There are regions within Indonesia that are not as developed as other parts of the country, but it still has a significant wealthy population and an overall abundance of cash that is just not distributed around the people well. Factoring my extensive time there, in comparison, I haven't seen anywhere quite as impoverished as Cape Coast and the surrounding areas. It was a moment of realisation for me just how thoroughly poor Ghana is, even when put into contrast with other countries that still might be considered developing.

The road gave a rough ride; it was a wide pothole-laden browny-orange dirt track that cut through the countryside, and the passing traffic (which seemed to only go 'fast' or 'faster') kicked up the dust into the air, creating a thick orange fog. Breathing left a faint grit in my teeth. The journey came to an end and the Tro-Tro stopped outside the entrance to the park — another wide browny-orange dirt road leading off into a deep green forest, with a man sat inside a little security hut at the junction. I was impressed with the journey here, not with safety as that had been horrendous, but rather in terms of cost. It was a full 35-minute drive from Cape Coast, and it cost us six Cedi (around

£1 in local currency). London Girl must have misheard the price when she got on and assumed they said four Cedi, and then there was another argument with her and the rusty door guy at the side of the road.

"YOU ARE TRYING TO RIP ME OFF!" she shouted. Passengers on the bus began to get involved after a minute of listening and started to argue with her as well; the goat herder guy in particular became quite agitated and even got up out of his seat to shout at her. Mel and I had reached a tipping point with her so we paid our six Cedi each, walked off and left her to it.

The highlight of Kakum National Park is the rope walks. Although a short activity, it is essentially several bridges constructed of wood and — you guessed it — rope, right across the tree canopies; twenty metres high at times, offering fantastic views of the African jungle in the early morning haze. Listen! Not a single music beat to be heard, just beautiful birdsong. Our guide led us down to the forest floor and showed us some cool stuff. There was a large type of tree which sounded hollow, it made a loud echoing sound when hit. We were told the Indigenous people of the forest used these for centuries as a method of communication with one another as the sound carries across quite some distance, like some sort of mad jungle Morse code type rhythm. So, there are still technically thudding music beats out here in the jungle! Then there was a tree which, when the base was cut, freshwater came out, which again kept those same people hydrated during the dry season. Rubber trees are indigenous here too, and these were fascinating — when hit with the guide's machete, a runny liquid came out which looked like milk initially, but became rubbery over a few minutes. Apparently, local people still to this day make footballs out of it if they can't afford a real one. There was a seed called a *pow pow*, so-called because of the noise it makes when it's stepped on. The contents of the seed act as a pain killer when ingested and are apparently still used in modern times as an ingredient in paracetamol today! I pocketed a couple of the seeds as I'd be needing them shortly for the headache of heading back to civilisation.

We were done by 10AM, leaving us with a whole day still ahead of us, so with the park ticked off the list it was back to Cape Coast to wander around the city in the safety of daylight. One of the stops included the Cape Coast castle, an integral part the slave trade centuries ago, used as a hub on the Atlantic coast of Africa to ship the slaves over to Europe or the Americas. For such a key part of human history (its dark side at least) it wasn't in a good state, sitting there looking rather neglected. We weighed up having a swim in the sea but there were signs up explicitly instructing visitors not to enter due to the strong currents. There were a few markets and other bits of mild interest, plus the novelty of just walking around somewhere completely new, but honestly; I was rather underwhelmed with it all and just couldn't seem to fully enjoy myself there. I was actually ready to go back to Kokrobite for our last night in Africa and go out with a bang, I mean we still had to go back for our stuff we had left in our room in *Big Milly's* anyway as we'd left most of our luggage there, and if we wanted to dance the night away it was probably the best place to go.

I sent a text message to one of the Rastas we had met on Christmas Eve, named Rice, and he was more than keen to meet up for a session when we got back to Kokrobite. We just had one more night to go in Hotel Hell (or rather Heaven given the hymnal output from local neighbours), then we'd be able to leave this place forever.

### Kokrobite, Ghana – Friday, 28th December 2018

We arrived back at *Big Milly's* around midday, after a long bus ride back along the bottom of Ghana's coast. Rice met us that afternoon on the "right side" of the beach with a bottle of locally-brewed rum, along with his young female friend Sam. Rice and Sam both had cool dreadlocks swinging down their backs, meanwhile Mel had been convinced to have her long hair braided on the beach not long after sitting down with them. I was left out, feeling a bit "square" with my normal haircut in comparison to the other three. We sat as a group idly on the beach, drinking the rum neat in little plastic cups. I got to know Sam a little; she told me she was close to breaking the music scene in Ghana, I told her there's definitely a market for it here as music is played on a fucking loop everywhere. Although an ambitious idea, if she made any real money, her and Rice had plans to transform Kokrobite into a real tourist destination, buying a large derelict building on the far end of the beach to turn it into a huge resort. I could see the potential I suppose, but there was a lot of work to do. The beach was definitely a selling point to the area, and unlike the one in Cape Coast, we could actually enter the water without the risk of strong currents. With that in mind, Rice and I entered for a swim in the late afternoon.

I hoped having been sat socialising with a couple of locals I might have perhaps now radiated some sort of street cred, enough to deter absolute strangers from coming up so close to me at least, but it didn't, and a small group of lads who appeared from nowhere followed us into the water. Being with Rice, who also worked as a part-time lifeguard on the beach, had me venturing out into the water further than I would ever dare by myself. Soon enough I got to the frightening point in the water where I was unable to touch the floor with my feet. One risk is of course currents, but out here in the tropics, God knows what sort of deadly sea creatures that can definitely out-swim me are lurking around in the murky depths. I wouldn't have thought there was much anti-venom on shore in the immediate area if something did have a cheeky nibble at my toe either — there was barely running water from the taps! One of the young lads who had followed us into the water began to flap violently, apparently struggling out of his depth.

"Boy, can you swim?" Rice shouted sternly at him. The lad tried to shout "No" through large mouthfuls of water. Truth be told, I didn't even initially recognise what was going on as I thought he was just being daft and showing off, but Rice's lifeguard instincts kicked in and he carried the poor lad back to shore. I think the lad just wanted to follow the white man but disregarded the fact that the white man could swim, and he could not.

The on-duty lifeguard, with his watchful eye, had seen this going on from the shoreline and stormed across the beach with a look of anger as our small group got back to land. The poor young lad was being forcibly dragged by Rice whilst still coughing up mouthfuls of water.

"What were you doing out there, you stupid boy?" started the lifeguard, who began hitting the poor lad several times across his head as soon as he was in swinging range. I could see Mel and Sam sat some distance away looking on, probably wondering what was going on seeing someone being dragged out of the water by the scruff of his neck then getting several sharp smacks to the head. I watched in as much amazement that the lifeguards in Ghana were apparently allowed to save someone's life and then deliver a few digs afterwards. Within this moment of drama, someone passing crashed his quad-bike metres away from us and landed in a heap on the floor. This was definitely the maddest stretch of sand I'd ever been on.

In the evening Mel and I were invited deep into the housing area surrounding the beach (a shantytown of sorts) to Rice and Sam's place where, like in the sea earlier, we would never have dared to venture this far without someone else. The streets were virtually pitch-black once night had set in, yet both Mel and I could tell after most of the day getting to know Rice and Sam that they were trustworthy people, so we felt we had a ring of security around us. The night ended with us partying with a group of local people outside Rice's place until sunrise. The night was incredibly fun but a bit of a blur if I'm being honest — still, it was a fair end to the time here, and I daresay I was actually finally enjoying the country properly for the first time.

Whilst it did have its moments, I found Ghana was my least favourite of all the places I've travelled to. I will admit things did pick up once we fell in with a group of locals, but other than some nice people, there wasn't much else that felt truly worth the extensive travel out for. I've been to hectic and somewhat unsafe places before, northern India springs to mind, but at least there are the big-ticket attractions like the Taj Mahal which are absolutely worth seeing. There are indeed things on Ghana's tourist trail, but I didn't find they were worth the trip out here for. The Cape Coast castle wasn't looked after, nor was the town that hosted it. The Kakum jungle visit, although interesting for a couple of hours, was expensive for what it was. There are far better and safer beaches in the world, ones that don't require the use of malaria tablets to visit. The tourism industry is growing in Ghana for sure, and there's talk of relaxing the visa requirements for foreign tourists in the near future (at the time of writing it is not 'Visa on Arrival'). Maybe in ten years' time, it could be better; Rice and Sam may have got lucky and managed to transform Kokrobite. But for now, us being part of the small wave of tourists going off the beaten path doesn't necessarily make the experience good. I can't recall ever getting back from a country and being so glad to be home, totally shattered from my time away. I was so thankful for the peace and quiet when I wanted to sleep. Will I be back? Probably not. But if anything, it made me appreciate my favourite places in the world even more.

# CHAPTER FIVE
# THE MIDDLE EAST

# JORDAN

**Amman, Jordan — Thursday, 11th April 2019**

There were a few people I know in my day-to-day life — friends, family, work colleagues — who all had some pointed comments about my trip to Jordan.

"You're mad!", "It's in the Middle East, why are you going there, will you be safe?", sometimes followed by outright rejection of the destination. A surprisingly common comment was, "What's wrong with goin' to Spain?" (or another equally sunny European country). I'll tell you what's wrong with Spain; where's the adventure sat around a pool for two weeks in Marbella? I get that some people enjoy the unwinding aspect of it, and perhaps my view will change in the future after Mel and I have had a few kids, but until that day, we're going to enjoy that sense of adventure to our getaways. I acted nonchalantly, saying that all was fine when asked about going to the Middle East, but I'll admit other people's reactions did have me spending some time researching to make sure it *was* safe, and I wasn't walking into a lawless madhouse. To be fair, the country lies next to lots of rowdy neighbours; Syria, Iraq and, to a lesser extent, Israel. And while mostly calm internally of its borders, its largest neighbour Saudi Arabia hadn't exactly been avoiding the news lately either as they were relentlessly bombing the shit out of nearby Yemen and its rebels trying to overthrow the government. From all reports, I was happy to read that Jordan was completely safe for tourists and offered a place packed with stuff to do for those interested in something a little different. Further research showed the nine nights we had booked were probably not going to be long enough to see everything there; there is ancient history, deserts, the Dead Sea and a world wonder to name just a few. Mel was sold on the idea of a visit, and we agreed to avoid doing it on a pre-packaged tour, instead doing it ourselves by renting a car as the attractions were found along the entire length of the country.

I'm pretty seasoned when it comes to driving abroad, but it had been a few years since I had last done it, and even longer since I'd used an automatic car. There's something about automatics that I can't really seem to gel with; perhaps its only because I see them as nothing more than big go-karts for people who can't be bothered to learn manual, but you can't beat the feel of the bite from the clutch kicking in with a manual car, or even the simple things to fine tune your driving experience like knowing when to adjust your gears for a big hill because you're not automated machinery. Manuals are arguably more optimal for fuel efficiency too, providing the driver doesn't drive like an absolute bellend. There's undoubtedly more effort to drive one versus an automatic, but both Mel and I prefer manual and seeing as we were planning on covering over five hundred miles across the country, we both wanted to drive in a style we were most comfortable with. I'd booked the car for this trip online some months before arrival, and the website offered "A Hyundai or similar", not stating either manual or automatic as options. When we finally came to the car pick up at the airport, the "or similar" part from the booking presented us with a brand of car I had never seen before, a rather sad looking automatic *Baic* with *Made in China* written in various places around the interior. Mel wasn't particularly fussed either way, but it left me with a moment of disappointment upon realising we had a Chinese go-kart for a driving holiday. I may have attempted to get something else at the rental shop had the flight not landed past midnight; but after clearing immigration and collecting our bags, we decided we didn't need the hassle of trying to swap cars at this hour so kept the *Baic*.

Mel will tell you she's a good driver, and I will give her that she might well be, having learned to drive on the congested streets of Jakarta, but she still insisted I was first up to try driving on this excursion as we had no idea what the roads would be like. After loading our bags into the car, I adjusted the mirrors, checked the location of the indicator controls and made sure the headlights were on. Nervously, I started the engine and off we set, leaving the brightly lit, huge arched road outside Arrivals, heading out of the airport grounds into the dark Jordanian desert. The hotel we chose to sleep at was purposely close to the airport to avoid any long distances so late at night — a mere nine minutes' drive away if *Google Maps* was to be believed.

It doesn't take long to pick up on the heavy police presence in Jordan. I compare it to home and there's always one or two police with guns dotted around at Manchester Airport, but beyond that it is rare to see them around the rest of the country. Meanwhile in Jordan, armed fellas were found everywhere, and presumably more so at the airport with it being a prime target for a terror attack. The link road between the airport and the main highway was filled with police too, like they were all urgently heading to or from somewhere; multiple police cars drove up and down the road, some of them heavy-duty armoured vehicles with mounted machine guns and large bars at the front of the grill. This was my first time visiting the Middle East and the initial impression of seeing these guys driving around at night-time unsettled me greatly, making me even more nervous having to drive around them all. It didn't take long to find ourselves on a public highway, a straight line that cut through the desert with a notable lack of street lighting, leaving me unable to see much of the road in front of the car. Although adamant to Mel I had put the headlights on the bright setting before we started, I realised it was possible I hadn't as the visibility in front of me was awful. Instead of pulling over and sorting the headlights like a normal person might, I began to flap a bit driving amongst the police wagons, panicking with switching the controls as the window wipers accidentally started and headlights flickered between dim, dimmer or off. In the rear-view mirror a large van belonging to the authorities appeared with strobe lights flashing, approaching closer at some speed. 'Oh crap,' I thought, 'the police have spotted me driving without the headlights on and I'm getting pulled minutes into the drive.'

I wasn't entirely sure whether the van was heading for me but slowed down just in case, worried that I might have also been unintentionally speeding. The van hovered behind me, so I pulled over, almost to a stop, as the blue flashing lights from their beacon engulfed the darkness of our car. The light was dazzling but I could just about see the van driver's annoyed face in the rear-view mirror. Well, he's obviously pissed off with me and I'm getting arrested then, I'm sure. To my surprise, the van overtook our Baic as soon as it could, clearly displaying the English word *Ambulance* written on the back as it drove off into the distance. I guessed the driver looked annoyed because I was in his way, dithering around in the road in my panic, and although thankful I wasn't being pulled up by the armed coppers, this first experience on the roads had rattled me. We sat at the side of the road for several minutes, Mel (who had been fairly calm herself until recently) shouting at me to get a grip whilst I was still messing around with the car's controls. It took a few passing cars to notice that they, too, had really dimmed headlights, like the lowest setting we have available on cars in the UK. We guessed that the dim lights might be the country's standard setting but weren't entirely sure about this, and if our car had a brighter headlight setting then the *Baic* was hiding it from me. Both agreeing this would be the only night driving we'd be doing for the entire stay, we set off again with what felt like a five-watt bulb lighting up the road in front. On the stretches of road with no street lighting I could barely see in front of me, causing me to swerve last minute around the potholes or rocks that had somehow made their way onto the road. Bloody foreigners and their weird ways of doing things.

The night-time driving fun continued. Turning off the highway and onto a slip road, the written signposts didn't make any sense as most of them were written in Arabic — even the universally understood signs of an arrow pointing us toward the flow of traffic would conflict; a signpost would tell us to drive one way, then on the lane floor itself would be arrows printed as if to suggest we were going the wrong way. There were no other cars around at this time of night though, so if we were driving the wrong way then at least there was no one else to crash into. It was a nightmare, and I began to worry if we had made a bad call deciding on a driving holiday out here.

We slept only a few hours, possibly due to adrenaline in my case, but mostly keen to make an early start in the morning to the first place of interest on the trip: the Wadi Rum desert.

## Wadi Rum, Jordan — Friday, 12th April 2019

If you think of the shape of the country of Jordan roughly as a lower case "r", the capital Amman, and its international airport, are found in the top left, with most of the tourist activity found along the spine of the "r" (the right part has little to offer tourists other than a long road along the desert direct to Iraq). We had a four-hour drive down the spine today; a single highway to the far south of the country through yet more desert, taking us near to the border with Saudi Arabia. Mel wanted to have a crack at driving which, after last night, was absolutely fine with me. We've both driven in countries with erratic drivers before (hell, I was one of them last night), and although not the worst roads we'd ever been on, Jordan was still pretty bad with its residents turning in junctions without indicating, or having them move straight into the fast lane of the highway at a slow speed without any thought of the surrounding drivers. Reckless overtaking is one that causes the most anxiety for me though; overtaking on bends is usually reserved for only the biggest wankers at home, yet it was commonplace here. The road was empty most of the time at least, so it was easy for Mel to navigate around the occasional drivers we'd come across. The road south went on for miles through much of the same scenery, cutting through the barren desert, covered in dull coloured rocks and, very rarely, dried shrubs poking through the sand. We saw occasional goat farmers dressed in traditional Arab clothing, wearing red and white head-scarfs and shawls, who would usher their cattle alongside the road with a stick. Breaking up the same surroundings would be the small towns we passed through which offered new things to look at. These towns were usually comprised of no more than a couple of hundred houses, styled like square yellow bungalows with small windows. As Jordan is a Muslim country, there was always a mosque in town, usually several; these seemed to vastly outnumber anything of more use, such as shops or post offices. These towns didn't look like they'd be fun places to live in unless you were really into praying and counting rocks.

Several hours into our day and ready for a break, our car pulled into a service station in the desert ready to have a stretch of the ol' legs and make use of a toilet. Wherever you are in the world, service station toilets always offer the lowest standard of toilets in the entire country. That said, the toilets on Jordan's Route 15 were particularly grim – dozens of flies buzzing around the stinking squat toilets with huge mounds of dried shit already in them. I'm guessing the limited water they have available around these dry areas are better used for drinking rather than pushing poo round sewers. Although the day's temperature was currently only in the low twenties, it was still enough to get the toilet smell really festering inside the building. I could barely hold my breath long enough for a wee, gagging when I had to breathe whilst trying to keep my aim, even though spilling my piss around would be the least of this toilet's worries. After using filthy toilets comes the classic dilemma— would it be more hygienic to not use the handwashing facilities here; is having touched my cock the cleaner option than having to touch these shite-encrusted taps? And, another factor with the desert location here; should I be brave enough to touch them to turn them on, would any water actually come out? I decided on this occasion that not washing was the safer bet. I met Mel outside who looked horrified at the similar stomach-churning experience she'd had in the ladies' toilets. Although grim, we'd not eaten since breakfast and it hadn't been enough to put Mel off the thought of food, having spotted a yoghurt drink in the outside shop adjacent to the toilet whilst waiting for me, and she said she wanted to try one. I said I could go for one as well. We bought one each and, to our disgust, discovered that salted yoghurt drinks are apparently a thing in Jordan. Having gagged twice in two minutes for two entirely different reasons, we promptly put them in the bin and hit the road again.

It was now my turn to drive again. I hated that car; I'd put my foot down to overtake, and the piece of crap would hover at the same speed in a low RPM, not deciding what to do, waiting a good four seconds at times before it registered that I wanted to accelerate. This was dangerous when attempting to overtake slow-moving vehicles on the road. Well, until it decided it did want to accelerate, so would max out, sending the fuel economy into overdrive and our speed along with it. When I took my foot off the pedal slightly in hopes of reducing the increasing speed, it was like putting the brakes on. I couldn't remember automatics being quite this bad, but this one wasn't fun to drive. I thought to myself that if we crashed into oncoming traffic now as I slowly overtook a rickety open-top truck carrying oranges, at least there'd be one less automatic in the world.

The Wadi Rum desert somehow manages to look even drier than the rest of the country, but if you're even slightly interested in remote, desolate landscapes, then it's hard not to be impressed by the natural beauty of it all. Huge orange cliff faces towered like skyscrapers from out of the sand, breaking any direct view of the horizon in all directions. The road cut through the desert but was sometimes lost from the sand blowing over which made it difficult to navigate. The car didn't like the sandy roads and juddered as it tried to adjust to the lack of traction that the sand caused. Central to this particular desert you'll find a small dusty village where some of the Bedouin are stationed (the word *Bedouin* was traditionally used to describe the native nomadic tribes right across the Arab world, from here right across to northern Africa); best known for herding cattle and living a humble lifestyle, although most have tended to settle at a location these days. There were a couple of shops at the village, along with a school, so it appeared to function as a hub for the locals who were living in the camps scattered further into desert. I understand most of the Bedouin lived in harsh conditions when their primary source of income was through cattle farming back in the day, but I'm guessing in the modern times almost all families in this region rely on tourism for their direct source of income. Why would anyone choose to live all the way out here herding goats that are prone to disease and hunger when you can be herding tourists with all their cash instead? There were certainly enough tourists around to sustain a thriving industry — in our short stop in the village we had spotted nearly a hundred tourists disembarking from tour buses, being collected by the Bedouin in their 4x4s to be carted off into the camps scattered across the desert. Mel commented we had definitely got the right idea by renting our car as we watched twenty tourists pile out of a van. There's a certain magic to a road trip that is lost when you're on a big tour bus. Sure, you don't have the worry of driving but that sense of freedom and adventure is gone when you're not responsible for getting yourself around; you can't beat the impulsive detours one might take, finding an unexpected treasure in the process which a tour bus would drive right by.

We found a spot to park our car in the village and were met by a guy called Mohammed, whose Bedouin camp we had previously organised to stay at. Mohammed looked older than me, perhaps in his early forties, wearing the traditional Jordanian Bedouin gear of white robes, hiding his thin build and facial hair. I was shocked to learn he was actually younger than me by two years at the age of thirty-two. I put his aged skin down to the hot, dry air around these parts, plus he was an excessive smoker and forever had a cigarette in his mouth as he spoke to us. After the introductions, we drove out of the village and into the desert in Mohammed's jeep, heading to his camp. It was a large 4 x 4 that was a pleasure to be in as it glided through the sandy terrain, and if you ask me, a proper vehicle unlike that shitty car we had left behind at the village.

Our camp and home for the next few nights consisted of sixteen four-walled tents for residents to stay in. These were small, especially compared to the huge communal tent at one end of the row. The communal tent was for people to pass the time at (although it was mostly empty in the day time due to the heat that trapped inside it), or to gather around its central fireplace at mealtimes. The interior was decorated with traditional fabrics and low beanbag-style seats. Impressively, there was even a washroom tent with a toilet and running water for a shower. Our only real instruction for the time here that Mohammed asked us to adhere to was to conserve the water where we could as he had to bring a big truck filled with water every other day to keep it all working. It was hot outside, but tolerable. Inside the tents it was unbearable, probably on par with a sauna. Not that the heat was around all day; whilst the temperature hit almost 30°C in the daylight, it dropped to near freezing at night — almost cold enough to see breath. The dry desert air was something else as well, that night I experienced a phenomenon that I had never seen before: the air was so dry that the big woollen bed sheets we were provided with would spark with static as we lifted them up, so much that they would light up slightly, crackling like a sparkler as we lifted it up from the bed. I must have been so positively charged with the static that as Mel and I kissed goodnight, a spark jumped between our lips which lit the room up and caused a bit of pain as thousands of volts jumped across between us. It was surreal. Another notable event with the location, which was miles from anywhere as you might imagine: there was no light pollution. I woke up at 4AM on the first night and couldn't get back to sleep, so I decided to take a short walk in the desert. It was a little spooky being in such an eerily quiet expanse of desert by myself, but the stars were something else; hundreds of thousands of them, enough to light up the entire sky. It was a moment when you really appreciate how small we are in the universe, and what I could see right now was a tiny fraction of just our own galaxy, never mind the other billions of galaxies that were out there. I woke Mel up to see if she wanted to share this existential moment with me outside and to ponder our place in the universe. She grumpily told me that there was no chance she was going out into the darkness, and not to wake her again.

## Wadi Rum, Jordan — Saturday, 13th April 2019

For the next couple of days, we would spend the daylight hours traversing the vast desert on hikes, filling up our backpack with several litres of water and some of the local staple of dried flatbread lifted from the communal breakfast table to keep us going. Occasionally we'd find little caves in the rocks, each and every one worth our time exploring. They weren't usually big, but must have provided shelter for the Bedouin during the frequent sandstorms that hit the area. Sometimes inside we'd find Arabic carved into the walls, leaving us wondering how long ago some of it was written. The exotic nature of Arabic symbols etched into a rock gave it the feel of being hundreds of years old, and it might well have been. Or it could be some local youth writing the equivalent of "*Karen woz 'ere*". We could often see several sandstorms being blown from miles away across the desert towards us, yet it would take so long to reach our position that it would give us time to plan a way around it. We still however managed to get caught out in one. The huge cliffs and rocks acted as good markers for our journey when the visibility was decent, but my phone's GPS had to come out when the thick of the sandstorm would reduce visibility enough for us to lose our bearings. Sand whipped our legs and stung as much as the static in the bedroom. We made it to a sheltered area (nothing more than a gap in the towering rocks) and as we entered everything became perfectly calm whilst the sandstorm carried on outside. I had been told that this desert is often used for scenes on the planet Mars in films, and I could see why as the red sand flew past our quiet little clearing. It really did feel like an alien world.

I noticed there were piles of rocks stacked upon each other in a mound around a foot high scattered around the desert. Back at the camp, I asked Mohammed if these were some sort of markers so the Bedouin didn't get lost. He said no, they were made by local kids as something to do for fun. As wholesome a form of entertainment as it is, how utterly boring must it get around here in the long term that the youth find rocks and stack them just to kill time? The youth round my way pass their free time by sniffing poppers, drinking *White Lightning* on park benches and fingering each other; the cultures of our two countries could not be further apart. Mentioning alcohol, it was as dry as the desert for getting a drink too — as mentioned with Jordan being a predominately Muslim country, it was hard to find in certain areas. Mohammed looked surprised one evening as I asked was there anywhere to get a beer. It was weird experience for me not having access to booze on holiday; usually three days into a holiday I've drank my body weight in beer. Sitting in the communal tent one evening with strangers relaxing on the seats, watching it slowly go dark outside across the desert, it would have been a perfect time to unwind with a drink. Fortunately for me, the next stop on our trip was a city called Aqaba on the south coast of the country which, from what Mohammed told us, was apparently a good place to party.

### Aqaba, Jordan — Monday, 15th April 2019

Jordan is a mostly landlocked country except for a small strip of the south coast which meets the Red Sea by the city of Aqaba (a lot of its western border does lie along the Dead Sea but in modern times this is, in essence, nothing more than a big salty body of water with no connection to the rest of the world's seas). As well as being a major destination for Jordanians who want to holiday within the country — with an arguably more liberal attitude to alcohol and partying than even its own capital, offering numerous bars and beaches — the city of Aqaba is also a major international shipping port for the country. Along the main motorway leading into the city we were met with a large cluster of police as well as a huge inland customs border too (which I found rather odd as it was located miles away inland from the city itself); once there we had to stop to get our car checked over by police. In some countries, a notable police presence does make you feel a lot safer, but in Jordan it almost seemed unnecessary. At no point had we felt we were at risk; the locals we had met were nothing short of warm, lovely people who generally just seemed rather honoured that we had chosen their country to holiday in. This was proved even more as we pulled up into downtown Aqaba and accidentally found ourselves on the wrong street for our hotel. A young guy outside a shoe shop who didn't speak much English (which had actually been a pretty rare occurrence), but fair play to him; he tried his best to get us to our hotel, even offering to walk us there. I can't fault the hospitality of the Jordanians: they genuinely are great hosts. Out and about on the streets later in the day, the locals would smile and wave at us as we passed their shops. The consensus here was that it was safe to walk around at night as well, which is something I just wouldn't have thought possible given Jordan's location in the world.

During the drive to Aqaba from the desert, we had passed through the town of Ma'an. It covered quite some area on the map and with a population of over 40,000, it seemed like it would be rather big in relative terms to the rest of the places in Jordan, so we hoped to stop for somewhere to have a coffee and a rest break. When we arrived, it was merely a few small shops and a petrol station. Other than that, just a built-up area of houses and a few mosques; just a larger version of all the small towns with nothing to do that we had passed through previously. Thankfully though, Aqaba did come as a welcome change in that there was a small but noticeable Western influence offering precisely the things that we were after for our time spent in the desert — activities, bars and proper restaurants (although, unfortunately for the town, a few Western fast-food chains had sneaked in, too). It all looked great. We stumbled across the *Rover's Return*, a rather strange *Coronation Street*-themed pub, and a nearby outdoor bar with a large, trendy outdoor seating area and several locally-brewed ales available, it all couldn't have been further away from Ma'an and the other towns we'd seen. A couple of drinks in, we began talking to the young barman who was originally from a small town in the countryside up north, but loved living in Aqaba since relocating here. Despite being Muslim, he boasted he enjoyed going out for a drink. "Aqaba is a great city!" he said, and whilst I had no doubt it was, coming from any of the towns I had seen on the drive down here really did make it seem good in contrast. He must have been chuffed that stacking rocks on top of each other is only an optional form of entertainment here; if he didn't fancy that, he could scuba dive, eat at an international restaurant, go shopping, have a spa day, or maybe enjoy a beer by the beach after an afternoon of water-sports. Boasting about his love of the town, he said the coastal weather is perfect as it only ever rains one day a year here. Well, I think that day may well have been today. On his recommendation, that afternoon we took a short taxi ride to the south beach at the very end of the country, and a light drizzle began. The beach itself would have been worth the trip in nicer weather — it was much better than the one in central Aqaba; there wasn't any litter lying around in the sand and the water looked much cleaner. On this beach, we were now a stone's throw from the border of Saudi Arabia and across the Red Sea channel both Israel and Egypt were in our sights, leaving us pretty much looking at four countries in one single frame.

The afternoon on the beach wasn't great. Most of the time was spent trying to protect ourselves from the wind and rain watching local women in *burkinis* getting battered by the waves in the sea. If you've not seen a Burkini before, they are a weird mash-up of the full body outfit that women usually have to wear outside in Arab countries (Burka) but refined to look a bit like swim wear (bikini). I'd seen with Jordan's more liberal view on Islam than say, Saudi Arabia; Burkas were allowed to come in some colours like pale blue or grey, rather than the standard black. These women had even gone full liberal with *blue burkinis*! They'll be allowing women to meet in groups next at this rate! That's a joke, by the way. Well, mostly; I'd come to find that, outside of the two main cities of the country, Amman, the capital and here in Aqaba, the country was still very Islamic / conservative, and yet Jordan is still one of the more liberal countries in the Arab world, if liberal is even the right word. Burkinis still completely cover the body so minimal skin is shown, but due to the nature of all cloth when it gets wet, it still has a habit of clinging to the shape of the human body, thus defeating part of the purpose (skin-tight clothing is also frowned upon). As weird as the whole thing looked to me and my Western viewpoint — I mean, being wrapped in a lot of material whilst trying to swim just doesn't seem at all practical, even if it has been modified to swim in — I suppose if wearing it allows an afternoon on the beach, whilst also serving its primary purpose of protecting the woman's modesty from the gaze of men, then fair play to them. I often wonder why it's only the poor women who are subjected to having their modesty protected from the gaze of men. Surely on this logic, men should also have to wrap themselves up to protect from the gaze of homosexuals?

Sat on wet sand, getting damp and cold from the wind and rain is something we can totally do back home on a beach in England. Therefore, we decided we'd had enough time out on the sand today and left the Burkini crew to enjoy the waves.

### Petra, Jordan — Tuesday, 16th April 2019

Monday nights in most places across the globe are usually lacking in any notable nightlife; this was certainly the case within Aqaba. Apparently, Sundays can get quite lively — go figure! Regardless, even though Monday was quiet there were still bars and restaurants open. To be honest, the pair of us got a bit carried away with it being our first access to alcohol in days. It resulted in a rather late night, but despite it, we managed to wake up early the next morning to continue our road trip, driving several hours back up to the north of the country. I was convinced the car was trying to kill me because it knew I hated it; it kept randomly deciding to slow down on the motorway despite me keeping my foot on the floor. Whether there was some sort of built-in hidden sensor that I didn't know about, or it was just falling to bits internally, I don't know — but it only ever seemed to do it when I tried to drive, it always worked fine for Mel. I can drive okay, get off my back! The next stop on our agenda (if the car would allow us) was one of the Seven Wonders of the World: the ancient city of Petra, located roughly midway in the country, deep in the hilly countryside. Despite Mel and I reading up about the site in preparation before we came, one fact had totally bypassed us — we really had no idea how big the place was going to be. I thought maybe it was a few carved buildings like those often seen in the tourist brochures, maybe a few other parts to it, but no; only once we were there did I really appreciate the scale of it all. The place was huge, a city literally carved within the natural rock formations. Originally dating back to 300BC, the native people carved many houses, markets, a theatre and places of worship out of the side of rock faces for day-to-day living. Sure, the majority of spaces inside the rock were usually nothing more than a basic four by four metre room once inside, but then the sheer number of the rooms was impressive — holes covered the side of the red rocks like Swiss cheese. Some of the more advanced sculptures for the temples and such were mind-blowing; how they managed all these intricate rock carvings, some twenty metres high, all those years ago was beyond me. The place was so big in fact that we spent an entire seven hours walking around, climbing partially up the rock where we were allowed. We covered six miles and we got to see maybe around half of it.

Back in the days of old, Petra was established by the Nabateans who were a large Bedouin tribe native to the area. Through a combination of luck and planning, the Bedouin grew the city and it became an important hub for trade in the region. After a good run of a few centuries, its fortunes changed after a huge earthquake struck, destroying parts of the city. This was then followed by changing trade routes, influenced by the takeover of large swathes of land by that pesky Roman Empire who loved getting involved with everyone in the region around that time. When the trade dried up, all of the residents ended up moving out save for a few hardcore shepherds, leaving it to lie in ruin for well over a thousand years. It was only rediscovered by the rest of the world outside of Jordan around two hundred years ago. Since then, it's become the massive tourist attraction it is today, and some Jordanians appeared to have moved back in too; selling trinkets and donkey rides from their homes, catering to the thousands of daily visitors. The scale of the whole place is something to behold, offering sculptures the size of buildings and huge caverns. I could imagine how life in the city might have been because of how it has retained its charm, and the site's layout and rooms are pretty much intact to this day. It is worth a visit to the country for Petra alone, which has trumped the other world wonders I've seen so far — even more so than Machu Picchu and the Taj Mahal. I'd argue that once a world wonder has been done, unless money is no object and there's available free time to boot, then there's not really any point in going back to them. Petra, on the other hand, was so impressive that it's one I'd certainly want to see once more before I take the ultimate dirt nap.

The town surrounding Petra, which was been built in more modern times, is sprawled across Jordan's western hills, itself busy with locals making a living from indirect Petra-related tourism. The town didn't offer a great deal for tourists other than a lot of hotels and restaurants, but I did note there appeared to be quite a lot of bakeries dotted around which I hadn't noticed passing through other towns in the country. One place processed dough in moving machinery underneath the ceiling, and freshly baked pitta bread would occasionally drop down onto the counter from it. It looked strange and was almost mesmerising to watch, but I was rewarded with a tasty pitta bread for my time spent watching the process. Incidentally, pitta bread and hummus is eaten with virtually every traditional meal in the country; it's pretty much a Middle East staple (if you don't know, hummus is mostly mashed chickpeas, olive oil and garlic). Mel and I had eaten it usually for breakfast and lunch since getting here and found, if done right, it's one of those foods that's pretty basic on the ingredients list but is somehow absolutely delicious. The residents of the town were again as friendly as anywhere else in the country — although I found it interesting that, whilst they were still Arab, they weren't necessarily from Jordan. I met a couple of friendly young Syrian males at the aforementioned bakery who told me their stories of how they fled from the Syrian civil war, crossed the border as refugees and settled here. They spoke English perfectly, were well-educated and had made a nice life for themselves in the country. There were other nationalities from the Arab world too. The guy who ran our hotel was a Yemeni, a really nice chap who couldn't have gone any further out of his way to make sure our stay was as good as he could make it, and again spoke English as well as me. Sadly, his great attitude wasn't matched by the quality of the hotel room; water leaked in the bathroom from a source in the ceiling we couldn't identify, and didn't drain away very well, meanwhile the bed was stinking away like the last booking for the room had been made by a wet dog. To be honest, at £50 a night it was a bit of a rip-off and yet it was still one of the cheapest places we could find. Generally, we found accommodation across the country to be quite expensive, like a lot of things were. I'd assumed before coming it'd all be wallet-friendly in the Middle East — true, food was generally cheap — but anything else was matching what you'd pay in England, like fuel, alcohol and accommodation. I'm guessing all that security in a troublesome region comes at a cost.

## The Dead Sea, Jordan — Thursday, 18th April 2019

The Dead Sea, so-called because of its extremely high salt content — ten times saltier than regular sea water — is so toxic that no life can survive in or around it. Well okay, apart from one species of hardy microbe that was discovered not so long ago, but even that is struggling with the ever-increasing saltiness. On the occasional days when Jordan does see rain, rainwater runs down from the surrounding mountains, gathering minerals as it does, and deposits them into the basin which holds the sea. The sea is usually sat baking under the hot Middle Eastern sun for most of the year, evaporating the water as time goes on, forever increasing the saltiness. The sea has constantly been lowering too, partially down to climate change and evaporation, but also down to people in the surrounding areas of both Jordan and Israel overusing the water before it has had time to replenish. Because the sea has become so low, it has effectively cut itself off from the rest of the world's seas, leaving it as its own entity with a salt content that is never diluted by other bodies of water. Further adding to the uniqueness of the sea, the surrounding land around it sits two hundred metres below sea level, making it the lowest dry land on earth.

Being in the sea itself is quite an experience. Whilst the water tastes worse than shit, and I cannot stress enough to avoid getting it in the mouth, the excessive salt content makes the water heavier than the human body and therefore impossible to sink in. Although, be wary; it is still possible to drown here, something I noted as I watched an old Indian tourist seem to oddly get stuck rolling around on an ongoing loop – Mel likened him to a spinning hog roast – and he couldn't get his face out of the water much to breathe. Luckily, lifeguards are stationed around the few sectioned-off areas where people are allowed to swim, and they were over like a shot to rescue to the poor chap. The coast along the Dead Sea stretches for miles but only a handful of places have been selected for people to enter; I assume that, because of the unusual properties of the water, swimming there generally requires being safely monitored. Normal swimming methods don't really work — trying a front crawl had my legs hovering above waterline with the rest of me awkwardly flapping my arms about trying to swim. I found the easiest method of moving around was as if on land, treading water in a walking motion. My method may have looked odd as the salt pushed my upper body out of the water with the waterline near my belly button, but I found it was the most energy-efficient way of getting around. Mel on the other hand was more keen spending her time rubbing the mineral mud onto her skin and lounging around the banks of the sea at the resort we were staying at, completely covering herself in the apparent rejuvenating properties the mud brings with it.

## Amman, Jordan — Friday, 19th April 2019

We were to finish our trip with a planned weekend of nightlife in the capital, but before dropping that horrible car off Mel wanted us to take a morning detour north from the Dead Sea to the place where Jesus Christ was first baptised. She thoroughly enjoyed her time wandering around the really old rock steps that led down to a pool of cloudy water, but for me personally, there wasn't anything that impressive to see there — it was just a few bricks and a puddle of algae soup; the area just happened to be where a deluded man two thousand years ago reckoned that taking a dunk in the water made him legitimate in the eyes of a man in the clouds. I was more interested in the geopolitics of the area and was excited that I'd be able to see Israel up close beyond the countries' shared border. This border closely follows the river Jordan in the desert, but at certain points we were able to walk right up to Israel, metres away in fact. The divide sometimes looked intimidating, with the barbed wire fences and Israeli military occasionally found walking on the other side. What I didn't expect was to find myself getting annoyed at the strikingly arbitrary lines that humans make for themselves which divide us as people. Maybe I've been spoiled growing up in Europe during a period of mostly free movement between countries, but it's not often I've come straight up to a fenced-off border I couldn't pass through. Although not quite as intense as the divide between North and South Korea, which was far more heavily guarded with its multiple rows of mesh fencing, the border between Israel and Jordan was still clearly marked by a tall line of fences. To see the entirety of the baptism site you'd have to make two trips to the same area; one to Jordan to see the church and exact spot Jesus was baptised (the river has naturally moved course over the past two thousand years from where the baptism supposedly took place, moving more towards Israel), and then another trip across the river but taking a loop around for miles via one of the few entry points across the border, assuming of course that getting baptised in the same river sounds appealing (which we could see people doing from Jordan). The core of what I'm getting at here is that the countries don't have a porous border, making land crossings a pain in the arse and only possible in a handful of places, of which one was not found at the baptism site. To add a layer of complexity for the people living here, the travel rights between Jordanian and Israeli passport holders are vastly different. Israelis are allowed to visit Jordan visa-free; Jordanians, however, have to go through an Israeli government-approved process to enter as a tourist which is more of an intense process than a standard tourist visa. I find it sad that two neighbours are like this with each other, but of course it's all drawn from religion as Israel usually tends to have an issue letting anyone into the country who originates from a Muslim-majority nation.

The same in theory applies to Mel travelling on an Indonesian passport — despite being Catholic herself, Indonesia is another Muslim-majority nation, meaning it's unlikely she will ever be able to visit Israel unless she is prepared to jump through hoops in the rare hope of obtaining a tourist visa. In this case they're judging people entirely on their country of origin rather than the individual, which I think is ridiculous. I'm not just having a moan about Israel's visa policy (let's face it, visas and travel restrictions are implemented worldwide), but they are no more than limits put on people by other people, lines drawn in the dirt from years ago, based on either religion or politics. I rarely feel it so much with my frankly superior British passport and the travel rights it gives me, I can visit both of these countries without having to apply for a visa first, like I can with many other countries around the world. Yet, the situation for humanity still annoys me. I stood close to the riverbank, surrounded by a dry, rocky scrubland without much else going on — and guess what! The land looked exactly the same across the river as well. The only thing that divided us was that on our side of the border, the natives believed in some ancient bollocks and across the river the people there believed in different ancient bollocks, causing tough borders between two neighbours. We could see other tourists in Israel waving at us across the border, all here to see the world like us, but we were still separated from going over to say hello by the convoluted restrictions of man-made borders and visas.

The afternoon had rolled around and the two of us had ditched our car for good, leaving us on foot for the remainder of our stay. We found ourselves wandering around Amman, the capital city, dressed up smart and looking for a good night out. The city is stationed across a region of nineteen hills and constantly had a feeling of being tightly packed with pedestrians and traffic, weaving up and down the steep slopes and narrow roads. It would be easy to get lost; there wasn't particular landmarks noticeable for people new to the city, and the buildings all looked the same — shops and houses made of the classic Arabian architecture: beige blocks of differing sizes stacked on top of each other with small windows puncturing the walls. There were a couple of other tourists, but not many, certainly none as dressed up as us two for our night out. Our first port of call in the city was eating something other than pitta bread and hummus, and we had our hearts set on something we'd recently seen on TV. There is an American TV show we both enjoy watching called *Bizarre Foods* presented by American celebrity chef / human dustbin Andrew Zimmern; a man who visits strange and wonderful places around the world, often eating equally strange and wonderful things which the locals offer up to him as supposed "delicacies" (hence the name of the show). Eyeballs, mold, bollocks and insects; he's had the lot. He also has a spin-off show for the weaker-stomached — *Bizarre Foods: Delicious Destinations* — which is much tamer on the foodstuffs, showcasing the incredible food of excellent eateries around the globe, interviewing passionate staff and a random customer at the end who says how good the food is. Mel and I are fans of both shows and there had been a recent episode in Amman recommending a restaurant in the city centre. Having never before had the opportunity to eat anywhere featured on the show, there wasn't a chance we were missing this one here.

We were excited by recognising parts of the restaurant from the show when we got there, but the buzz quickly wore off as we struggled to find somewhere to sit due to it being filled to capacity (which to be fair is usually a great sign that it's a good place to eat!). There were tables and chairs inside the building and the restaurant had even utilised an alleyway to the side of the building, but this too was all filled with Ammanis who sat cramped around the small wooden tables eating exotic food like off the show. Little pots of the local mezze scattered around the tables, savoury bites like falafel with sauces and dip — simple, but again like hummus, a top-notch scran. We stood to the side of the restaurant looking both lost and to be honest, a little bit over-dressed for eating here. After several minutes of waiting around (we'd have gone elsewhere if it wasn't for the programme) a waiter rather rudely grabbed my arm and pointed us to a table positioned sadly not in the slightly breezy alleyway, but rather in the middle of the hot restaurant. It didn't take long for the ambient heat of the air to make me uncomfortable once we sat down, but it was all going to be worth putting up with to try the food off the TV.

We ordered and sat in silence as we waited for our food, the lack of anything for us to do contrasted against the bustling restaurant, people were deep in loud conversation trying to talk over other tables whilst the waiters darted around clearing plates and fetching bills. To be honest, we were too tired to engage in any conversation between ourselves as our few days out on the road was beginning to catch up with us both. In this kind of situation where conversation isn't flowing, we'd usually probably be glued to our phones. I'm generally against using a mobile phone at the dinner table as it's rather unsociable to be looking down at a screen, but, having been alone in each other's company for over a week, it can sometimes be nice just to catch up on the news or look at shit on Facebook rather than engaging your brain into conversation. In Jordan, data-roaming wasn't an option for our mobile networks, so our usual fall-back had been removed. Too tired for conversation nor mobile phone data for distraction, it left Mel free with her keen eye on the restaurant operations (a hangover from her old job waitressing in fine dining establishments). After a few minutes of observing she nudged me and told me to watch the waiters, which I'd have been oblivious to otherwise — any leftover food from other customer's plates when they got up and left was being put to the side and then recycled back onto new customers' plates. I'm not sure if its normal practice here in Jordan to reuse food, and I don't particularly like the idea of food waste, so I could almost see a positive towards the practice; still though, I'm paying to eat fresh food at a restaurant, not for someone else's leftovers. It didn't help watching the waiter transferring falafel or pitta breads around with his bare hands — the same unwashed hands that had just been handling cash and emptying an overflowing bin about a minute before. What had been the history of the food too? Sat out for an hour already with unfettered access for the local fly population to come and have a good crawl over first before it's my turn, never mind other people and their germs. Is it not within the realms of possibility the food could have made its way to three or more customer's plates? They weren't even hiding the low standards of hygiene at the front of house, so Christ knows what was going on in the kitchen. This wasn't *Delicious Destinations,* this was a full-on episode of *Bizarre Foods!*

I picked at my mezze when it came out. The falafel balls looked fresh, but I couldn't be entirely sure and the lumpy bits of veg I managed to swallow didn't sit right. I felt uncomfortable and hot in my nice clothes. Mel ate a bit more than me — she grew up eating the street food of Jakarta, evolving her immune system to a near-immortal level of resistance against food poisoning. I like to think that generally I have a high tolerance too, but sometimes the psychological aspect can overwhelm me. Even the bit I nibbled at churned my stomach. We turned the corner after leaving the restaurant and it didn't take long to find myself throwing up in a quiet side street in the few available moments when nobody was around, splattering flecks down my nice clothes. I didn't have any clean clothes left to change into for our last night in the country so I was stuck looking like a mess. How the fuck can the guy off *Bizarre Foods* eat all the grim stuff he does, when a few dirty hands wrapped around my falafel was enough to have me blowing chunks?

Being sick had killed the mood for getting involved in the evening's nightlife straight away, so we took a walk around the city first to settle my stomach. We had a romantic walk as the dusk set in, taking us down little dimly lit alleyways and climbing up along huge ancient ruins stationed high in the hills with a nice view out over the city. I won't go into detail about all this though as I doubt it would be particularly interesting to read about. If you want tales of romance or ancient history, like I said earlier; you should have realised by now you're reading the wrong travel book.

There had been quite a noticeable number of bars and — dare I say it — a drinking culture in Aqaba on the south coast, but the same couldn't be said for Amman. It was a realisation for the pair of us that the capital city of a country isn't necessarily the primary place for its nightlife. There were some bars that we found ourselves hopping around that evening, but any of the apparently "decent" ones required taxi rides between them, and once we got there, all were slightly on the quiet side and lacking an atmosphere for a Friday night. It didn't help that alcohol was expensive and a pint of beer could sometimes cost as much £8. It was well into the night by the time we had settled at a rock bar somewhere in the city centre. A band was on which offered a little bit more atmosphere than the other places we'd been, but for a Friday night in a capital city, Muslim or not, I cannot really recommend Amman as a place to party. The rock bar was fun though, and finding a cosy little table by the entrance gave me a good look at everyone walking into the bar for a drink.

Life is full of crazy coincidences and unusual events, but I believe getting out into the world by travelling throws up these moments with even greater odds of happening. They happen with such frequency too. You might have heard stories about people on holiday in a foreign country randomly meeting acquaintances from their lives back home that they didn't know were there. I'd once bumped into one of my English friends at a festival in Koh Phangan in Thailand in 2014. I usually struggle to find my friends at a festival in England when I *know* they're there, so what is the probability of locating someone I didn't even know was in the country, at a jungle party on an island on the other side of the world, amongst thousands of other attendees?! It's not just chance meetings. Happening to be somewhere at a certain time can have profound consequences along the road. I once met a backpacker sat in a hostel's social room when travelling through Asia some years ago. He was an Australian lad doing a similar trip to me but on a different route, by chance both crossing paths at this small hostel in north-west Borneo. I clicked with him, kept in touch after going our separate ways, and when he moved to London some years later I took a visit to see him, bringing one of my friends from my hometown. My friend ended up hooking up with his friend on a night out in the capital; fast forward some years later and they're now a full-on couple and have several kids together. Because I decided to stay at a hostel on the other side of the world at a certain time in my life, the following chain of events caused brand new people to exist in the form of my friend's new children. I know my involvement's rather indirect after a certain point, but I ponder this sort of stuff sometimes. The chances of this all happening must be astronomical. And whilst I am still amazed by it, in a way I now half-expect them to happen because of the frequency in which they've occurred in the past. So, to my (sort of) great surprise, the door opened in this random bar in Amman, and in walked someone I knew. Bert, the Californian scientist who I had last seen shitfaced in Korea, by himself, and dressed in pretty much the same smart-casual clothes I remembered him in. He recognised me, and I him, and for a moment with him stood by the entrance we both locked eyes onto each other without saying anything, each wondering what the fuck the other was doing in Amman and obviously processing the extremely small chance of anything like this happening. Only one sentence was uttered for the whole reunion, which was from Bert, looking rather agitated after noticing the flecks of dried sick on me, who said: "Holy shit, what are you doing here? In fact, don't answer; don't take offence, but I am never drinking like that again." He turned around and left the bar before I even had chance to reply. I thought he was making a joke and waited for him to come back inside, but he had genuinely departed and I never saw him again. I have a strange feeling my story with Bert isn't over and that I'll see him again once more — some strange chain of events over years that will lead us both to another chance meeting in some random country we'll both visit in the future. If it does happen then surely that would be a sign to get fucked up with me again, although he would have been in safe hands had he stayed around that night in Amman to be honest. The night we had was enjoyable, but a little too quiet and a little underwhelming for our tastes. It was certainly no Seoul when it came to partying.

Our time in Jordan had come to an end. I can't emphasise it enough as a destination to anyone thinking of dipping their toes into something a bit different for a getaway. Sure, it still feels like it is developing in certain areas as some of the infrastructure looks like it's currently getting overhauled, and there are long expanses on the road without much to do for tourists on their way between the highlights. But there's still lots to see. The country is embracing parts of the modern world, like the Bedouin still living a relatively traditional lifestyle in the desert hooked up with smartphones and Wi-Fi. Plus, in a region of troubled countries, they're doing something right. Friendly locals filled the streets of the towns, adding a complimentary layer of security to an already safe country. The only exception to safety was maybe the roads, where people sometimes drove a little on the erratic side; although I wonder in hindsight whether they might have all been struggling with the controls of their shitty little *Baics* too.

# CHAPTER SIX
## EASTERN EUROPE

## ROMANIA

**15th April 2022**

In late 2019, if you watched the news, you might have picked up something about a disease. Brief news cycles about diseases flare up all the time around the world, so pretty much everyone thought this one was nothing to be taken seriously. How many times do you see outbreaks of Ebola, bird flu or some other similar disease that makes the news for a week or so, an outbreak in Africa or the Middle East, but never really travelling far beyond the place of origin? This one was proper foreign this time; all the way in China, in a city that no white person had ever heard of before, thousands of miles away. It'd be the same sort of outbreak as the others no doubt: trouble an area for a bit, a mention on the news at home for a few weeks, then it'll all simmer down. Some weeks passed as we entered 2020, with the story bubbling away in the news — developments that it had leapt over to South Korea, which was even further away from home than China and therefore nothing to worry about. I can attest from my own visit that the South Korean disease-monitoring stations at immigration were a bag of shite anyway, so there was no surprise something had snuck through. Then an outbreak of the same virus hit Italy, with videos on the news of people in full hazmat gear wheeling dead bodies out onto the streets. It then became a collective "Oh shit!" moment for the rest of the world when we all realised this wasn't just confined to East Asia, and a huge wave was about to knock the stuffing out of us in Europe.

The subsequent months were spent confined at home through worldwide government-enforced lockdowns. Being unable to travel was a relatively minor casualty in the grand scheme of things, I suppose; certainly when compared to the hardships that were being endured globally from having economies shut down or by catching the disease itself. Still, having the realisation that our 2020 travel plans were ruined as the year progressed was upsetting. First, our plans around the Stans — Uzbekistan, Kyrgyzstan, even possibly Afghanistan, and then, later in the year, Japan — were all cancelled one after another. We struggled to get the money back from the flights over the rest of the year. Fortunately, the UK had a record-breaking summer of baking hot weather so it wasn't a total loss sat in our back gardens during lockdown — at least we're getting a few nice summers in England as life on the planet slowly dies from overabundance of greenhouse gases.

2021 was pretty much another write off for international travel (even for the handful of holiday-makers that managed to get to Europe; they had to endure shit like sitting in groups of no more than six at the bar, or wearing face masks on the beach!), but upon the arrival of spring 2022 things finally felt like they had taken a cautious step back towards normality. The virus lingered in the background but collectively the global community started to move on — I'm not sure why I'm telling this like you haven't all experienced it, but anyway; at the start of 2022 I began to prepare trips ready to get myself back out there into the world. To kick the new freedoms of travel off, Mel and I had an exciting group holiday with our friends organised to Ukraine, visiting the capital of Kyiv, along with the nearby Chernobyl power station (known for the nuclear disaster in 1986) and Pripyat, the neighbouring town that was left abandoned in the wake of the nuclear fallout. The town hasn't been inhabited since the disaster, and other than time slowly breaking down the abandoned buildings, it's a complete snapshot of life preserved from nearly four decades ago. It amazes me that tourists are allowed in due to the relatively high levels of radiation that are still present even after all these years. Interestingly, since being abandoned by humans, lots of wild animals have apparently moved in and flourished, although they probably have two heads or something. Then, typically — because one huge, historical global event of our lifetime wasn't enough — a fucking European war broke out between Ukraine and Russia, causing a fresh round of global disruption after the virus. It began early in the year with Russia amassing troops at the border of Ukraine and Putin releasing a few statements about their small neighbour being an existential threat to his country or some rubbish. Having not learned my lesson from the earlier threat of the virus breaking out, I naively thought that it would never develop into anything serious. Then Putin made a dramatic televised address and the Russian troops entered Ukraine. *'Surely things will never escalate that far,'* I kept telling myself, and by early February (firmly on the hope train) I guessed Putin would have officially been given Crimea and the whole thing would be over before Easter. By late March, a few weeks before our date to travel, things were worse than ever with tanks and missiles shamefully flying into the country. It looked like our whole trip was going to be cancelled. Crimea river, some might say, especially those who love puns.

I phoned the famous Irish airline who are notoriously not keen on refunds, asking for an alternative flight to anywhere. Based on our existing ticket value, in place of Kyiv, they offered up the town of Suceava instead; a quaint town in the Romanian countryside with a few castles around. It was certainly somewhere different and it was absolutely anywhere away from the extended Covid-induced stays at home, which was all we were really after. After the call with the airline ended, I realised this was the first time in my life I had flights booked to somewhere without being able to locate it on a map. When I checked where the town was out of interest, I was startled to see the how far north it was — half an hour's drive to the Ukrainian border. Further research into the area said the town was experiencing a heavy influx of refugees from the war, so even having been sent to a new place in a different country, the war would likely continue to impact the trip. Consequently, several of the original group pulled out from fear that trouble may spill across the border, leaving only myself and my two friends Kieran and Oli willing to go. The war wasn't stopping us. And if there was any trouble, I'd be going with two big lads at least. Oli equals my height, Kieran's a bit shorter, but between the three of us we were big guys.

A taxi had been pre-arranged to pick the three of us up early morning to take us to the airport. I was fresh for it. I'd had a nice bath and an early night, anticipating a heavy few days ahead with the trip becoming a bit of a beery "boy's one" since Mel and the other female were amongst those that had pulled out of coming. Kieran had a few beers the night before but was still fine for the morning. When group holidays are mixed-gender affairs, certainly within my circle of friends, they tend to be a bit tame, with the girls often tempering the lads' behaviour. With boy's holidays on the other hand, the chains are off and they have in the past become a festival of debauchery, times often spent with very little clothing on, and of course involving a lot of drink. Aptly kicking things off for the next few days, Oli turned up having just been awake on a twenty-four-hour bender. He didn't look fit to fly, and things were to go downhill for him from there.

Airport security cleared, we made our way to the airport bar to find an abandoned bottle of vodka, still wrapped in its duty-free bag, left on a seat. We kept our eye on it for a solid ten minutes, watching anyone walking into the bar to see if they were going to claim it. No one did, so it was now officially ours. At the time, finding a whole bottle of vodka seemed like a huge blessing. People give the booze prices in places like Scandinavia a hard time for being expensive, but even mere tap water at Manchester Airport costs money and a beer can be upwards of £7, which is a ridiculous amount to be forking out. We devised a crafty plan around our new find which entailed ordering cheaper orange juice from the bar then discretely tipping the vodka into the juice under the table, resulting in us getting get pissed for a fraction of the price of the beer. The problem for Oli at this point was that a third of a bottle of Russia's finest was enough to tip him over an edge he had been already teetering on for several hours. He quickly became outright too pissed to be allowed to fly; swaying, slurring his words and on occasion falling over. Kieran had boarded well before the two of us when the time came to enter the plane, leaving me to deal with Oli's future as my negotiating skills with the air stewardesses were about to get a full workout. As you might imagine, they were not keen on letting someone in that state on board to fly. I did something I'm not particularly proud of, but it was out of desperation given the fate of my friend: I lied. And I lied about something bad, too. I lied that Oli couldn't stand straight and spoke weird because he had brain damage after a bicycle accident years ago, and a "couple of pints" at the bar before we had got here had set him off into a bad mental state. Even in his drunk state, Oli managed to realise what I was up to. Instead of just being quiet and leaving me to deal with it, he thought continuing to act up would help his situation and so pressed his tongue under his bottom lip and let out a loud groan in front of the whole plane. I wanted to crawl up my own arse to escape the embarrassment. Either the airline staff bought the act (they probably didn't) or they just wanted us to go away and sit down, but to my surprise they actually let him on (I think my charm did it) — but with the condition that if he acted up on the plane then it was on my head. I knew he'd be fine once sat down; he was a bit of a mess but never an aggressive drunk, all he needed right now was to just sit down, drink half his body weight in water and then sleep it off. I appreciate neither of us will be allowed into heaven now for a lie like that, but at least for today, we were allowed onto the plane.

The drama was over and for the first hour or so, aside from Oli thrashing around in his sleep trying to get comfy, the plane ride was mostly quiet. It was great while he was out cold; I could relax for the flight and started to read a magazine to pass the time. With me in the middle of the three, sat on my other side was Kieran who had been pretty quiet thus far, although drinking steadily throughout the flight. In the corner of my eye I could see him roll up a cigarette. I assumed it'd be for outside the airport terminal later and didn't think much else of it. Then he put it in his mouth, got up out of his seat and walked to the back of the plane. He wouldn't, would he? I mean, he'd gone three ways on that bottle of vodka and then some extra, but *everyone* knows you can't smoke on a flight. I went back to reading my magazine. A minute later I could hear a commotion at the back of the plane. I knew exactly what was going on, got up quickly and ran to intervene.

"Sir, is this your friend?" the camp stereotype of a male air steward said.

"Umm, depends what he's done," I replied, looking at an annoyed Kieran.

"I have just had to hit a cigarette out of his mouth, he was about to smoke it on here!"

"Dickhead," Kieran replied, rather drunk, aggravated that his smoke had been taken away from him.

"I've told him already that if he doesn't sit down right now, sir, the police from Romania will be waiting for him when we land!" He begrudgingly sat down after some convincing, leaving me to once again turn on the charm with another air steward to diffuse the situation (thankfully without the lies this time) and managing to save him a €3,000 fine in the process. Hell of a trip this was turning out to be already.

Oli had gathered himself with a couple of hours' sleep on the flight. As we disembarked from the plane and queued to enter the airport on the runway, the Romanian word for "Arrivals", "Sosiri", glowed as a big sign above the terminal door. Oli pointed to it, looked at me and said, "Mate, I'm 'sosiri' for before." It was a poor joke, but the timing was funny so it made me laugh.

If you ever find yourself on your first visit to a place and are trying to gauge how populated it is, the size of an airport is a good indicator of how big an area it's servicing. The number of booths at border control and the overall terminal size all are clues to the amount of foot traffic that passes through and whether you're going to a major destination or some backwater spot on a map. Suceava Airport felt more towards the latter; it wasn't much beyond a small wooden building adjacent to the runway. It was easily the smallest airport I'd ever been to in Europe, reminiscent of those I'd been to in rural south-east Asia rather than anything I'd seen before on my own continent. Only two booths existed at passport control and the queue still didn't take long to make our way through. There's nothing wrong with smaller airports mind, in fact I usually prefer them — processing just three or four planes a day means they can efficiently deal with each plane, compared with flying into big international hubs with their hundreds of flights an hour and the big immigration or baggage queues that come with them. As far as I could tell, we were the only British people on the entire flight, notable by the drunken behaviour of course, but still; it was interesting that the entire flight was made up of returning Romanians. It was an exciting thought stepping outside the airport, thinking this is really a place that tourists don't venture to and wondering what could lie in store for us in town. Outside a big 'Sosiri' sign were several taxi drivers looking for fares. We approached them and out of all of those we spoke to, we met a young man named Eddie who (along with his decent sounding Anglican name) also spoke English; that alone was enough for us to go with him for our lift into town.

"So, Ed," began a sobering Oli making conversation on the ride, "What's it like in Suceava?"

"Nothing to do here, but you can find cheap drink and good woman!" Big Eddie replied in his good, but not quite perfect grasp of English. Ah, the universal male common ground of alcohol and "woman" — this can sometimes mean prostitutes. I hoped it wasn't prostitutes. They are like sport to me, one of those things that some males seem to enjoy, but it's nothing that appealed to me even in my single days.

"Why do you come here?" he carried on — the five words that would follow us over our time in Suceava by every English-speaking local who couldn't believe we had picked one of the most unusual tourist destinations in the whole country. We didn't really have an answer to this, other than the war stopping us flying directly into Ukraine, and the interest of the subsequent replacement's obscurity. We had toyed with the idea of still going into Ukraine over the weeks leading up to this trip due to the proximity of the border; it'd be a 'fuck you' to Putin in our own way, and our chance meeting with Eddie seemingly fit in with our warped sense of danger as he was apparently up for enabling us. "I can take you, no problem," he said after answering a myriad of questions about the local situation and his take on what the Romanians thought about the war in general (which was a resounding "Meh, it's a great shame, Putin sucks, but it's not happening to us; we're in *NATO* so we're protected."). Would we actually go over there during our stay here though? Big Eddie made it sound like it wasn't a big deal to venture in for a few hours.

"Can I smoke in the taxi?" asked Kieran, who had been dying for a cigarette since flying over Hungary. He was in luck — you could apparently both smoke and drink in taxis here, legally or not I'm unsure, but Big Eddie certainly didn't give a shit.

I had my apprehensions about what small-town Romania would be like. Would it be rough, a bit dodgy with groups of gypsies on the prowl perhaps?

157

Gangs of Romanian youths ready to mug me the second I stepped outside of the taxi? Who knew? For a relatively well-travelled guy, I couldn't recall ever meeting a Romanian, so I didn't know what they or their country represented. Perhaps I had only picked up on the endless negative tripe few permeating society from what the largely Rupert Murdoch-owned British media pumps out, which has done a good job of portraying Eastern Europeans in a bad light over the years, certainly well before and after the Brexit vote. This is where Johnny Poland has come to England and somehow managed to steal our jobs and claim unemployment benefits *at the same time!* Crime on the up at home? That won't be because of the Tory government making huge funding cuts to the police, oh no — apparently, it's because a Romanians and Bulgarians have set up home in England. I should have known better really than to just assume the worst; I know plenty of Eastern Europeans in the form of Polish people who are fantastic and they get tarred with Murdoch's same shitty brush. From the airport and into the countryside it was so far so good, Romania looked charming in the dusk of an early spring evening. The road was new with freshly painted lines and cut through long fields as far as the eye could see, with large six-bedroom houses stationed at the far end of them and the residents within surely enjoying a bucolic lifestyle. As someone who enjoys hiking as a pastime it might have been the sort of place that would be great for it; the country offered long stretches of almost wilderness, although the building density quickly increased the further we got into Suceava's centre. It was actually quite a large town which I didn't quite expect, we appeared to drive through built-up streets for at least a quarter of an hour before getting to the hotel. We passed little parks, fountains and shops. It actually looked like a nice town.

The hotel for our stay was called *Balada*, one of the nicer ones in town hosting the handful of international visitors that Suceava receives. Perhaps, in hindsight, not the best place for three rowdy lads to stay when any cheap shithole would have sufficed. Stood in the hotel car park Edward read out his phone number so we could contact him for the trip into the country at war tomorrow. It had been suggested in the pub a few weeks back as something bit daft to do for a laugh but now, actually having the opportunity to do it had me thinking that perhaps it was just a daft idea and should have been left at that. I mean, it's Ukraine, a country whose troubles had been heavily reported in the news over the past few months; an illegal invasion with refugees, burnt out buildings, missiles and worse. Why would we go there? But, on the other hand, why *wouldn't* we go when we have the opportunity? It would be an interesting experience. The south of the country where we'd be entering into from Romania is considered relatively safe, plus, we now have a guide in the form of Big Eddie. Going would be the ultimate defiance in our small bubble against Putin for spoiling our original plans.

Even after meeting Eddie, I think we might have left it at that but, being the social animals that we are, we happened to meet a group of American aid workers at the hotel's reception whilst checking in. They'd just come back from Ukraine and leapt on our interest about visiting. I can't quite remember the uniform, but it was definitely *Red Cross* style — eight almost retirement-age Americans that were talking about their time in the country together having done a few days across the border. They looked a little bit dirty, like they'd had a long day.

"Excuse me," I said, putting on the charm once again, "Have you all just come back from Ukraine?"

"Yessir," one of the older blokes said in his deep southern accent, "We're helping with the aid efforts. Why, you thinking of goin'?"

"Well, actually yes. Could we go there as tourists?"

"I suppose so, but why don't you help out whilst you're there?"

"Help out with what? Aid?"

"Yeah. You can help with our group. When you arrive into the country at the border, turn straight to the right after the barrier, you'll see some tents there. Go to them, they're part of our group. They'll show you how to help."

Meeting Edward, and now these guys, the stars had aligned. We were in all likelihood going to Ukraine tomorrow, and now we'd agreed to help in the aid efforts too. One of the older aid women who had been talking to Kieran throughout our group conversation grabbed his hand with both of hers and said God had truly blessed him by putting him here to help the refugees. I could see it in her eyes that she meant it about the God part. As far as I was concerned, he had already been blessed by God by narrowly missing a €3,000 smoking fine earlier, so I guess it was time for him to do some payback.

Suceava is not renowned for its tourism, or much of anything as far as I could see. We passed lots of closed shops and buildings that I couldn't tell what they were for. It wasn't bad to walk around, quite pleasant in fact, but for lads on the piss there's not really a "main street" with bars, nor any sort of main hub for activity, the town instead opting for individual shops and bars sporadically scattered across a wide area. There is a large square with a big *I love Suceava* sign and a few public benches around it which might have been considered the town centre, but still; it was all very quiet for a Friday night. Our chat with Big Eddie during the taxi ride earlier had enlightened us to the places to look for, however it did mean whipping out *Google Maps* on the phone to find them as we wouldn't have had a clue otherwise. Some places were clearly bars, but others looked like someone decided one day that their house was going to be a bar, so put out chairs and tables in their living room and garden and started to sell beer from there. These sorts of places wouldn't have been obvious to passing tourists as they didn't have a sign on the front, or the entrance may have been hidden around the back. It was getting late in the day, so not wanting to wander off too far we picked a bar close to *Hotel Balada*. The lads had sobered up from their few hours' break, but they were quickly back into the swing of things once the vodka shots came out.

A small group of locals (two couples in fact) sat on the table next to ours and, after picking up we were English, invited us to move tables and sit with them for a drink. The locals asked the question again: why did we pick Suceava to visit? Of all the places in the world, hell, even all the more interesting places in Romania, why pick somewhere with nothing to offer tourists beyond a few castles in the countryside? We could only really answer "why not?", but honestly, the unusual places to go can be just as enjoyable. From personal experiences, the well-trodden tourist paths usually have local people who are either fed up with the amount of people passing through, ruining their town the noise and litter and so have little to no tolerance for them, or they perhaps work in the tourism industry directly and only see them as a source of income. Yet when you come to these places that tourists rarely venture to, the people you meet are often keen to interact with the novelty of a foreigner around, and therefore usually show warmth and hospitality. It happens where I'm from. I remember a South African guy wandering into my local pub in my small town some years back who was in the area for a wedding, and just the fact he was a bit new and foreign to the town saw him make an instant group of friends who gave him a great night. He was probably struggling with a hangover for the wedding the next day but I bet he enjoyed his night with us. I'm not saying this wouldn't happen if he'd been English, although I doubt he'd have got a reception like that in some pub in London. There's something about the otherness of someone coming to places where tourists don't normally travel being an ice-breaker with the natives. Case in point: the strangers we had only just met tonight had, within minutes, kindly organised a taxi to buy and drop off cigarettes for us as a gift, as most of the shops were shut, with a couple rounds of drinks with it to boot. For a first impression to a country, these lot were a great bunch to start things off with.

It had been a good session. We left early morning thanking the Romanians we had met for a good night and, without having really got our bearings, when the time came to leave weren't quite sure which way we were going. Just walking in any direction was too much for poor Oli, and save a couple of hours' upright sleep on the plane, he now had over two days of drinking under his belt. He lost his footing and crashed head-first onto the floor. The sound of his head smashing against the asphalt of Suceava will stick with me forever; imagine a coconut shell filled with jelly being hit with a hammer. Oli lay on the floor not moving after his fall.

"Oli, are you okay mate?" I said, giving him a nudge with my foot. He didn't move. Blood began to pour out onto the road from his head.

"Oli mate, are you okay, what the fuck mate?!" He still didn't move. The blood puddle became bigger and bigger. We managed to peel him off the floor (once Kieran managed to get the pointing and laughing out of his system, that is) only to discover Oli's face a total mess, blood gushing down onto his clothes. He was surely in the throes of an initial concussion, although somehow was coherent enough to understand what had just happened to him. I had convinced Kieran to help me support him for the first few steps, but not wanting to risk getting the handful of clothes I had brought out soaked in blood, we left Oli to fend for himself after we realised he could just about support himself. He staggered along like a zombie with us until we got back to the hotel, somehow managing to get past the staff stationed at reception without getting stopped, who definitely would have had their concerns if they had noticed the amount of blood pouring out of his head. One of my last memories of the day was lying in bed thinking about how he'd certainly have some blood to deal with on his pillow in the morning.

### Suceava, Romania — Saturday, 16th April 2022

I had woken up in Kieran's room without Kieran around, accompanied by a dry throat and headache. Both the lads' phones were off and I wondered if they had made it to their rooms okay — well, Kieran obviously hadn't as I was somehow in his room without him. Only when I checked Oli's room after several minutes of banging on the door to be let in did I find he and Kieran had been sharing a bed together in one of the biggest messes I had ever seen — I expected a bit of blood, but it was everywhere; the bedsheets were soaked, never mind the pillow. It looked like a murder had taken place. It was quite the irony that the hotel was called *Balada*, as it appeared Oli in had, in his concussed state, also emptied his *bladder* in the bed overnight too, soaking partially into Kieran's clothes. I don't know if it was the blood, the piss, the smell of the two lads sweating away overnight or what, but the room's air made me feel sick to breathe in. It was grim. Anticipating the maids coming in and screaming in horror at the mess, we decided to turn the "Do not disturb" sign on the front door and intended to leave it on for the remainder of the stay, kicking the proverbial can down the road as long as we could, but knowing Oli would have to deal with the cleaner's fury eventually. His only pair of pants covered in blood and piss and therefore rendered unwearable, Oli opted for wearing the only other legwear he had brought with him and put on his swim shorts for the day around Suceava. It was eight degrees Celsius outside.

I messaged Big Eddie to see if he was still keen for our run into Ukraine but he didn't reply, leaving us at a bit of a loss on what to do for the day. Surely the day would likely revolve a bit around drinking later on, but at 10AM it was a bit too early for it. We took a walk around the town trying to find something of interest without the use of any maps, and ended up in a small residential area adjacent to the city centre. It has to be said that even something as mundane as walking around a residential area can be fun when you're abroad, and this was especially so in Romania. Each and every building looked completely different, small buildings with huge upstairs extensions that didn't look supported properly. Small wooden buildings that people lived in next door to towering mansions with tiny gardens, long bungalows next to trendy block-style housing. Blocks of Soviet era flats. Some painted white, others beige or grey. There was no uniformity to them like the houses back home, and with all the different styles of buildings next to each other it looked like a free-for-all on a *Minecraft* server rather than a housing estate. There was absolutely no standard style the buildings, and I suspected not a lot of planning permission processes used along with the construction of them either. Interestingly, the residents seemed to be big on growing their own crops in their gardens; most appeared to utilise garden space on growing food, often guarded with flimsy barbed wire as a token gesture to keep people out, when in reality it was quite easy to walk around to gain access. Maybe due to financial reasons, but likely enjoyed culturally too, it did seem like people were more used to growing their own crops in Romania and they were probably quite efficient at it by judging the rows of neatly mounded soil and netting waiting for spring to properly kick in. I compare that to my foray into growing my own crops for something to do during the first Covid lockdown; I spent close to a hundred quid on soils, fertiliser, pots, seeds and tools. I got about a tenner's worth of carrots and peas to show for it come the Autumn.

In the gaps between buildings, any unclaimed land would allow vegetation to grow long and wild, unlike back home where the council is normally on a long bit of grass like a shot. Where we did share common ground though was the excessive number of potholes in the street, quite literally common ground in that aspect. There was a heart-breaking amount of stray dogs around, either idle or running around in small packs. I'm a big fan of man's best friend, perhaps excessively so, and I wanted to pet the strays. Even the sick-looking ones missing their body hair still need some love. They'd usually run off if the three of us got too close though.

With half an hour spent on the tamest sightseeing expedition ever done in the history of tourism, and Oli adamant he didn't need a trip to the hospital to get some stitches put in (he definitely did), it was time to get a drink somewhere. Virtually everywhere was shut at ten thirty in the morning, but we did find a little pizza place which sold beer. Not local stuff mind, stuff we can get at home like *Moretti* and *Stella* — it dawned on me at this point that this probably wasn't going to be a very cultural holiday. The other guys didn't seem bothered about it; they were here solely for fun, and honestly, I was okay with it too. I've had my fair share of cultural holidays over the years, if I were to practically spend the whole three days inside a bar then so be it. The weather wasn't particularly encouraging us to spend time outside either, it was a cold and overcast day, threatening rain. Three beers in as midday approached, Big Eddie finally texted, firstly apologising for the delay and then to say he was ready to pick us up to go to Ukraine. It was quite a surreal moment where the three of us had to decide if we were actually going to do this now, sat in the safety of Romania with a mouthful of pizza and *Stella* deciding whether to get in a taxi and drive to a country that was actively at war with another. I started to get cold feet about it, as did Oli, although in his case it might have been down to wearing swimwear outside. I texted Edward back saying we'd consider doing it tomorrow if it was better for him, hoping our non-committal response might be enough for him to drop it, but he replied saying he'd rather do it today as he had the free time to drive us around a bit once we were in the country. We finally agreed to do it after settling on a price. His car pulled up at the pizza place shortly after and just like that, we were heading to Ukraine.

Suceava sprawled on for some time as we passed through it — I was actually surprised to see how long it carried on for, there was a whole other part to town across a large river that we wouldn't have known was there had Big Eddie not taken us. Hell, who am I kidding, we wouldn't have even seen outside of a couple of streets with the pace we were going at things this morning. Then, Suceava ended, leaving us on a long, straight road in the countryside with nothing more than the occasional large house stuck in a field somewhere.

"This is a bit mad isn't it, what we're doing?" said Oli, who had literally just read my mind. It was for many reasons, and more so that we didn't really have any sort of plan once we had crossed the border. Didn't the American oldies yesterday say something about some tents after the border, someone we could speak to about helping out or something? Out of the three of us, Oli really didn't look up for it either as he must have had lingering concussion from last night's fall, and had certainly done a poor job trying to clear his blood off his face in the shower earlier in the morning. Dried blood remained around his ears and partially in his hair and the wound continued to weep slightly. No wonder the stray dogs kept running away from us earlier. When most lads go on holiday together, they go on a city break for a few days, perhaps participating in activities such as paintballing or go-karting. Not us; we're off to a country at war for no reason aside from possibly doing some aid work. At the very least we had good old Eddie with us, the friendly local who seemed nonchalant about the whole thing. Any time we tried to gauge his thoughts on entering Ukraine, he'd shrug and say it's "all fine".

We were ten minutes' drive away from the border when Big Eddie's phone vibrated with an incoming call. His wife was on the other end of a video, speaking for some time in Romanian, then Eddie started to swear in English. His wife waved a small book around on the video call; it took me a moment to realise she was showing us he had left his passport at home. The whole thing looked completely staged. His passport was one of only two things he needed today, the other being his car. Eddie must have thought entering Ukraine wasn't a good idea after all. We were so close now though, were we going to turn back around after getting this close? During the last few miles of the drive up to the border, a plan was thrashed out with Eddie that he would take us as far as he could, and we'd walk the rest and come back in a few hours whilst he waited in Romania. Eddie admitted he hadn't been to Ukraine before so he potentially would have been as lost as us even if he had come, but he was still our man; our local who at least spoke one language from around here, who we had now lost. I didn't want to alarm anyone back at home with our ever-changing plans for the day, least of all Mel, but messaged one friend, Rob (who I had shared eventful times with abroad previously), and told him what we were up to. He said he would sound the alarm if he didn't hear back from us in a few hours. What the fuck were we doing?

The view out of the window suggested we might have still been in the countryside, yet Eddie's taxi halted on the muddy embankment of a wide road. He wasn't able to continue any more due to the trail of cars ahead leading to several small buildings in the distance, which I had no doubt were part of the border control. Running parallel to the road were small square tents catering to refugees that had already crossed the border; first aid, free food, meet-up points, SIM cards for phones — all quite impressively providing a host of services for those in need. Several refugees were already spread along the entrance of the tents, I found it heart wrenching to see them carrying all of their belongings in several carrier bags, although I expected to see more refugees given the millions that had reportedly left Ukraine in the news. The tents had mud in front of them, indicating a lot of footfall had been here previously, so perhaps the bulk of them had already made their way through. There were whole families travelling in small groups, although mostly without the young, fit men who had to stay back to fight. Some refugees stood around a fire, warming up alongside the embankment as the smoke poured onto the road, giving the air a slight haze. Others stood around idle like they were waiting for a lift or were not sure what their next steps were now they had crossed the border into safety. And then there stood us three piss tanks, completely out of our depth, not really sure what we were doing here or why. It was a bizarre moment in my life, absorbing this environment, the first safe destination for those fleeing war, walking through the line of aid tents and against the direction of incoming refugees.

There was no clear direction to follow for us to reach the border, certainly no signposts or arrows pointing us in the direction we should be walking to the border control. Following this stationary queue of cars and lorries was the only indicator on where to head, and being on foot allowed us to weave through them with ease. It was interesting to see people were actually heading back into Ukraine as well as coming into Romania; usually it was just a couple of men in each car (I wondered if they were expatriates returning to fight), but occasionally there would be a full family in a people carrier. Other than our shuffling feet, no sounds could be heard as we had cleared the tents area. Cars had their windows up to keep the heat in from the cold outside and, presumably due to the slow-moving queue, all of the engines were off too. The surrounding silence made what we were doing feel a lot more intense than it needed to be. We came to a building which looked a bit like a petrol forecourt, a roof with open walls with a small building underneath with a couple of men stationed inside at the Romanian border control. A small group of people on foot were in the queue before us, several scruffy Eastern European men with dirty clothes who looked almost as lost as we did. They fumbled for their documents and pulled out all sorts of papers, finding their passports buried amongst it all.

I was nervous. The reality of where we were and what we'd seen already had been quite a sobering experience, but now we were actually doing this — entering the country — and if we carried on any further, we'd be past the point of no return. I expected a couple of questions from the Romanian border guards about what we were doing here, I definitely expected a few questions about Oli's head or about the dried blood on him, but they didn't seem phased; they stamped our passports without comment and ushered us through. We then came to a large expanse of concrete with lines of mesh and barbed wire fencing, corralling us into small walkways. A huge man wearing military fatigues with a large rifle strapped to his chest was stationed shortly after Romanian border control. We nervously smiled and walked past him, only to have him begin to shout at us in a foreign language trying to get our attention, making a gesture with his hands for us to walk over to him. *'Oh God, what does this fella want?'* I thought. The words he spoke sounded different to Romanian even to my untrained ear, so he must have been Ukrainian. The three of us obeyed his command and, upon reaching him, he scribbled a symbol down on a slip of paper out of a book, tore it out and handed it to me. It had pre-printed Ukrainian writing on it next to the symbol he had written on it. I had no idea what it was, but assuming it was part of the border control, I put it in my passport for safekeeping and we continued on.

We had now entered an effective no-man's-land between the two countries — an open area of concrete between Romania's petrol station looking border control and Ukraine's large concrete Soviet blocky one. As far as I understood how borders and passport control works, we couldn't re-enter Romania now without entering Ukraine first to get a stamp in the passport; there was literally no going back at this point. I took the lead, being perhaps the more travel-savvy of the three of us, but deep down I was thoroughly nervous. I think all three of us had said "This is mental!" at least once.

We came to Ukrainian passport control. There was a large white building, and two windows to the side in a tight walkway created by a chain-link fence close to the windows. The windows looked like they did different jobs, one was perhaps passport control whereas the other may have been a security point. To be honest, we weren't sure as the signs above them were all written in Ukrainian for a start, and both windows appeared to service pedestrian traffic both ways. When our turn came, we handed our three passports in one go. There was an attractive young woman sat at a desk, wearing military fatigues, next to a man dressed like he might have been a doctor. They took a look at our passports and then up at the three English lads they represented. Three scruffy twats who probably shouldn't be here, attempting to enter on English passports. Was she going to be at all suspicious? She might have been; she asked us something in Ukrainian and I didn't have a clue what she meant. I pointed towards the three of us and said "English", prepared to do the classic English tourist abroad thing and say it again, although louder this time if she didn't understand me the first time around. I found in Romania there had been a large number of people who spoke English and I think even those that didn't really speak it knew a few words to get by. Everyone we had met so far under the age of thirty we could communicate with on some level. I could instantly tell that this wasn't going to be the case in Ukraine and that the ability to communicate in a meaningful way had shifted. "English" definitely wasn't the answer she was after given the look on her face, but she still stamped our passports and waved her hand for us to move on.

The next booth had another military woman in it sitting on the other side of a small window, a much older one this time.

"Get on her, she looks like your mum Oli!" blurted out Kieran quite loudly and with the worst comedic timing when he got a look at her, breaking the quiet we had been in for the past half hour. I'll admit that she did look incredibly similar to Oli's mum — a Ukrainian military version of her — but it probably wasn't the right time to be cracking jokes given where we were (although I was unsure if she had even picked up on a joke being made as her facial expression didn't change). After a tense study through our passports, particularly mine with its pages filled with visas and stamps from around the world, she looked up from the counter and said a whole sentence to us in Ukrainian. Again, no fucking clue what she meant, but I thought I'd picked up the words "*NATO*" and "Russia" amongst it all. At a guess, this might have been some sort of security question to see where our allegiance lay so speaking for the three of us, I repeated the word "Russia" and gestured my thumbs down and pulled a bit of a face like I had licked a lemon. The woman said nothing but gave us our passports and waved us through with her hands. I guess that was the security interview over with! Perhaps they don't have the resources to properly interview everyone coming across, but it was certainly easier than expected to pass through the security booth. There had been reports in the news about groups of British people flying out to Ukraine and taking up arms to help with the fight, so I wonder if she thought we might have been here for this purpose. In fact, she almost certainly must have thought that given the amount of dried blood on Oli, looking hard as nails and like he'd been in a war even before coming to Ukraine. Putin would take one look at him and call it a day. There was a final stretch of walkway to a final gate with another military man holding a rifle. He took our slip with the symbol on that his counterpart had issued at the start of the process and then that was it — we took a step around the barrier and finally made it into Ukraine. I'd seen no more than eight Ukrainians serving at the border and really had expected to see more of the army around. Only two of them seemed to be carrying guns. I suppose the majority were off fighting elsewhere in the country, and in hindsight it is a bit pointless having too many men stationed at the border of a country that is mostly peaceful to you.

## Ukraine — Midday, Saturday, 16th April 2022

After the border we came to a wide straight road with a long queue of lorries waiting to come into Romania, carrying on as far as the eye could see. It was the same situation we'd come seen before crossing the border; all had their engines switched off like they knew they were in for a long wait. Copious amounts of trash lay around like in the aftermath of a festival and there were a couple of skinny stray dogs rummaging around for something to eat. To the side of the border lay an expanse of tarmac housing many vehicles which looked like they had been abandoned having been parked haphazardly. Several cars had people in like they were waiting for someone, one of which looked like a taxi with a hairy old man sat in the driver's seat having a cigarette out of the window. We approached him and I asked, "Taxi?", but he wound his window up and shook his head.

"Okay boys, we're here," said Oli, "What are our plans now?"

I wasn't sure. We couldn't see any of the tents that our American chums had mentioned yesterday. We all agreed they'd said last night we needed to visit the tents on Ukrainian side of the border, but perhaps we had misheard as there was nothing around other than litter and empty vehicles. This had somewhat pulled the rug from under us, as we'd hoped this would have given us some direction once here — what to do and how to help. We also assumed we'd at least be able to get a lift off someone, a couple of taxis waiting perhaps, but without having any wheels (or indeed a purpose), the only option available was to walk down the long road alongside the lorries and head deeper into the country.

The people we had seen at the border had thinned out, leaving only the three of us to our walk along the long road. Of course, the country was at war and the people we had seen close to the border genuinely looked tired and sad; it was a day and night difference between here and Suceava, a mere half hour drive away, where life was normal and everyone seemed content. But even so, the mood just felt bleak — it was so overcast it appeared almost dark despite it being only midday, the thick clouds threatening rain. Other than the lorries, the only other thing following parallel to the road was an endless row of leafless trees, with hundreds of crows swirling around and building nests at the top of them. They constantly cawed between themselves, filling the otherwise silent surroundings. The call of a crow is sometimes used in movies around graveyards or outside haunted houses to set a certain spooky tone, and it was something which was in high abundance here. It truly felt unsettling walking along that road.

There had been a considerable drop in air temperature in the twenty-four hours since coming here. Arriving late last night we had caught the back end of a day that had reached 20°C, but being outside today it was bitterly cold and the rain we had seen was almost sleet. Oli's bollocks must have been clobbered by the temperature, poor lad, having only a thin piece of cloth to protect them. The road continued with the three of us walking along with our heads down. Anyone we had seen on foot going in our direction had lifts already waiting for them at the border, so for the lorry drivers watching us pass it may have seemed odd for the three of us to be walking into the country on foot. Some of the lorries looked unmanned, like they had been left there for a long time. Occasionally fellas could be seen sat inside, asleep. I wanted a photo of myself and the lads in Ukraine to prove we'd been but at no point did it feel appropriate to be taking selfies in front of people who have been heavily impacted by this war, whether they be fleeing families or these lorry drivers merely transporting goods between the two countries. I loaded up a map on my phone to see what we had coming up, noting a town called Terebleche a couple of miles down the road, but also noticed that Big Eddie had messaged asking how long we were intending to spend in the country. I don't think he was keen to wait all day; we'd already been pushing two hours to get to this point. The three of us decided we'd see if the nearby petrol station further up the road offered a beer (because there was a significant risk of sobering up), then we could decide what the plan was after that.

The petrol station was dazzlingly bright upon entry, a huge contrast to the grey surroundings outside. It was well staffed, modern and new, offering an array of freshly-made sandwiches along with an astonishingly large variety of beer and crisps. I was touched to see staff were painting fresh lines on the forecourt in an effort to keep it looking nice; one side of the country was literally getting pummelled into dust by the Russians, yet over on this end of Ukraine the people were still making an effort to keep what they had looking welcoming. We grabbed a handful of beers from the fridge and attempted to pay for it on my card, handing it to a man wearing dark green military clothes at the counter. I couldn't quite tell if the military were running the petrol station or this individual had an unusual choice of fashion, because surely his presence would have been optimal on the forecourt with a gun protecting against theft of the fuel rather than sat behind the till with the cigs and chewing gum. After some waiting, Ukrainian text flashed up on the card reader and it was rejected. I had read the West had recently cut Russia off from the *SWIFT* global banking system as retaliation to the war, basically stopping anyone within Russia from making external electronic payments from out of the country, but I'm not quite sure why a visa transaction didn't work in Ukraine. It could have been anything: the phone lines were down perhaps, or my bank declining the transaction on the basis of what the fuck was I doing in a Ukrainian petrol station when a war was on. The burly army man slapped the card reader, then spoke in Ukrainian and pointed for me to turn a corner. Having no idea what lay in store, I was delighted to see a tiny currency exchange bureau where I was able to get some Ukrainian currency with the Romanian Lei I had on me. With a fresh wad of Ukrainian Hryvnia, and still feeling out of place, I sheepishly bought our beers and our small, bedraggled group sat at a table outside the petrol station and quietly supped.

Other than telling my friend Rob earlier about being here, no-one else back home knew I was here. Kieran, on the other hand, couldn't wait to call his mum to tell her; winding her up to say he was sat having a beer in Ukraine, trying to get a reaction out of her. After sufficiently annoying his mum, he turned to Oli and said he didn't need to call his mum as she'd already seen him at the border checks before.

A large people carrier pulled up outside the petrol station and a family piled out of the car with what I assumed was a mother, father and two teenage daughters. The two daughters honestly didn't look too phased by what was going on and were at one point posed for a quick selfie together at the petrol station before entering the building. They looked like a normal family, and yet here they were with all their important belongings stuck in the back of the car. From what I understood about emergency Ukrainian laws imposed during the war, the father would be unable to leave the country and so he'd only be escorting his family to the border. From there he'd then have to return, possibly to fight. I believe that people are born where they are by chance, with no predetermined reason like fate or divine intervention. By this chance the three of us sat at the table with British passports, free to turn around and go home whenever we're ready. And the poor Ukrainian family, they're going through likely one of the toughest times of their lives; the mother and two daughters were now refugees, likely parting ways with their husband and father when they reached the border just up the road. This was just a snapshot of one family, but the thought of the Ukrainians that had been displaced and lost their homes and loved ones because of the war is alarming to think about when ramped up to the scale of the millions that have been affected. What breaks my heart even more with war is all of the lost pets that have had to be dumped by their fleeing owners, and those poor animals stuck in zoos — whether they're not being fed due to the zoo's income being cut off, or even just being abandoned in their cages. The human tragedy is sad, but gets the coverage it rightly deserves; however, the poor animals that are just as innocent are still affected by war, and their tragic plight is often overlooked in the coverage. Seeing those lost dogs at the border tugged on my heart strings — I hoped they were at least strays who are more adapted to living on the streets, and not those left by the Ukrainians unable to bring their pets across the border.

It was such a surreal feeling to be in a country that was at war with another, even in the far west, away from where the real trouble was. There was a strong underlying feeling like life wasn't right. In just a couple of days' time, Ukraine would sink Russia's flagship navy vessel, the Moskva, in a successful counterstrike. In retaliation, Russia would fire a long-range rocket that would hit several buildings in the relatively safe city of Lviv, far in the west of the country; close to the Polish border and only a hundred and fifty miles up the road from where we currently sat. Firing that rocket would drill into the people of Ukraine that anywhere is a potential target, even on the side of the country furthest away from Russia. I took a short wander by myself around the petrol station whilst the lads finished up their beer. Away from the long road with the lorries I could see for miles across the countryside, but it was rather unremarkable — just flat fields that went on and on, and the sky's grey colour palette didn't improve the overall view of the terrain. Big Eddie messaged again, and although being polite, I think he had been growing a touch impatient with waiting idle (that said, he did forget his passport, so it was his own fault!). Without any solid plans to carry us on, we decided that we'd probably be better off heading back to Romania. I still felt defiant against Putin despite only having spent a few hours in the country. We'd had our holiday plans cancelled directly due to the big knobhead's antics and yet we had still made it here, and in our own little way had put a little bit of money into the Ukrainian economy. We necked the rest of our beers and hit the road, realising that we must now be part of only a handful of people ever with the noble accolade of going into a country at war for a single pint of beer.

We knew the score now, so were slightly more confident approaching the border this time. Oli's mum waved us through again and we reached a queue at the Romanian border control, this time behind several refugees. A large security man approached us and, whilst examining the state of Oli's head, asked in English whether he was a refugee and if he wanted medical aid. A short conversation left him amazed that we were three English lads coming in from Ukraine on foot. He was not from round here himself and was in fact a member of the Swedish army, designated as part of a programme around the European Union to protect its borders. I had already thought to myself that his grasp of English was just a touch better than everyone else I'd met on this trip, and him being Swedish explained it — they speak better English in Sweden than the English themselves do.

"Wait a minute, you guys just went into Ukraine for a beer, then came back?" he exclaimed. The three of us nodded sheepishly like we were about to get into trouble.

"That's fucking crazy, I love it! I thought your friend might have been a refugee with all the blood on his head!"

It appeared that we had made a new friend here. He then insisted we follow him to get Oli's head treated up at the medical tent. Oli protested that surely the service was reserved for the refugees, but our new friend said not to worry about it; the service is for all, plus they were having a quiet day today anyway. We cut across the border's frontier, surely passing alongside security buildings that most people are not usually allowed to go near, then to a small red ambulance with several medical staff sat within it. They were right on the job as soon as Oli's big, battered head appeared. I've had some wild lads' holidays abroad over the years, seen and done some crazy things in the process — but it's going to be hard to top seeing my friend in his swim shorts getting medical treatment at a refugee centre on the border of a country at war.

The medical staff were great, professional and friendly. Not only that, they also gave the cut in Oli's head the deep clean that it was desperate for, wiping away the grit from the wound and clearing the excess blood around his head that had been missed by his half-arsed shower in the morning. I'd told Eddie once we'd passed the border we were only five minutes away, but this medical detour ended up adding another fifteen minutes before we got back to his taxi.

"'Where were you guys?" He asked where we arrived.

"'Oli was just mistaken for a refugee," Kieran replied, half joking.

"You guys are fucking crazy!" Eddie replied laughing. Yep, we had literally just been told that at the border.

I called Mel and informed her what I had just spent the last few hours doing. She called me something I cannot repeat, using words a lot stronger than "crazy". I'll give her that English is her second language, but she doesn't half know how to string several expletives together in a sentence!


## Suceava, Romania — 7pm, Saturday, 16th April 2022

Big Eddie dropped us off in down-town Suceava after the drive back, the streets of which were getting soaked with the heavy rain that had been threatening to come all day. We thanked him for his time (after paying him for it too) and ran across the pavement to the town's Mexican restaurant that he had recommended. Come all the way to Romania to end up in a Mexican restaurant! Although, after the eventful past twenty-four hours with those two, I just fancied some comfort food — something I knew I'd like. A huge taco with spicy beef and salsa, washed down with a bottle of *Corona* or something. The menu wasn't in English but fortunately one of the waitresses was able to translate the menu for us, giving us a run-down of the offerings. All three of us settled on the beef burrito and a margarita cocktail.

Back home in England, we are perhaps guilty of Westernising Indian food; to the point I'm told certain dishes are wholly different to their namesake back in their land of origin — originally due to our colonial past and strong links with India, then adapting the flavour over the years after the recipe was first brought over. They're still a curry, but the Brits are terrible for adding too much cream into a Korma or Masala, or for compromising on herbs or spices that are traditionally usually used. It appeared to be a similar idea here in Romania, but their take on Mexican food was on another level. The burrito was similar to a minced beef stew with some of the liquid boiled off to thicken it up. There was absolutely no spice or Mexican flavour to it, I could only taste beef stock. The salsa was merely chopped tomatoes and kidney beans. It didn't taste *bad*; it just didn't taste *Mexican*. The only thing even remotely Mexican about the whole affair was the tortilla, but even that just looked like it didn't fit in with the rest of the offerings on the plate. Where had the guacamole got to? No sour cream? Spice? At least we had the margaritas, we thought — until they came out, and they were essentially fruit smoothies with a shot of vodka in them. Again, nothing wrong with them on face value, just not what I was expecting. We might have our own take on Indian food in England, but I'm pretty sure we get Mexican right. Hey, maybe we don't, but it's a lot closer to authentic than this beef stew on a tortilla. I put it down to the complete lack of foreigners I'd seen in Suceava and the outside influence they bring with them. Walking the streets earlier in the day, there were no African or Asian people and definitely no Mexicans. Compare that to my small town in rural Cheshire with a population six times smaller than Suceava's 96,000, where even we have small communities of Bangladeshi and Chinese people living there. Hell, Mel isn't even the only Indonesian, a country which is over sixteen hours of flight time away! A neighbouring town to where I live which has a similar population to Suceava has in the past put some of its road signs in Polish because so many of them live there. There's a couple of great Polish restaurants in that town, not to mention an authentic Thai and Italian all on the same road. I don't have a problem with how either country runs itself, whether mixed nationalities living in England or the clearly homogeneous set up in Romania, it's just the way things are. But it's interesting then that the locals of Suceava have just had a stab at producing foreign food like Mexican, must have thought it tastes okay and not too dissimilar from an Eastern European style stew; the key part here being: no one is any the wiser — so they stuck a tortilla on it and flogged it off as Mexican. The formula obviously worked though as the restaurant was packed with people, so who am I to judge?

Stew masquerading as burritos aside, I couldn't fault the town itself nor the hospitality of the residents. Throughout the remaining two nights we had in the town, we met welcoming groups within the small and interesting bars we wound up at — Romanians who'd get us a round in before we'd even had chance to put our hand in our pockets. I felt partially guilty accepting beer from people. Even though prices were extremely cheap (on a par with south-east Asia rather than somewhere that's part of the European Union), I felt like I should have been the one buying as a thank you for encouraging us to sit down with them. English was surprisingly prevalent here, so we'd usually be able to talk and on occasion have a few laughs in between. I found Romanian humour similar to British; witty, often daft, but it could get a little dark too. I was to learn that the monthly minimum wage here worked out at about £400 a month so if any of these guys were earning this sort of money then it was quite costly for them to be buying rounds in for us. I genuinely got the impression that the local people just wanted to make sure you enjoy the time in their country and company, and if that meant forking out money as well as giving us their time for conversation, then so be it. To give a further sense of perspective on the price of things, Oli's completely soiled duvet and bedsheets only cost £30 to replace on the morning we left, which I thought was a bargain.

Oddly, I find some Romanians, particularly the younger generation I would meet throughout the trip, would undersell their town or country and talk about it like it wasn't a pleasant place to be. "Suceava is a shit hole!", "It fucking sucks here all year!"; these sort of comments. Whether I needed a few years under my belt to truly get the vibe of living here to qualify to comment on this, I don't know. Okay, there wasn't loads to do; there's not in my hometown either but it's still a nice place to be. The people here were friendly. There was a lot of green open space around. It didn't feel unsafe to walk around at night (from a male's perspective, anyway). Cars drove sensibly, obeying the red lights and road signs. Local markets sold quality fruit and vegetables, far superior to the supermarkets back home. I had come with fresh eyes to the place after having seen my fair share of the world, so I think it qualifies me to say that Suceava is nice, and all the Romanians shitting on it will just have to deal with the praise. As I've got older, I've started to appreciate places for the subtle things you don't think about when you're younger — factors like air quality or decent walks in the countryside. Suceava ticked a lot of these "adulting" boxes which perhaps the younger generation will appreciate more when they're older. Speaking highly of the place to the locals, not just to be polite but out of genuine appreciation, was something our new friends struggled to wrap their heads around, but I hope our "outsiders" take on things gave a sense of perspective for them. Although that said, I mocked some of the younger guys a bit when they talked about their bleak existence, drinking heavily and smoking because they'd lived a hard life. I said they were too young for a hard life, but they replied with, "We grew up in Romania, my friend," which kind of took me back a bit. I didn't want to rock the boat too much on this one because for all I know, living in the country in the years after the Soviet Union fell might have been a different story.

It's strange how the war affected us in this sense; we had inadvertently come to a small town because of it and had ended up loving the place. Upon reflection, Putin's war had brought me personally closer to Eastern Europe as a whole too, more than I ever could have imagined. The sympathy for the plight of the those displaced by the war and the awareness raised for the country was a start, and then learning about the towns across Ukraine in the news that I would have never heard of otherwise. But then disrupted travel plans taking me elsewhere, becoming friendly with groups of people from two countries of the region (having lengthy conversations with the Ukrainian refugees we later met in Suceava and lengthier drinking sessions with the Romanians), all giving me a good understanding of the way of life in both places, with people that I wouldn't have met if the war didn't happen. It's worth mentioning that the people there are keenly aware of the image they have in Western Europe; that they bring crime with them, that they're not well-educated or whatever. There are definitely more unusual characters wandering the streets than back home, but honestly; I found the people there broke the stereotypes that our media likes to portray them as. And as for education, many more spoke a second language there than back in England. Ultimately, we enjoyed Romania so much by the end of the stay that we returned later in the year — not once, but twice — this time with Mel and my dad in tow. Not bad for a town off the beaten path, managing to pull me in three times when for me, usually, one visit to a place is enough. The next time I'm over, I think a trip across the border for more than a pint of beer is probably in order too, war on or not.

# CHAPTER SEVEN
# SOUTHEAST ASIA

# THAILAND

## Koh Samui, Thailand — Friday, 26th September 2008

You may have noticed in the heading there that the timeline has taken a significant step back into the past. Allow me to tell you about a tale from my early days as a backpacker during my very first time out of the 'Western Sphere' of Europe and the States. I wasn't always the travel- savvy guy that you've read about amongst these pages, and was in fact completely green to the way things worked abroad. You might not think I'm even that savvy reading the above, but trust me; things used to be a lot worse. We've all got to start somewhere though. The following is a weird tale, but one worth telling as it was the first time that I went through an extended period where things had slipped out of my control whilst abroad, therefore writing about it here would be a fitting end to this read (it definitely has nothing to do with me wanting to increase my final word count for the book!).

I consider travelling with Mel in recent years to be enjoyable, and aside from the rare argument when we're hot and tired after going through a day spent in transit together, generally we get along very well. This wasn't the case travelling with my first long-term partner with whom I went backpacking in the late Noughties. If I'm being entirely honest with myself, things had slowly broken down between us even before we embarked on the trip. Our arguments and ongoing upset were a regular occurrence right up to the day we set off on that plane to Bangkok. Evidently, the trip was the sole thing keeping us together, as once we had actually made it out there and spent some

176

time on foreign soil, it took only a week to split up as a romantic couple. Wanting to still see Asia for the first time having saved up for over a year prior to leaving, we begrudgingly continued to travel together, heading up to the rural north of Thailand and crossing into the small, underdeveloped country of Laos. We spent two days on a longboat travelling along the Mekong river, seeing remote and highly interesting tribes living alongside the water. Things may have changed in the region in the many years since I was there, but even to this day I can't recall ever seeing such a basic way of living; people's homes made from tiny bamboo shacks stationed on the muddy banks alongside of the river. No running water, roads or electricity. Compared to the people of the Kenyan countryside (which is perhaps closest to anything like what I'd seen in Laos), the rural Kenyans still had roads and means to get around, but the residents of the Mekong riverbanks were largely isolated due to the inaccessibility of the surrounding dense jungle and fast-flowing water of the wide river. In the town of Luang Prabang further up the river where we could find a bed for the night — and reportedly the only cash machine outside of the country's capital — the military-enforced curfew at 10PM saw intimidating security vehicles patrolling the streets to ensure nobody was wandering around. A few hours later, rows of monks lined the streets and chanted prayer at the crack of dawn to wake up tourists and residents alike. I had certainly thrown myself in at the deep end of Asia for a first visit, but I absolutely loved it all. It sparked something within me to see more of the world. I couldn't believe there were people living like this in this day and age, or how hot other countries could be, or new foods to try that had never made it back to restaurants at home. Our trip continued after Laos, bringing us back to Thailand; visiting the southern gulf tropical islands, the infamous Koh Phangan to start us off, and then a few days' stint in the neighbouring Koh Samui.

The Ex and I had tolerated each other throughout the journey, and in fact since the split things had begun to go well, having the pressure to be a romantic couple taken away. But, after an afternoon spent drinking at various bars on Samui's west coast one afternoon, we had a fresh, blistering argument over nothing in particular that saw me storm off in a bad mood. With the Ex left at the bar, I walked up and down the streets looking for somewhere she wouldn't be able to find me at; perhaps a nice quiet bar by the beach or, ideally, one of those bars that were styled like a pub at home I'd occasionally come across throughout the country. I was fed up of her company and was ready for some alone time, but leaving her had placed me by myself properly for the first time since coming to Asia. It was rather intense. Thailand is a fun place and on the rare instances I get to go back and visit these days, it's great to unwind and catch up with people. I would come back to this region in a few years to find an affinity with the island of Koh Phangan, living there for several months and enjoying the laid-back lifestyle. However, this was all yet to come, and back at the young age of 23, whilst in complete awe of Thailand and Asia in general, I did find it overwhelming. Not to mention I was completely naive to how things worked anywhere outside of England. Young tourists — particularly those who spend a great deal of their day with alcohol in their system — can easily get eaten alive in country if they're not careful. Thais are great people generally, but there's a high concentration of bad eggs in the touristy parts of country (they bring crime), along with countrywide police corruption (which isn't great if you've been a victim of crime). There's a surprising amount of the life-wrecking drugs around like methamphetamine, despite the country issuing the death penalty for hard drugs. If you're lucky, you might get to see two lady-boys knock the shit out of each other outside of a bar, because chicks with dicks are weirdly iconic for the country, but those rare fights between them outside of bars are truly something to behold. There were people living in extreme poverty; shacks next to skyscrapers, chasms of wealth division. Four people crammed on a single motorbike without helmets. Monkeys running loose. Elephants used for labour to move heavy stuff. Heat, humidity, mosquitoes, white sand beaches. Cheap beer and bars filled with prostitutes. There's a lot to process for the first-time tourist.

The heat of the argument leaving me without clear head, I decided having more drink would be a good idea to help me out of my low mood. I found a bar, choosing it based on nothing other than I was fed up with walking, and entered to find vibrant strobe lights and loud dance music pumping through the air like it was catering to a room full of people dancing rather than the actual handful of tourists and Thais sat around tables. I wondered if the owner might have been British, as oddly there was also a TV in the corner of the room with *EastEnders* on, showing Ian Beale's big miserable mug looking wholly out of place at a bar in the tropics – yet (perhaps being a touch homesick) I found seeing something from home, even something as shit as *EastEnders*, oddly comforting. I sat down and ordered several drinks over the course of a few hours, happily alone at first, but once the alcohol level in my blood picked up I felt like I wanted to converse with someone, or better still, try and meet a girl. It didn't take long. A resident Thai girl who appeared to have been several years older than myself, and quite attractive, pulled up a chair and sat down next to me after she'd spent some time watching me watch EastEnders from across the bar. She introduced herself as Lei and after about half an hour was able to coax what I was doing out here. I said I had just split up with a partner some weeks ago but was travelling with her still. Lei said her relationship with her partner had recently ended too, and she was after the same thing as me. The timing worked out well for us both I suppose.

At 2AM, following a blur of late-night bar hopping, we were God-knows-where on the island, stood outside the door to Lei's place whilst she fumbled with her keys to let us in. We entered a basic single room on the ground floor of a short apartment block, the sort of place I'd only seen in Thailand where everything is en-suite including both the kitchen and bathroom. It was dimly lit due to a single low wattage bulb that struggled to light up the room, accompanied by a blade fan that whirred around above the bed. After opening a beer from her fridge we lay down in bed together. I assumed sex was going to be a feature of the night at some point, but it was rather pleasant to find that we spent the first hour on the bed opening up to each other and learning about each other's lives. We touched on relationships again; I said how I had come out here backpacking to see the country but as the trip had become a mess with my ex-partner I honestly didn't know if we could continue travelling together much longer. She told me about how her last relationship ended, where her partner's head had come clean off in a motorcycle accident on Tuesday.

"I'm sorry, what happened? Did you just say Tuesday?" I said, sitting up out of bed.

"Yes, that is correct," she replied nonchalantly.

"You mean like Tuesday as in three days ago?"

"Yes. I saw his head come off his body after motorcycle accident with car."

This girl was wasting no time in moving on, three days after her partner had died she was out on the pull again. The thought of a decapitated head rolling down the street did spoil the night's mood for me if I'm being honest, not to mention the thought of his ghost who was probably stood in the room with us now, holding his head under his arm, soon to be watching a sweaty white lad humping away at his missus. One hell of an accident that must have been to take a head *clean off*. It was time for less talking now, I thought, and a bit of kissing in case she started saying more weird stuff. This of course led onto the real business. I insisted on using a condom which she didn't seem keen on, I didn't have one on me either as the last thing I anticipated doing on this entire stint in Asia was meeting another girl. Fortunately, after some rooting around, she happened to find one in her bedside draw. The composition of the condom was a strange material which I had never seen before, quite thick compared to the translucent ones we have back home. It was also rubbery as well as a bit too small for me and I struggled to slide it on. There's a stereotype that Asian lads have small cocks which I don't want to perpetuate, however it was hard to ignore the small piece of rubber partially cutting the circulation off once it had been fitted. As I mentioned earlier, she was a bit older than me, and this evidently came with more experience in bed, certainly compared to any of my ex-girlfriends. I was already anxious about my first one-night-stand and nervously tried my best to perform and match her experience by sending my arse up and down on top of her as quickly as I could. I must have been a complete stallion, as after about five minutes of use the condom had shredded in half (or, rather, it was made from the cheap material I suspected it was before I'd put it on). Hell, I was so drunk that it could have just been a white party balloon we had been using. I was so alarmed seeing my skin unprotected, I quickly pulled out in a panic.

I realised I had just had unprotected sex with a one-night-stand for the first time in my life, and the worry I might have caught some sort of sexually-transmitted disease flooded me instantly. This fear was compounded by being constantly sensible and precautious throughout my teens. Being cautious in the past had paid off by proudly keeping myself disease-free, which was notable compared to some of the stories I'd heard from my friends who had picked up all sorts of gross shit over the years, but having my good run broken and possibly sticking myself in the same camp as them now, I wasn't sure what the standard practice was once exposed. I'm sure the odds were that Lei was clean, but then she was the type to jump straight into bed while her partner was still warm in the morgue. I bolted out of bed, leaving Lei bemused and ran to the bathroom where she could see me flapping around, looking for things to clean myself with. There was no soap in sight; the only thing in the realm of sanitation was a container of bleach (which may have been the desperate option), but up by the sink lay a bottle of extra-strength *Listerine*. I grabbed it, unscrewed the top as quickly as I could and doused my bellend in it, hoping it would kill any bugs before they could take hold. It stung the very tip enough to make my eyes water. Lei sat up on the bed and shouted what the fuck was I doing pouring mouthwash over my cock, and I replied almost in tears that I honestly didn't know. Upsetting her panicked me more so I grabbed my clothes and ran out of her apartment stark naked. I'm pretty sure stuff fell out of my trousers but fuck it, I'd deal with whatever it was in the morning. I dressed myself in the alleyway around the side of her apartment building, luckily my frantic re-clothing session was still pre-dawn so there wasn't anyone around to witness my exposed pale arse and minty fresh penis. Once clothed, I walked home a bit upset with myself, getting worked up over the past few hours. I'd gone out as a single guy for the first time in years and potentially exposed myself to something harmful.

### Koh Samui Thailand — Saturday, 27th September 2008

Money wasn't going great for me and the Ex. Having spent well over our budget on the trip up to this point, money was dwindling away so we had made a conscious choice to do a budget room for a few days in Koh Samui to try and level our finances out. The problem with budget rooms, particularly in Asia, is sometimes they can be tucked out of the way of the main roads and along dirt paths to the side instead. Because of this it took me hours in the dark to find where I was staying. 2008 doesn't seem all that long ago but proper smartphones were still years away, and it just shows how handy they are today as I'd have been tucked up in bed in no time aided by a detailed digital map had this happened now, rather than wandering the streets of Samui until daybreak looking for my shitty bungalow. In budget rooms you'll rarely find an air conditioner either and instead will only have a fan whirring around at the top of the room that does nothing for the humidity. The room was hot even in the early hours of the morning and after a minute of lying down on the bed attempting to get some sleep, the Ex began to stir and asked where I had been all night. She was unhappy that I had gone off by myself for a start, then was away for the whole night; she would have undoubtedly been even more annoyed if she'd have known what I had really been up to. I couldn't sleep, it was hot anyway, but she kept talking to me about the night which started to annoy me. My mind was locked on the fear of what I might have exposed myself to a few hours ago. I obviously couldn't talk to my Ex and explain my quandary; this revelation would have surely been enough to end the trip and we would have lost the months we still had ahead of us. We were dependent on each other financially to carry us through the trip and in all honesty, I don't think at 23 I would have had the nerve to go off all by myself to the next stops of Australia, New Zealand and Fiji, so I decided this was something that I'd have to keep a lid on for the time being. Having had no sleep after a couple of hours in the room, I told her I was going to go for a walk to clear my head, while actually my plan was to get a taxi to the nearest clinic for a STD test.

Alone again for the second time in two days, I hailed the first taxi I saw and jumped in. The taxi driver, a young Thai chap, was beaming and said through broken English that today was his birthday, and as his first customer of the day he would give me a little gift. He handed me a little wooden emblem with Thai wording engraved into it, held in a square clear plastic container, no bigger than a couple of inches across. He said it would bring me luck today. I said thanks very much, and thought to myself if there was ever a time I needed luck it'd be for the next few hours. As giving this gift had broken the ice slightly between the two of us, asking him to take me to a STD clinic wasn't as awkward as it could have been. His English was okay, but not great. I think he understood as he said, "Ah — you had fun last night?" and winked at me. Say no more lad, get me to a clinic!

After several minutes of driving inland from the coast, Mr. Birthday pulled up outside a huge shop window alongside a main road. He pointed and said to try here, and he would wait for me if it wasn't what I was after. Still naive and scared of being out in Thailand all by myself and putting my trust into Mr. Birthday's knowledge of Samui, I nervously left the taxi and entered the building. Something didn't look right about the place, it was unusual; all very white, bright and clean, a large room but with nothing much in it other than a long reception desk at the opposite end of the entrance with three Thai women behind it, all in their early thirties. I was the only "customer" in the room. I approached one of the women and said in the most shy, awkward voices I think I've ever said,

"I... umm... I think I had unprotected sex last night."

"Excuse me, what did you say sir?" the lady replied loudly, obviously trying to bring the volume of the conversation up so she could hear.

"I, uh, had unprotected sex last night. Can I get a test here?"

"Oh," she replied, pondering for a second on what I'd said, and then moved away from her position at the desk. She walked over to her nearest colleague and spoke to her in Thai. Then they both burst out laughing. I stood there for about a minute with two Thai women laughing hard at me. Then the third one joined in with the laughter. I didn't appear to be at the right place, fuck knows what this place even was, it probably wasn't even a STD clinic judging by the laughter, it might have been a hairdresser salon in the back room behind the counter for all I knew. After realising I wasn't getting served here, I turned around walked out of the shop and I re-entered the taxi and told Mr. Birthday to put his foot down and drive away somewhere. I looked back at the shop window as we pulled off and the women were still laughing. For the final insult, while using one hand to cover her mouth from the laughter, one of the women used her other hand for pointing at the taxi and followed it with her finger as it drove off.

I think the taxi driver had finally understood what I meant and pulled up at what looked like a proper hospital this time. If it wasn't a clinic then honestly, he's had two chances now, birthday or not I was done with him. I still gave him a bit of extra cash when it came to payment because he was a nice guy, despite exposing me to a level of humiliation I didn't know was possible, then bid him farewell and entered the hospital. I had already been to a Thai hospital earlier in the month from picking up a fever, having spent some time out in the rural northern Thai countryside not long after arriving in the country. The worry when fever comes while out in the tropics is that it might be something more sinister due to the prevalence of mosquitoes and the tropical diseases they bring, particularly when they feast from the unguarded rear legs of the tourist that has forgotten the mosquito repellent. I have been unwell a few times in the tropics and it genuinely scares me every time, but that one hit me particularly hard as this was only within my first ever few days of being here. All was fine though; I had picked up a mere fever and I bounced back after a week. Had I managed to avoid a scary blood haemorrhaging disease like Dengue fever in the north only to be then taken down by a bought of crotch rot on the islands?

Like the hospital in the north I had been to, the doctors and nurses in Samui had a superb grasp of English and it was nice to be able to explain my situation without any ambiguity. I was moved into a small clinic where a doctor took a sample of my blood, and then he had me spend an hour in the waiting room. Once again, this is another time that a smartphone would have come in handy; I would have enjoyed having it to take my mind off my current situation by offering something to read and pass the time. But no, because 2008 feels technologically prehistoric the more I think about it, I just had to sit there with a stack of magazines written in Thai and stare at the walls and worry what lay in store.

Here's a fun fact that I didn't know at the time: most STDs don't show up right away, and things like HIV can take a whole three months to show up in the blood! I had this huge wait ahead of me that would dwarf my hour spent waiting for answers in the hospital waiting room. Three months! Lurking at the back of my mind for quarter of a year worrying whether something minging was brewing inside me. I discussed all this with the doctor when I was called back into the room. The doctor also said unprotected sex with a one-night stand wasn't a good idea – I know mate, I'm usually careful! – and the only way to be sure right now was to go and find Lei, bring her here, so they could do a blood test on her. There was absolutely no chance this was happening; I had already burned my bridges with her by using up all her mouthwash and leaving without an explanation. During this talk with the doctor, another doctor barged through the door into the room holding some papers (presumably my test result), looked me in the eye dramatically and said I had hepatitis B. The two doctors discussed the situation in Thai, and I sat there stunned. So, I had actually managed to pick something up then? What the fuck even is hepatitis B?! That's it then, I'm going to die, I'm sure of it. The doctor I was sat with took the papers and read over them carefully. After some time, he apologised for his colleague's presumption and said what they had actually found was the antibodies for hepatitis B — because I had been vaccinated against it before I'd started my trip. Thai people with antibodies for the disease are apparently quite rare as vaccination in general isn't that common, which is why their system flagged a positive after my blood test. Immediate panic over but not particularly wiser on my overall health situation, there was nothing else I could do for now, so I headed back to the bungalow. I found locating it much easier this time in the daylight.

I entered to find my ex looking around the room, highly focused and yet as irritable as always.

"Never mind where you've been all day. Do you have our passports? Because I don't have mine!"

I wasn't sure. I hadn't carried it all day. The only thing I had carried on me all day apart from my shame was the weird wooden birthday emblem thing. After tipping the room upside down, we came to the realisation that we must have taken them out with us last night and lost them. Fuck me, could the day get any worse? The first port of call on the hunt for them was the bar we had separated at last night where the bar staff had found and thoughtfully kept the Ex's safe with them. But alas, mine was not to be seen. I stomped off again, leaving the Ex alone for the third time (making excuses for my reasoning why but entirely for fear of her and Lei bumping each other) and retraced my steps as well as I could remember. There was only a couple of places I could recall being at, so shy of dropping it on the street, it was either at the bar I met Lei at, in Lei's apartment or, if not either of those, then it was gone for good. The thought of going back to her apartment straight away was very off-putting, so I decided checking the bar would be the best bet.

I entered and the bar was far more lively than yesterday, with many more people up and dancing even though the music wasn't quite as loud. A lot of these touristy towns around Thailand feel like they're perpetually on a weekend, forever catering to the next batch of passing backpackers and holidaymakers that want to drink and party and so, being out there for weeks on end, days of the week become a loose concept, although tonight in the bar actually felt like a Saturday night for a change. There were more Thais sat around tables in particular, perhaps enjoying their weekend which might have explained why. And amongst them all, there was Lei with several of her friends sat around a table across the room, almost like she had been waiting for me.

"I have something of yours!" she excitedly shouted over, pulling my passport out of her handbag then waving it in the air when she saw me walking to her table.

"You can have passport back, but I want to kiss first!"

Her table of friends giggled. She was getting that kiss — obviously. I wanted my passport back if only to get off this fucking island, plus, I don't think I could have really picked anything else after I'd already had it away unprotected with her. I leaned over, kissed her cheek and several of her friends cheered and then started laughing. I think today's total of Thai women laughing at me was now at eight. I didn't wait around after I got the passport back, I was thoroughly embarrassed and half of the bar (even the other Westerners) erupted in cheers as I passed through the exit. I'm not entirely sure the others knew what was going on, or if they were just getting involved once they noticed Lei's friends laughing, although I swear I thought I heard the word "mouthwash" shouted by one of the crowd.

I managed another three months of travelling with the Ex and we ended up mostly having a good time as friends, however everything between us fully fell off the rails towards the end, leaving me with the headache of being homeless in The States for a short time without the money to get home (this is a story for another time!). My first foray into travelling had been rough at times, more so than I expected it was going to be before I set off, really. I thought travelling would just be a big, long enjoyable holiday, but that wasn't the case. Earlier in the book I mentioned about getting lost in Fiji which had also been another traumatic time on this trip. Not to mention the countless bouts of the shits without access to a decent toilet, or falling ill. You hear of backpackers coming back from their months away saying how good it all is, but there are also shitty bits no one is as keen to talk about. The trip still resonated more with me though — all that I said at the start of the book; sitting on a beach at 5AM to watch a sunrise after a party, a day spent with villagers in rural Asia, or meeting all the interesting people on the road who then become lifelong friends. It still rings true even to this day and it all stemmed from this first trip I embarked upon. Honestly, it was great then and I still love it now.

I eventually managed to get home from The States in the end, and after arriving had a proper test and received the all-clear. It's good to know *Listerine* works to stop STDs as well as prevent tartar build up, although I'm not sure whether they'll be putting that one on their adverts.

Printed in Great Britain
by Amazon